101 DRILL TEAM EXERCISES
FOR HORSE & RIDER

DEBBIE SAMS

Storey Publishing

ACKNOWLEDGMENTS

Writing this book has been an exciting adventure for me! I am grateful to everyone who so graciously helped in so many ways, including Stephanie Dobiss, who proved to have a wonderful talent for critiquing drill team exercises; my husband of 25 years, Dan Sams, who encouraged me to try my hand at writing and diligently proofread the book for me; Katrina Springer, my sister, who also proofread the book; my drill team, students, and boarders, who patiently rode through many exercises and helped to tweak some of them; and the Storey Publishing staff, who were so helpful. I am blessed to have such wonderful support.

The mission of Storey Publishing is to serve our customers by publishing practical information that encourages personal independence in harmony with the environment.

Edited by Sarah Guare and Deborah Burns
Art direction & book design by Cynthia N. McFarland
Text production by Liseann Karandisecky

Cover & interior photography by © William Shepley, except for back cover & page 1 by © Phelps/Hathaway Enterprises, Inc.
Arena diagrams by Chuck Galey, with additional illustrations for Exercises 8 and 16 by Bethany Caskey
Riders in chapter opener photos: Riata Ranch Cowboy Girls

Indexed by Christine R. Lindemer, Boston Road Communications

© 2009 by Debbie Sams

Special thanks to Heather Comerate of Drill Fever!, www.drill-fever.com, for initial photography research.

All rights reserved. No part of this book may be reproduced without written permission from the publisher, except by a reviewer who may quote brief passages or reproduce illustrations in a review with appropriate credits; nor may any part of this book be reproduced, stored in a retrieval system, or transmitted in any form or by any means — electronic, mechanical, photocopying, recording, or other — without written permission from the publisher.

The information in this book is true and complete to the best of our knowledge. All recommendations are made without guarantee on the part of the author or Storey Publishing. The author and publisher disclaim any liability in connection with the use of this information. For additional information, please contact Storey Publishing, 210 MASS MoCA Way, North Adams, MA 01247.

Storey books are available for special premium and promotional uses and for customized editions. For further information, please call 1-800-793-9396.

Printed in the United States by Versa Press
10 9 8 7 6 5 4 3 2 1

LIBRARY OF CONGRESS CATALOGING-IN-PUBLICATION DATA

Kay Sams, Debbie.
  101 drill team exercises for horse and rider / by Debbie Sams.
    p. cm.
  Includes index.
  ISBN 978-1-60342-143-0 (paper with comb bdg. : alk. paper)
  1. Horses—Training. 2. Horsemanship. I. Title. II. Title:
  One hundred one drill team exercises for horse and rider.
  III. Title: One hundred and one drill team exercises for horse and rider.
SF287.K29 2009
798.2—dc22
                                    2009001485

CONTENTS

INTRODUCTION

DRILL TEAM EXERCISES are fun and a good way to improve your riding skills and to enhance your horse's training. They foster commitment, leadership, teamwork, and good horsemanship.

Riders of all disciplines with horses of all breed types can use the exercises in this book, which have been designed for groups of four to twelve riders. These exercises can even be used in designing individual freestyle patterns.

Components of a Good Drill

Riders know that their drills are done well when they look easy to the audience. Drills should flow smoothly and evenly from one exercise to the next. Riders should exhibit even rating and spacing. Thread the Needle, for example, should look as if two very straight, evenly spaced lines mysteriously penetrate each other and then emerge as straight as they were. For a magical look, riders should avoid swerving, yanking, or kicking.

The bobbing heads of posting riders detract from the vision of unity. Riders should sit the trot or jog for a uniform look, unless a beginning rider has to post. The riders should practice good sitting form so that the exercises are easy on both riders and horses.

Riders should be BRATTs, reminding themselves often of the following: **B**end your horse; **R**ate your horse; be **A**ccurate; and emphasize **T**iming and **T**eamwork.

Keys to a Successful Practice

Riders remember the patterns best when they practice at least twice a week. You may throw together a simple drill with a couple of hours of practice and be able to present it decently right away. The more frequently you practice, however, the more polished your team will be.

The Arena

A good size for a small drill team's arena is 20 meters by 40 meters (65 feet by 130 feet). A useful rule of thumb is that all riders should fit in open formation on one long side. If the arena is so large that the team looks lost, use barrels, cones, or rails to section off an area for the drill.

Tape up dressage letters. They give reference points that indicate where the team has to go. It's easy to tape letters quickly to posts or cones. The letters used in this book are traditional dressage letters. The "centerline" goes the length of the arena from **A** to **C**. The letter **X** denotes the center of the arena.

STARTING A DRILL TEAM

It is essential that your drill team have:

- Committed members who will be at every practice and work hard
- Members who are leaders, and members who know how to follow
- Suitably matched horses and riders: green horses with experienced riders, and green riders with experienced horses
- Members with good attitudes; complainers and blamers won't fit in with those who are there to have fun and enjoy the process. If someone messes up, laugh and then work on how to do it better next time.
- Horses who do not bite or kick

Ground Work and Direction

Walk through the drill on the ground to learn new moves or to refresh the riders' memory before the mounted practice. This is a good time to go over adjustments to improve the visual or technical aspects of the drill. On the ground, it's easy to stop, back up, or reposition partway through an exercise.

An unmounted drillmaster is crucial. She is the team's eye on the ground. Riders are directed through the pattern by the drillmaster, who must have a view of the team as a whole.

At difficult spots, break down your steps and do the exercise several times until everyone feels comfortable performing it. The drillmaster should remember to solicit feedback from team members, who will often have great ideas for improving the drill.

Most importantly, remember to laugh at yourselves! Your drill practice is guaranteed not to go perfectly every time, but that's part of the fun.

Place Safety First

When you are riding a drill, safety should always be paramount. Here are some rules that will help keep you safe.

◆ Always wear a helmet, long pants, and shoes (*not* open-toed) with low heels.

◆ Be aware of the body language of the horses around you. Take proactive measures, such as moving your horse away, when his body language indicates that he is agitated, nervous, or otherwise distracted. (Biters, kickers, and those who dislike being in close proximity to other horses should not be part of a drill team.)

◆ If your horse threatens to kick, drive him forward. Signs that a horse is preparing to kick are swatting his tail up and then straight down, pinning his ears stiffly back, wrinkling his nose and turning his head

---

HOW TO USE THIS BOOK

I recommend doing the basic moves in chapter 1 first. These exercises will help you learn the basic rules of drill team riding, which you can then apply to other exercises. After chapter 1, you do not need to follow the chapters in order. Each chapter contains a unique type of exercise, and using as many different types of exercises as possible in your drill will make it more interesting and entertaining.

The diamonds next to the chapter titles (◊) indicate the difficulty of the exercise, with one diamond signifying the least challenging and five diamonds signifying the most challenging. In general, the exercises become progressively harder within each section of a chapter.

---

sideways, raising a hoof in a threatening manner, and slowing down to prepare to kick.

◆ When your horse shows signs of preparing to bite, such as pinning his ears and baring his teeth, move him away from the other horses by slowing him down or moving farther to the left or right, away from the potential victim.

◆ Be aware of where the other riders are in the arena. This will help keep you safe and give you the ability to perform the drill more accurately.

◆ Take note of objects or shadows that might cause alarm or spook your horse inside or outside the arena, so that you will not be caught off guard.

◆ Remove all hazards, such as jump standards, rails, cavalletti, and farm equipment, from the arena.

◆ Make sure all tack is in good repair and is properly fitted.

A drillmaster helps you perfect your performance. This drillmaster is indicating an abreast halt.

CHAPTER ONE

BASICS OF DRILL TEAM RIDING

AT EACH OF YOUR TEAM'S first few practices, you will do well to go over the basic exercises outlined in this chapter. Review them again every year and every time a new member joins your team. They will help your team to ride with accuracy and precision.

Once you've mastered the basic moves, you can increase the level of difficulty. For example, a simple centerline move could incorporate haunches-in, shoulder-in, or tempo changes. A straightforward serpentine could become a counter-canter. Small circles could become rollbacks, turns on the forehand, turns on the haunches, or spins. Obliques could become leg yields, haunches-in, or half-passes. You can also increase the speed at which you perform it to make an exercise more difficult.

Follow these five tips for mounted work:

1. Walk through the first four or five exercises.
2. After riding through several exercises in a drill, such as numbers 1 through 4, begin again with Exercise 1 but go through to Exercise 7, and so on, increasing the number completed each time.
3. Ride the entire drill at a walk.
4. After the riders have a good general idea of the exercises, trot the simple exercises and continue to walk the more difficult ones.
5. Gradually work up to doing the whole drill at performance speed. This can be entirely at trot or canter, or you may choose to mix it up.

RULES FOR DRILL TEAM RIDERS

- ◆ Listen for instructions.
- ◆ Do not stop unless the leader tells the whole line to stop.
- ◆ Do not pass another rider unless instructed to do so.
- ◆ Do not pull out of line unless a collision is imminent; rate your horse, increasing or decreasing your speed as needed.
- ◆ If you make a mistake, perhaps turning the wrong way or starting to perform the wrong figure, don't stop unless the mistake has disrupted the movements of others. Just catch up or improvise with a new maneuver. Your audience may never suspect the mistake.
- ◆ If you are the caller, ride at or near the end of the line.

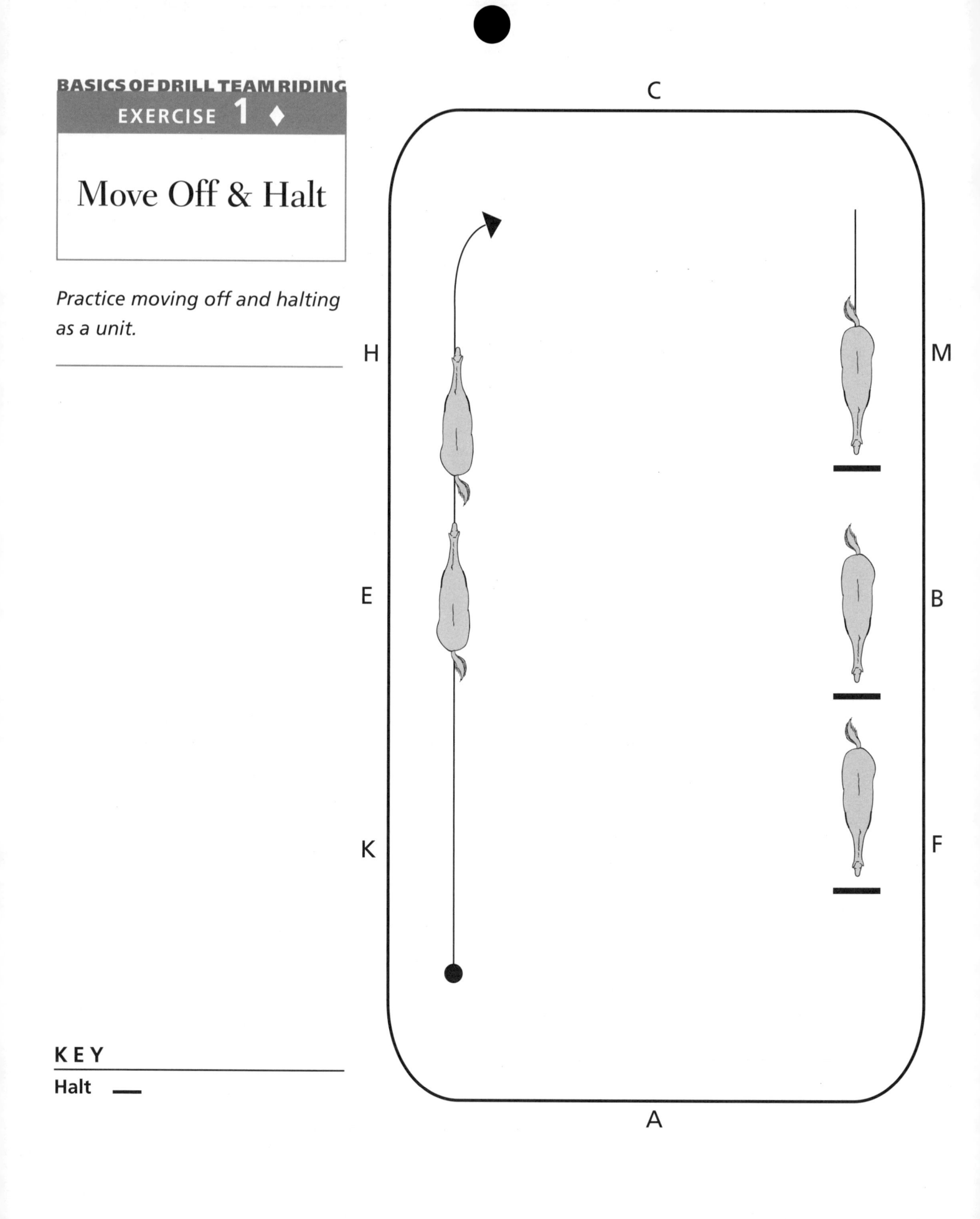

EXERCISE 1 ♦

Move Off & Halt

Practice moving off and halting as a unit.

K E Y

Halt ▬

C

H

E

K

M

B

F

A

1. Move Off & Halt

STARTING POINT

● Form a single-file line along the rail.

HOW DO I RIDE THIS?

MOVING OFF

1 The caller, mounted at the rear of the line, gives a preparatory signal, which can be a whistle or a voice command.

2 When the caller gives the signal to move off, everyone moves into a walk.

HALTING

1 The caller gives a preparatory signal.

2 When the caller gives the signal to halt, everyone halts.

KEEP IN MIND

◆ Faster horses are placed at the front of the line.
◆ Horses who are uncomfortable near each other are not placed together.
◆ Trying different orders to find the one that best suits the team's horses can be very helpful.

INCREASING DIFFICULTY

◆ Do transitions into and out of different gaits.

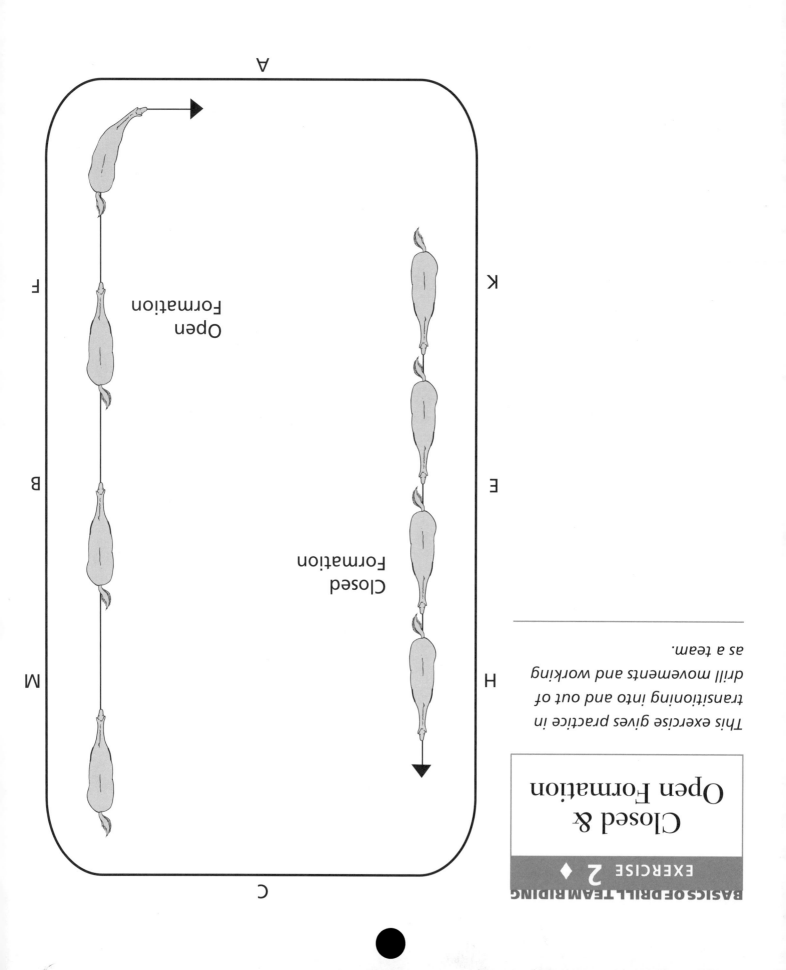

Open Formation

Closed Formation

This exercise gives practice in transitioning into and out of drill movements and working as a team.

Closed & Open Formation

2. Closed & Open Formation

SETUP

Closed Formation. Horses stand about 1 meter (3 feet) apart. When riders look between their horses' ears, they should see the top of the tail in front of them.

Open Formation. Horses stand about one length apart. When riders look through their horses' ears, they should see the fetlocks of the horse in front of them.

STARTING POINT

● Ride a line in open formation.

HOW DO I RIDE THIS?

CLOSED FORMATION

1 The caller gives the signal to close formation.

2 Riders in front slow down.

3 Riders behind increase their speed to close formation. Riders may cut corners a bit to catch up.

4 Practice keeping the spacing equal.

OPEN FORMATION

1 The caller gives the signal to open formation.

2 Riders in front increase their pace but stay in the same gait.

3 Riders behind slow their pace to create more space while staying in the same gait.

4 Practice maintaining the spacing.

Practice closing and opening the line formation. Open on one side of the arena and close on the other.

KEEP IN MIND

♦ For the horses' comfort, kickers and horses who are uncomfortable in a close formation are not ridden too close to each other.
♦ The drillmaster helps to keep the spacing even by telling the riders when it is correct.
♦ Horses who need more space between themselves and the horses in front of them can be ridden deep into the corners.

INCREASING DIFFICULTY

♦ Increase the speed.

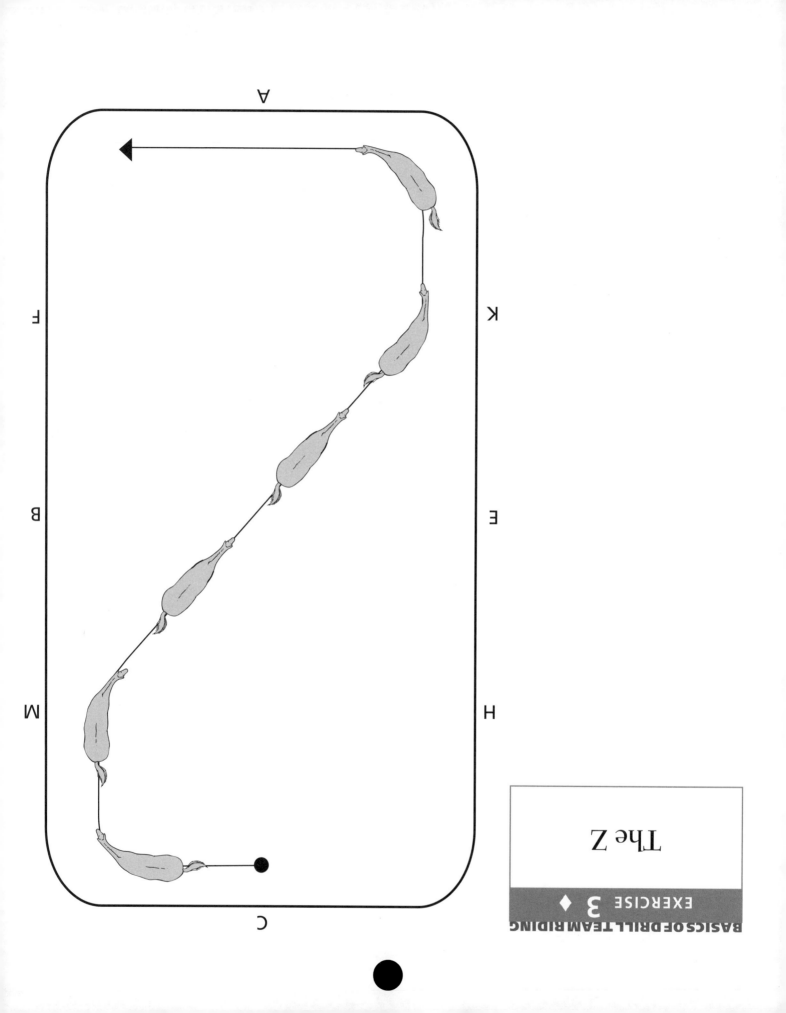

A

F

K

E

B

H

M

C

3. The Z

STARTING POINT

● Form a single-file line at **C** facing **M**.

HOW DO I RIDE THIS?

1 Ride forward through the corner on the rail. At **M**, turn across the diagonal.

2 Ride to **K**.

3 Turn left along the rail at **K**.

4 Turn the corner.

KEEP IN MIND

◆ Horses bend through the corners.
◆ Horses are rated to match the speed of the other horses.

INCREASING DIFFICULTY

◆ Increase the speed.
◆ Try the exercise in pairs.

TIME YOUR TURN

Here are a few pointers to aid in maintaining correct timing on the turns:

◆ The turn at **M** is made when the rider's body has passed the letter.
◆ The turn near **K** is made when the horse's nose reaches the section of fence before **K**.
◆ The horse is parallel to the rail after he turns.

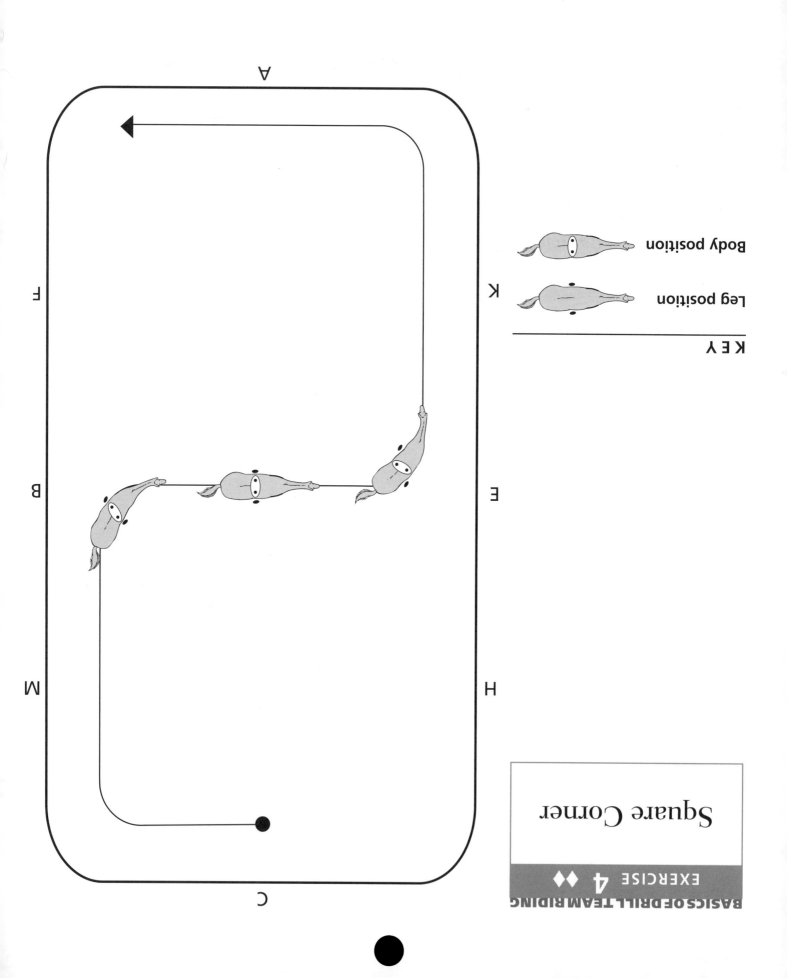

A

F

B

M

C

H

E

K

K E Y

Leg position

Body position

Square Corner

4. Square Corner

STARTING POINT

● Form a single-file line at **C** facing **M**.

HOW DO I RIDE THIS?

1 Move straight ahead and around the corner.

2 At **B**, turn toward **E**.

3 When the horse's nose reaches **E**, turn toward **K**.

4 Follow along the fence.

KEEP IN MIND

♦ Through the turns, the rider's inside leg is at the girth and the outside leg is behind the girth.
♦ The rider's body is positioned as though imaginary eyes in the chest and hip bones look in the direction of travel.
♦ The inside leg and the body position are used to prevent the horse from falling in.

INCREASING DIFFICULTY

♦ Open and close formation.
♦ Increase the speed.
♦ Add a flying lead change in the center of the arena.

pro tip

In order to keep single-file lines straight, you must remember to rate your horse so you can maintain a straight line. Look ahead and stay directly behind the horse in front of you.

— **Stephanie Dobiss**
Keystone Dressage and Combined Training
Association of Central Pennsylvania

EXERCISE 5 ◆◆

Partners

PAIRS ON CENTERLINE

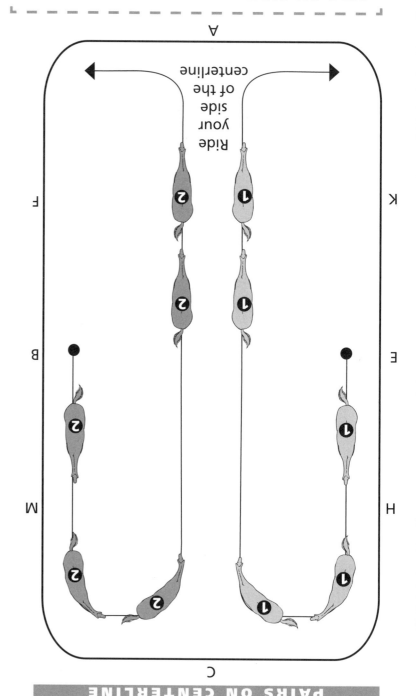

Ride your side of the centerline

SIDE-BY-SIDE

When an audience looks at a drill team, it looks at the riders' heads. For the best effect, partners should be side-by-side with bodies aligned.

PASS ON THE RIGHT

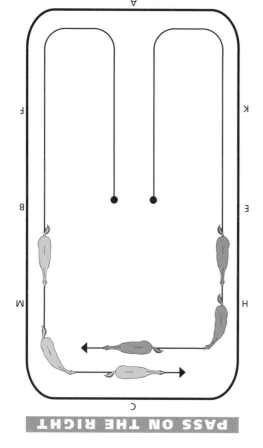

PAIRS ON FENCE

5. Partners

PAIRS ON CENTERLINE

STARTING POINT

- Line 1 forms at **E**, facing **H**.
- Line 2 forms at **B**, facing **M**.

HOW DO I RIDE THIS?

1 Ride along the wall, keeping the horses' bodies parallel.

2 Turn in pairs and come down the centerline at **C**.

3 Look at **A** as you ride your side of the centerline to **A**.

PAIRS ON FENCE

STARTING POINT

- Pairs line up at **K** facing **E**, with number 1 horses on the outside and number 2 horses on the inside.

HOW DO I RIDE THIS?

1 Ride in pairs along the wall with riders' bodies side-by-side.

2 Outside horses should pull ahead about one head's length on the corners as inside riders slow down.

3 After the corner, riders watch their partners' bodies and remain aligned.

PASS ON THE RIGHT

STARTING POINT

- Pairs line up on the centerline facing **A**.

HOW DO I RIDE THIS?

1 Ride toward **A**. At **A**, partners split away from each other.

2 When passing **K** and **F**, rate your horse so that partners pass each letter at the same time.

3 At **C**, pass your partner left hand to left hand.

KEEP IN MIND

- Riders watch their partners' bodies out of the corners of their eyes. Looking straight ahead, they remain aware of their partners' bodies' locations as an aid to staying aligned.
- Practicing pair work improves alignment, precision, and accuracy in all drill exercises.
- When practicing on foot, high fives are done each time partners come together. This reminds riders that they need to come together at the correct place and time.
- Riders pass head-on left hand to left hand.

INCREASING DIFFICULTY

- Ride triples or quads abreast.
- Increase the speed, but only as much as the weakest rider can accommodate.
- Try riding shoulder-in or haunches-in.

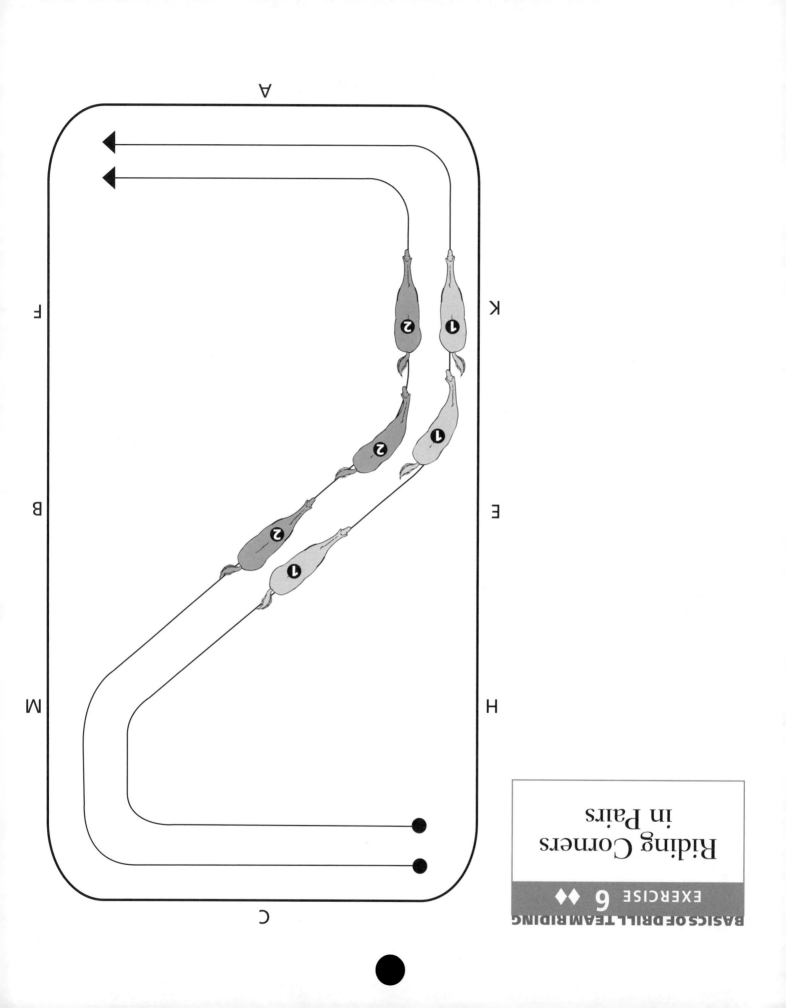

6. Riding Corners in Pairs

STARTING POINT

● Form two lines at the corner between **H** and **C** in pairs facing **M**, in closed formation.

HOW DO I RIDE THIS?

1 Ride forward.

2 At **M**, turn and cross the diagonal.

3 At a point before **K**, turn left.

4 Follow the fence.

KEEP IN MIND

◆ The turn is made after the rider's body has passed **M**.

◆ As a pair enters the corner, the outside horse pulls ahead and the inside horse slows down. The inside horse's nose is parallel to the outside horse's throatlatch.

◆ The outside horse must take more steps than the inside horse. When they finish their turn, the pair is even again.

◆ Practice rating horses through the corners to improve their performance.

◆ Crossing the *school* (the arena or pen where both the horse and rider learn) on the diagonal (the Z) enables partners to practice moving ahead and slowing their horses.

◆ Cross the diagonal to a point before **K**. At **K**, the horses are parallel to the fence.

INCREASING DIFFICULTY

◆ Increase the speed.

◆ Do other figures, such as figure 8s, circles, and serpentines, in pairs to practice corners.

VARIATIONS

◆ Have several pairs ride Zs together on the diagonals **M–K** to **F–H**.

◆ Turn to cross the diagonal, facing the long side, at any of these spots: **H**, **F**, **K**, or **M**.

Tricycling

Ride this any time when you are doing pairs but have an odd number of participants.

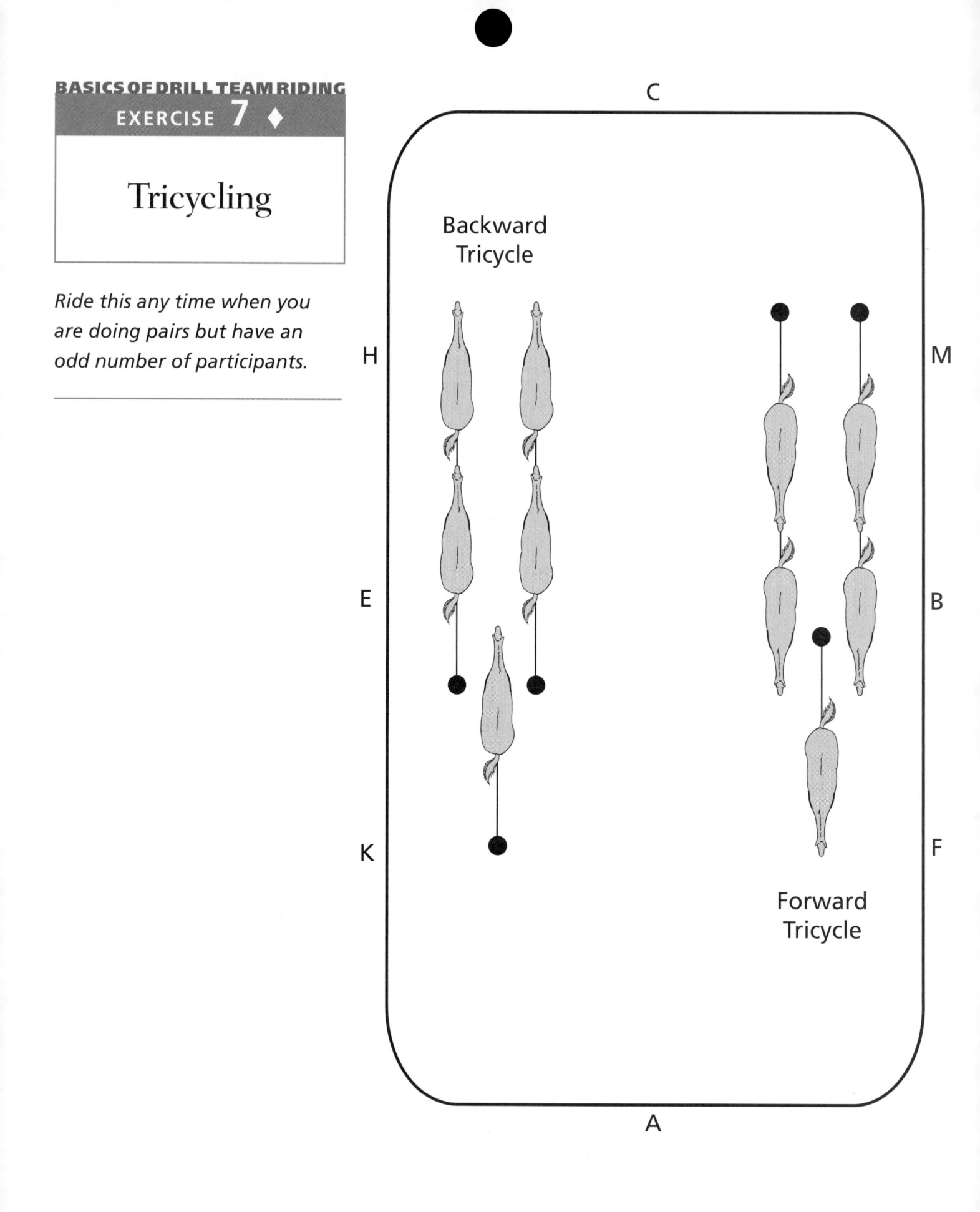

Backward Tricycle

Forward Tricycle

7. Tricycling

BACKWARD TRICYCLE

STARTING POINT

● Form pairs in closed formation at **H** facing **C**.

HOW DO I RIDE THIS?

Place the extra horse behind the line of pairs in such a way that his nose points between the last pair of horses. Maintain this formation as you ride along the rail.

FORWARD TRICYCLE

STARTING POINT

● Place a single horse at **F**, facing **A**. He should be about 1 meter (3 feet) off the fence line.

HOW DO I RIDE THIS?

Place the first pair slightly behind the horse in front. Remaining pairs should be fully behind the pair in front. Maintain this formation as you ride along the rail.

KEEP IN MIND

◆ All of the horses, including the tricycling horse, are spaced at an equal distance from each other.
◆ The tricycling horse does not ride even partially alongside the pair ahead or behind him.
◆ The tricycling horse stays centered between the pair he precedes or follows.

VARIATION

◆ If there is an even number of riders, place a tricycling horse both in front and behind for a unique effect.

pro tip

Ride your line! Drills are all about precision and timing. To achieve this, each rider needs to pay attention to exactly where she is riding.

— **Stephanie Dobiss**
Keystone Dressage and Combined Training
Association of Central Pennsylvania

These riders are bending and rating their horses to produce the accuracy and timing necessary for good teamwork.

CHAPTER TWO

CURVES

To correctly ride a circle, bend the horse along the arc of the circle to create balance. To ensure that your horse is balanced, communicate **B**ending, **R**ating, **A**ccuracy, and **T**iming, which will improve overall **T**eamwork (BRATT).

Bending

When your horse is bending, his spine should follow the line of travel. Keep in mind that the *inside* is the side closer to the center of the circle or turn and the *outside* is the opposite side.

- Turn your chest and hip bones in the direction you want to turn.
- Keep your outside arm next to your body to give the horse more contact with the outside rein.
- Put your inside leg on the horse at the girth to keep the horse in the bend.
- Keep your outside leg slightly behind the girth to control the bend and prevent the haunches from falling outside of the bend.
- Step into your outside stirrup to keep your weight slightly to the outside and to help your horse to balance.

Rating

When you rate your horse, you are either slowing him down or speeding him up. This controls the space between you and your teammates' horses.

- To create more space between horses, you can ride deep into the corners; make a slightly wider circle than the one being made by the horse directly ahead; bend and move your horse to the outside of the circle using a leg yield; slow your horse with a deep seat; check and release on the reins (half-halt).
- To close up space between horses, you can allow your horse to cut the corners; make your circles a little smaller than those of your teammates; or urge your horse forward.

Accuracy

Be sure that your moves are accurate, so that your drill will look crisp.

- Practice keeping the tempo steady, both on the straightaway and on turns.
- Stay directly behind the horse ahead of you.
- Practice bending correctly when following the lead horse, so that you do not fall in on the corners.

Timing

You must be in the right spot at the right time.

- Stay aware of everyone in the arena.
- Begin your turn *after* you pass the applicable letter.
- When approaching a letter head-on from the centerline, begin to turn about 3 meters (10 feet) before your horse's nose reaches the letter.
- When crossing on the diagonal or the oblique line, focus on a point roughly 3 to 5 meters (10 to 16.5 feet) before the letter. Your horse will then be parallel to the fence at the letter.

Teamwork

Work together as a team.

- Communicate!
- Determine who is going to do what before you begin the exercise.
- Help each other during the performance.

Circle/Turn through the Circle

CIRCLE

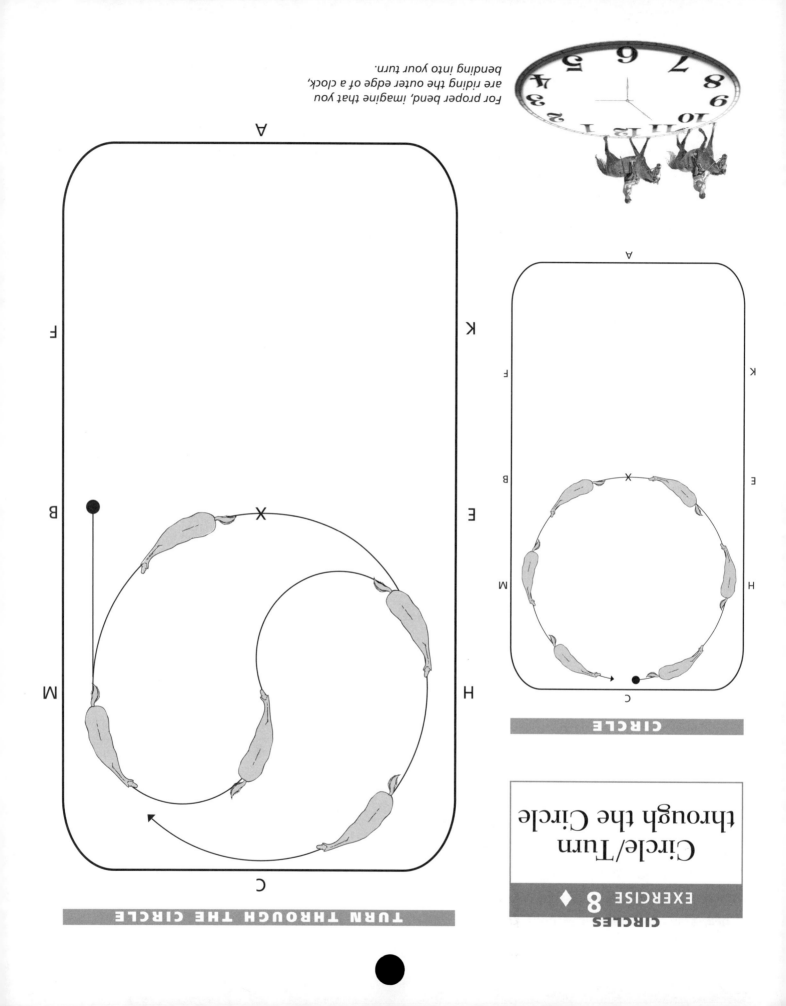

A

K   F

E   B

H   M

C

TURN THROUGH THE CIRCLE

A

F   K

B   E

M   H

C

X

For proper bend, imagine that you are riding the outer edge of a clock, bending into your turn.

8. Circle/Turn through the Circle

CIRCLE

STARTING POINT

● Form a single-file line at **C** facing **H**.

HOW DO I RIDE THIS?

1 Ride counterclockwise to **H**.

2 Make a large circle between **H**, **X**, **M**, and **C**.

TURN THROUGH THE CIRCLE

STARTING POINT

● Form a single-file line at **B** facing **M**.

HOW DO I RIDE THIS?

1 Ride to **M**.

2 Ride a full counterclockwise circle, beginning at **M**.

3 Back at **M**, ride counterclockwise to the center of the circle.

4 Ride clockwise from the center of the circle to **H**.

5 Circle clockwise from **H** to **M**.

KEEP IN MIND

◆ Be a BRATT (see page 23).
◆ The legs, seat, and rein are all aids for keeping the horse bending on the circle and not falling in or out of the circle.
◆ To help visualize the circle, imagine riding on the outer edge of the face of a clock to each quarter hour.

VARIATIONS

◆ Ride a circle at the other end of the arena or in the center.
◆ Vary the size of the circle. If there are not enough members to make a large circle, you can make your circle smaller so that the front of the line meets the back, or spread out the riders (open formation) more evenly.

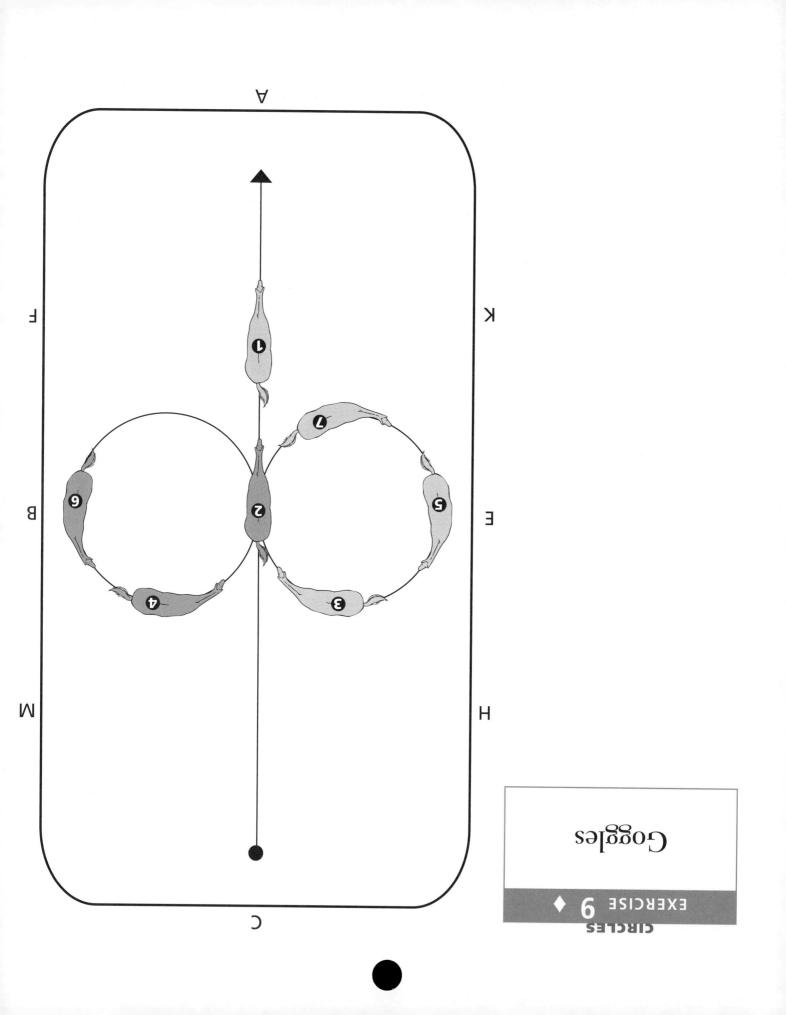

9. Goggles

STARTING POINT

● Form a single-file line at **C** in closed formation.

HOW DO I RIDE THIS?

1 Ride down the centerline.

2 When the first rider reaches **X**, circle right. When the second rider reaches **X**, circle left. Continue alternating riders to left and right.

3 The first and second riders arrive at **E** and **B** at the same time.

4 Circle back to **X**.

5 At **X**, come together in a single-file line.

6 Continue down the centerline to **A**.

KEEP IN MIND

◆ Open formation is maintained while riding the circles.
◆ The first rider times it to arrive back at **X** just before the second rider falls in behind him. The third rider paces her horse to fall in behind the number 2 horse, and so on.
◆ Partners watch each other in order to be at the same points through the exercise.
◆ Everyone must fit on the circles at the same time, so large groups may not be workable. (See suggestions below.)

VARIATIONS

◆ Ride down the centerline in pairs. Split and reunite at **X**.
◆ When riders reunite at **X**, you can split again and do larger circles that intersect (see Exercise 28: Wedding Ring). Meet again and form a single-file line at **X**.

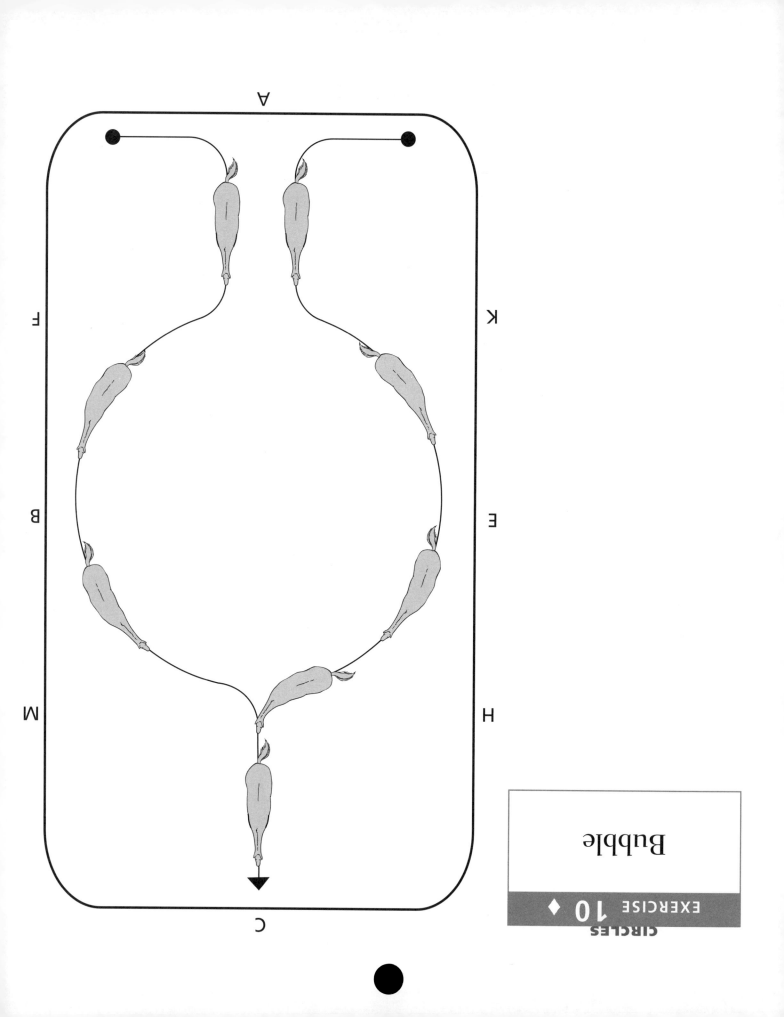

A

F

K

B

E

M

H

C

Bubble

10. Bubble

STARTING POINT

● Form two single-file lines facing each other along the fence at **A** in open formation.

HOW DO I RIDE THIS?

1 Ride down the centerline and form pairs.

2 Proceed down the centerline, passing **K** and **F**.

3 Immediately turn away from your partner and make a half-circle toward **B** or **E**.

4 After you pass the letter, continue on the half-circle back to the centerline between **H** and **M**.

5 At the centerline, every other horse will merge into a single-file line.

KEEP IN MIND

◆ Riders keep their eyes on **C**. At the beginning, they ride their side of the centerline.

◆ Riders watch their partners out of the corners of their eyes as they proceed down the centerline and around the circle to be sure that both are at the same point throughout the exercise.

◆ As riders approach the merge point, they rate their horses to arrive at the appropriate time to merge into the line. Riders take turns alternating sides as they merge (one from the left, one from the right).

◆ Decide ahead of time who is to go first in the merge.

VARIATIONS

◆ Start in one line and alternate left and right splits with every other rider.

◆ Start or end in pairs, fours, or sixes.

pro tip

Always smile, have good posture, and be in control of your horse at all times.

— The All-American Cowgirl Chicks
Fort Worth, Texas

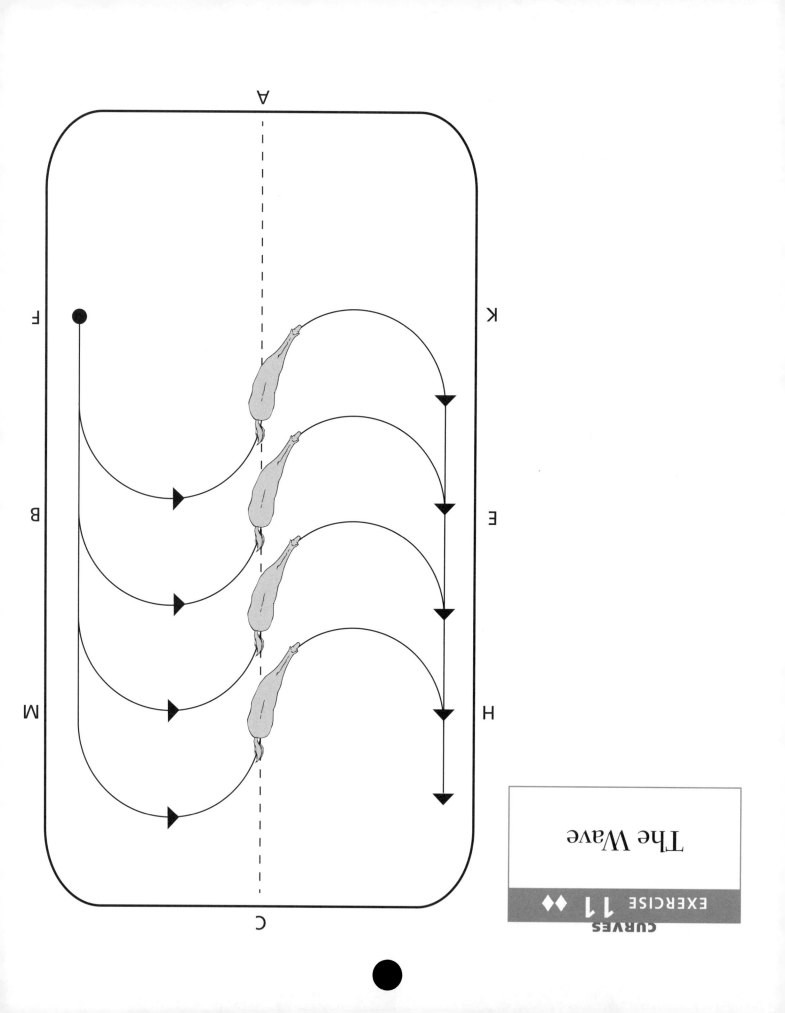

11. The Wave

STARTING POINT

● Form a single-file line, in closed formation, at **F** facing **B**.

HOW DO I RIDE THIS?

1 When everyone is centered on the long side (not too close to either end), the caller signals.

2 Ride a half-circle to the centerline.

3 Everyone forms a single-file line on the centerline, facing **A**.

4 The caller signals. Riders ride another half-circle to the opposite fence.

5 On the fence, riders ride single-file toward **H**.

KEEP IN MIND

◆ The rider at the end of the line is the best person to give the signal for the first turn since she can see when the line is centered.
◆ Riders are side-by-side during the half-circles with bodies parallel.
◆ During the half-circles, riders watch the riders on either side of them and regulate the pace accordingly.
◆ The horses may move several steps ahead on the centerline before the caller signals for the turn. This gives the caller a better vantage point, and it is more appealing to the audience to see the line curve, straighten, and curve again.

VARIATION

◆ Turn so that two riders ride the same path (riders 1 and 2 would be together, as would 3 and 4, and so on). The initial spacing must be great enough to accommodate two horses falling back into line on the centerline.

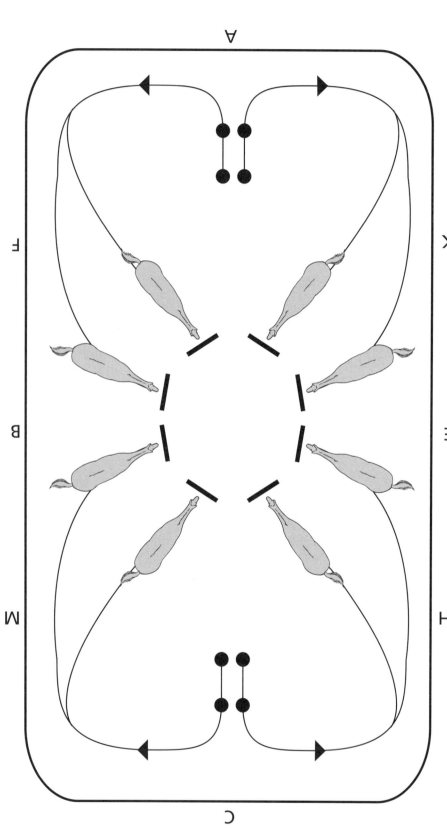

CURVES EXERCISE 12 ◆◆

Powwow

INCREASING DIFFICULTY:
SLIDING STOP

12. Powwow

STARTING POINT

● Form two sets of pairs, one facing **C** and one facing **A**, in closed formation.

HOW DO I RIDE THIS?

1 Ride toward **C** or **A**.

2 At the letter, pairs split right and left into single-file lines.

3 Move toward the center of the arena on your own path, with about 3.3 meters (11 feet) between you and the horses next to you.

4 You and the other horses halt in a circle at the same time.

HOW DO I GET OUT OF THIS?

- ◆ Circle Right (see Exercise 16).
- ◆ Try a weave. Divide the circle in half. Two curved lines facing each other move forward and pass left hand to left hand (see Exercise 94).
- ◆ Try Opposing Carousel Turn-Through (see Exercise 23, step 2). Every other rider moves forward and turns in front of the rider to the left, forming a clockwise circle. The riders left behind turn right, forming a counter-clockwise circle.

KEEP IN MIND

- ◆ Spacing and timing are very important because everyone arrives at the circle at the same time.
- ◆ Riders remain aware of where the other riders are and pace themselves accordingly.
- ◆ Riders are BRATTs (see page 23).

INCREASING DIFFICULTY

- ◆ Increase the speed.
- ◆ Perform simultaneous sliding stops to make this drill more complex and exciting. Be careful; no crashes allowed!

VARIATIONS

- ◆ Pairs head toward **C** and **A**. At the letter, they all turn right, merging every other horse into a single-file line next to the rail.
- ◆ Horses turn and move independently toward the center of the arena to form a circle.
- ◆ Halt with about 3 meters (10 feet) of space beside each horse.

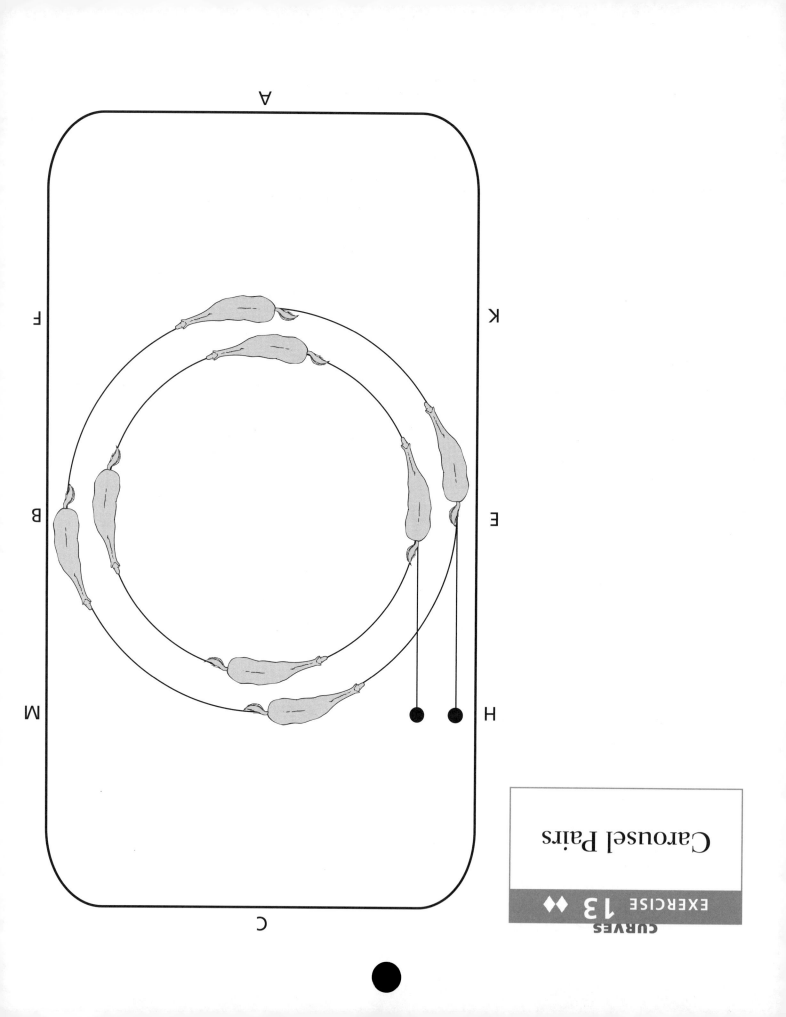

A

F

K

B

E

M

H

C

13. Carousel Pairs

STARTING POINT

● Pairs line up at **H**.

HOW DO I RIDE THIS?

1 Ride down the rail to **E**.

2 Make two large circles to **B** and back to **E** again as pairs.

Try to perfect one routine.

— **Sergeant Mayo**
Royal Canadian Mounted Police
Ontario, Canada

- - - - - - - - - - - - - - - - - -

KEEP IN MIND

◆ The outside horse is slightly ahead of the inside horse, as he has more steps to take.
◆ Partners watch each other's bodies to stay aligned.

VARIATIONS

◆ Vary the speed. Have the inside horses ride one gait slower than the outside horses. Try inside halt, outside walk; inside walk, outside trot or jog; or inside trot or jog, outside canter or lope.
◆ Resume pairs before exiting the carousel or have riders in the outside circle peel off to the wall, followed by the inside circle, forming a single-file line.

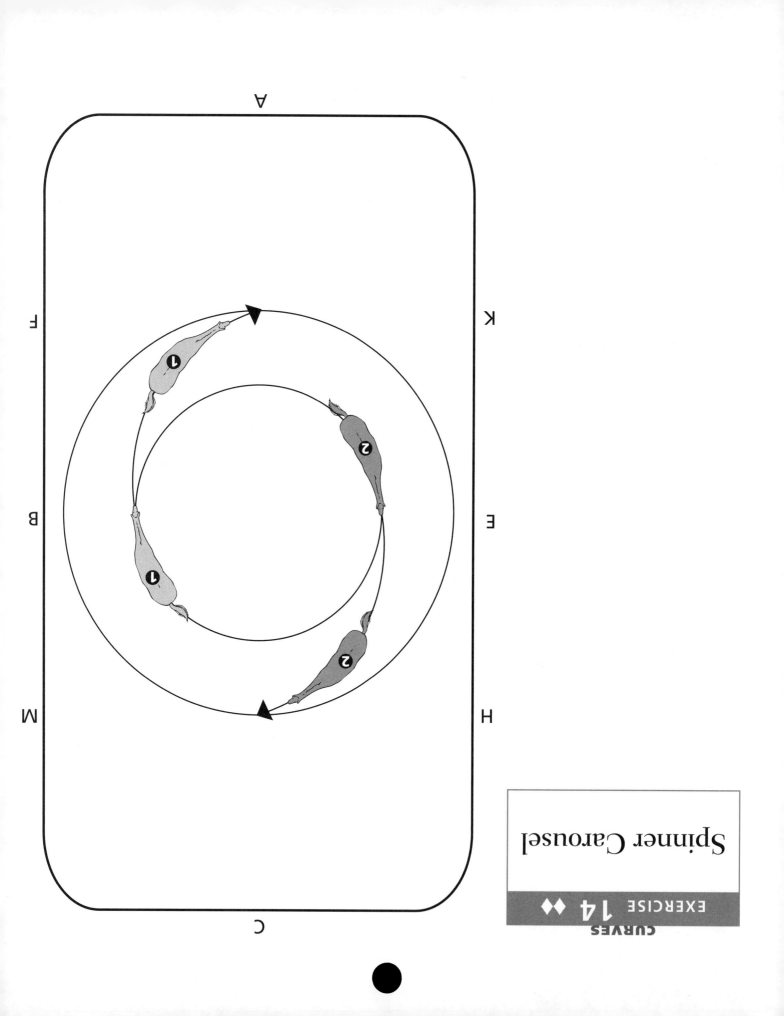

A

F

K

B

E

M

H

C

Spinner Carousel

CURVES   EXERCISE 14 ◆◆

14. Spinner Carousel

STARTING POINT

● Start with everyone in a small circle in closed formation. Line 2 follows line 1.

HOW DO I RIDE THIS?

1 The caller gives the signal.

2 Each line spirals out to a larger, open-formation circle until everyone is working on the larger circle.

KEEP IN MIND

◆ Riders move into open formation as they move out to the larger circle.
◆ Spacing is kept even.
◆ The size of the circle may need to change in order to look like a continuous circle.

VARIATION

◆ Start with a large circle in open formation and spin down to a small circle in closed formation.

pro tip

Place safety first: Always check your tack and have the proper tack to avoid any accidents. Always use your head.

— **The All-American Cowgirl Chicks**
Fort Worth, Texas

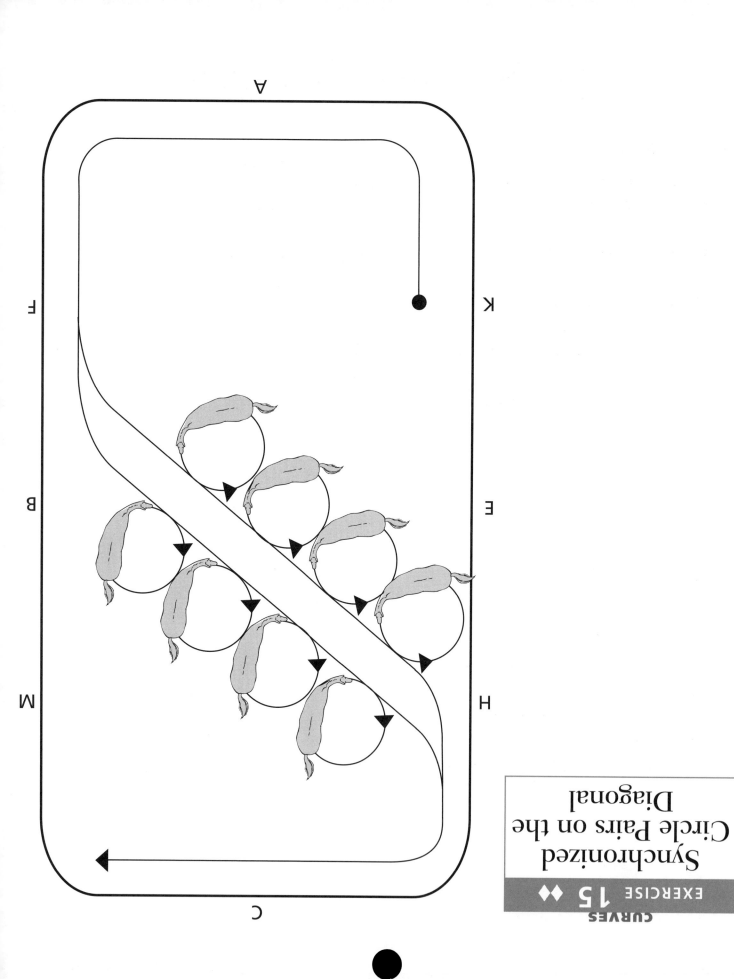

15. Synchronized Circle Pairs on the Diagonal

STARTING POINT

● Form a single-file line in closed formation at **K** facing **A**.

HOW DO I RIDE THIS?

1 Ride in a single-file line to **F**.

2 At **F**, riders turn to form pairs across the diagonal in open formation.

3 When all pairs are on the diagonal, the caller (at the back of the line) signals.

4 Partners immediately turn and make a small circle away from each other.

5 When pairs come back together, they continue across the diagonal.

6 At **H**, every other rider merges into a single-file line.

KEEP IN MIND

◆ When turning across the diagonal in pairs, riders focus on a point before **H**. Riders ride their side of the diagonal line, keeping the line straight and staying directly behind the rider ahead.

◆ All riders finish their circle at the same time. Riders watch the riders on either side to ensure this.

◆ On the straightaway, riders' bodies align. While practicing on the ground, riders give each other high fives when they return to their partners.

INCREASING DIFFICULTY

◆ Increase the speed.

◆ Do turns on the forehand, turns on the haunches, pivots, or spins instead of the circles.

VARIATION

◆ Do the exercise down the centerline to make it easier.

View of sidestep. To do a turn on the forehand, your horse's inside hind leg crosses in front of his outside hind leg.

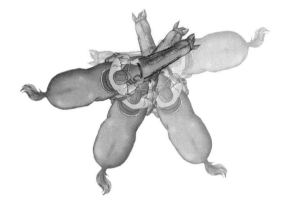

Turn on forehand. Your horse's haunches move around his outside front foot until you are lined up clockwise on the circle.

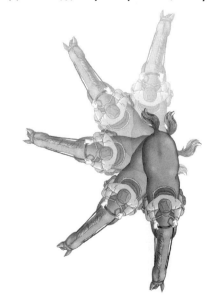

Pivot, spin, or turn on haunches. Western riders ride a pivot or spin. English riders do a turn on the haunches or a pirouette. Both English and Western riders turn on the right hind leg.

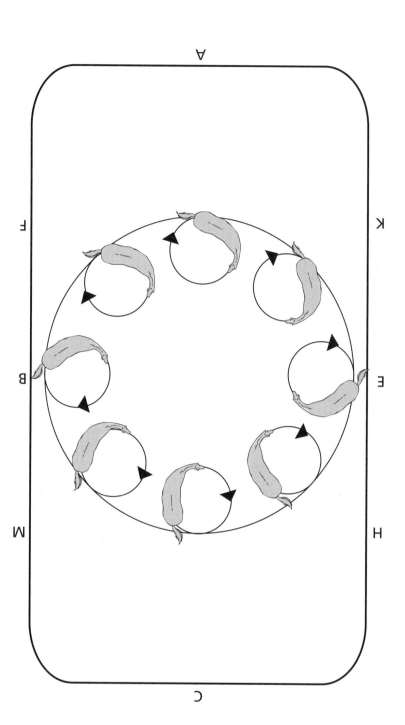

A

K

F

B

E

M

H

C

Circle Right

16. Circle Right

STARTING POINT

● Begin in a circle, with everyone facing the center. There should be about 3 meters (10 feet) between horses.

HOW DO I RIDE THIS?

1 The caller gives a signal (voice or whistle).

2 Riders turn right to form small clockwise circles.

KEEP IN MIND

◆ If the spacing is too close, this exercise descends into chaos.

◆ Everyone moves off at the same time.

◆ Sluggish horses need earlier signals than do the faster horses.

◆ Riders on hotter horses (horses who respond more quickly than average to cues) wait to give their signals until the slower horses appear to be ready to move.

◆ Riders watch the riders beside them to help stay in the same position on the turn.

VARIATIONS

◆ Instead of small circles, do pivots, spins, turns on the haunches, or turns on the forehand.

◆ Start on a single-file circle. At the signal, everyone circles right at the same time and then continues on the circle.

◆ At the beginning or end of a drill, have all horses circle and end up facing outward as they halt and salute.

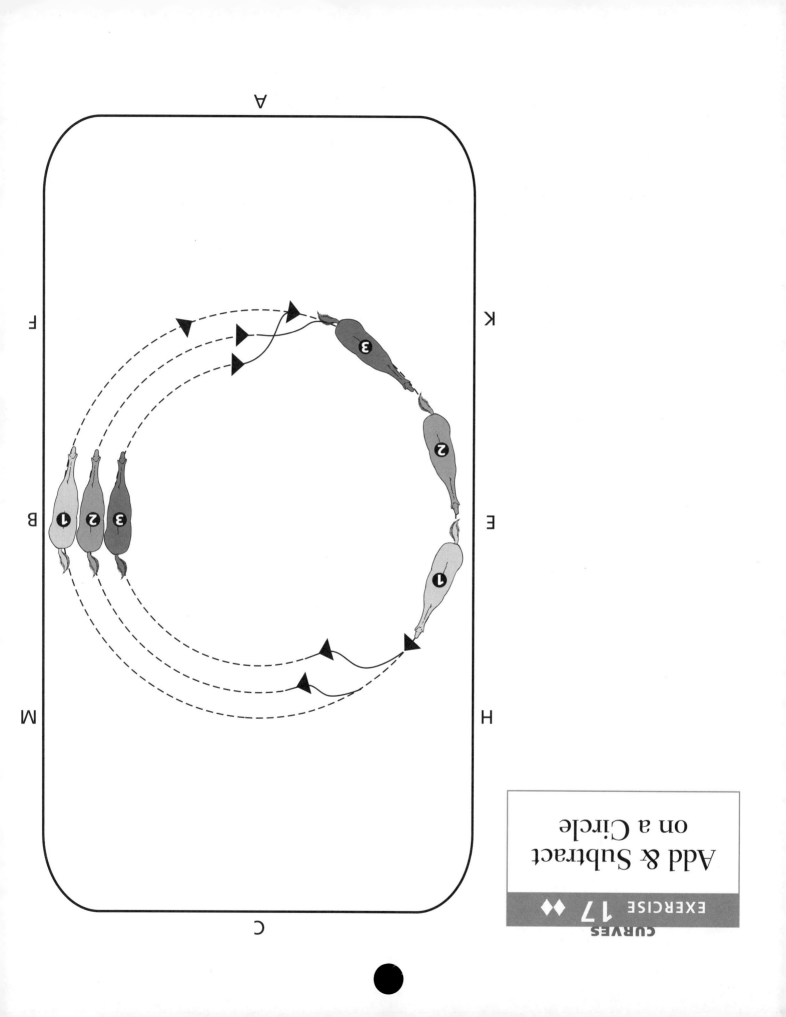

CURVES
EXERCISE 17 ◆◆
Add & Subtract
on a Circle

17. Add & Subtract on a Circle

STARTING POINT

● Form a single-file, closed-formation circle between **E** and **B**. Count off the riders by threes.

HOW DO I RIDE THIS?

1 Ride a large circle.

2 The caller gives a signal.

3 Number 1 riders stay on the outside track. Number 2 riders pull to the inside of the number 1 riders. Number 3 riders pull to the inside beside the number 2 riders.

4 Continue riding side by side around the circle for one complete revolution.

5 The caller gives a signal.

6 Number 2 horses fall back into place behind the number 1s as the number 3 horses move back into place behind the number 2s.

7 Continue circling in single file for one revolution.

KEEP IN MIND

◆ The number 1 horses keep a steady pace while the number 2 and 3 horses increase their pace to move alongside the number 1s. When it is time for number 2 and number 3 riders to move behind number 1 riders, they slow their pace.

INCREASING DIFFICULTY

◆ Use a leg yield to transition to the new track.

VARIATIONS

◆ Increase or decrease the number of horses to suit your needs.
◆ Stagger the groups on the inner circles to form a sweep.
◆ Have a rider in the middle carry a flag and do a spin or a pirouette.

pro tip

Use proper flag etiquette. Always be respectful of the flags and their purpose.

— **The All-American Cowgirl Chicks**
Fort Worth, Texas

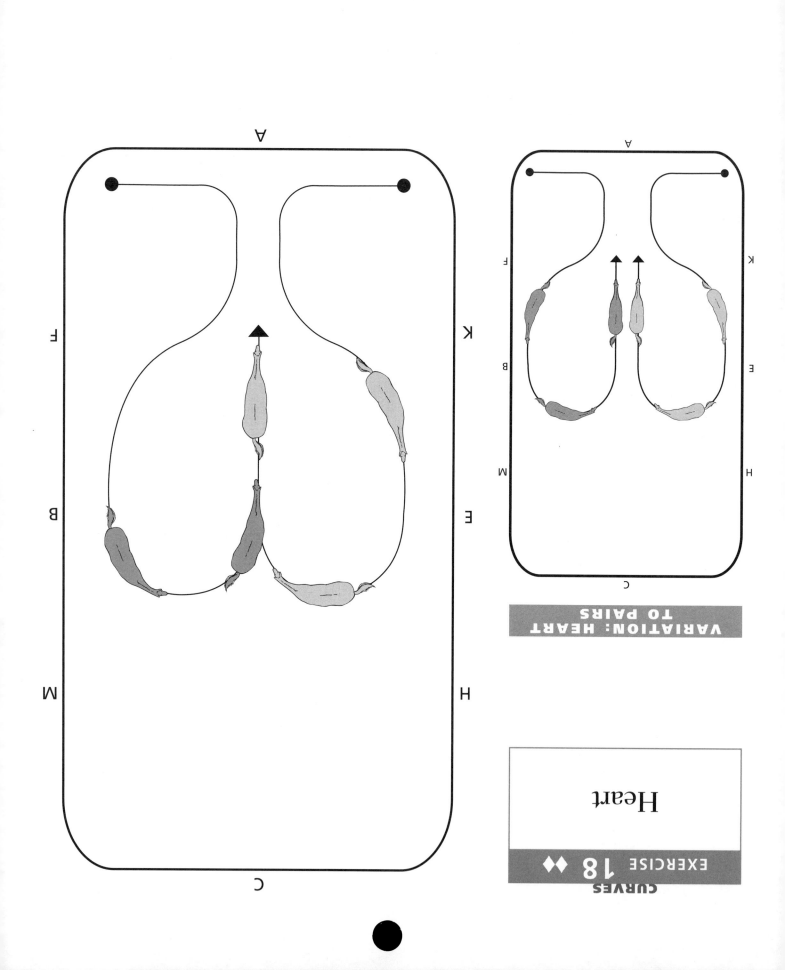

Heart

18. Heart

STARTING POINT

● Form single-file, open-formation lines facing each other along the fence at **A**.

HOW DO I RIDE THIS?

1 Turn down the centerline in pairs.

2 Proceed down the centerline passing **K** and **F**.

3 Turn away from your partner and make a half-circle toward **B** or **E**. Each pair of horses turns at the same location as the first pair.

4 After you pass letters **B** and **E**, turn toward the centerline, moving back toward **A**.

5 Merge into a single-file line at **X**.

KEEP IN MIND

◆ Partners pair up as riders turn down the center-line. Riders look at **C** and ride their side of the centerline.

◆ Riders watch the whole team to make sure that their half-circle synchronizes with the other half-circle.

◆ After passing **B** and **E**, riders watch the other line and rate their horses to fit into the single-file line at **X**.

INCREASING DIFFICULTY

◆ Ride in pairs, threes, or fours.

VARIATION

◆ Begin or end this exercise in single file, in pairs, or in threes, fours, or sixes.

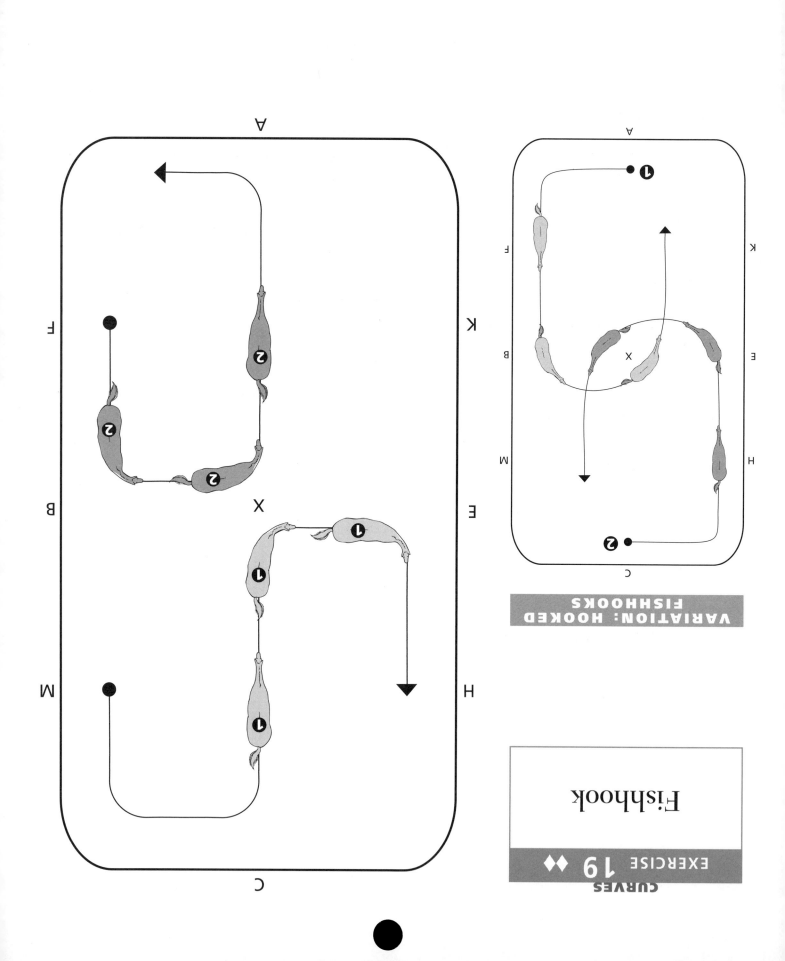

VARIATION: HOOKED FISHHOOKS

19. Fishhook

STARTING POINT

● Number 1 riders stand at **M** facing **C**, single file in closed formation.

● Number 2 riders stand at **F** behind number 1s, single file in closed formation.

HOW DO I RIDE THIS?

1 Number 1 riders ride to **C** and turn down the centerline. Number 2 riders ride to **B** and turn toward **X**.

2 Partners pair up momentarily at **X**.

3 Number 1 riders turn toward **E** and number 2 riders turn toward **A**.

4 Number 1 riders turn right at the rail, number 2 riders turn left.

KEEP IN MIND

◆ Partners keep watching each other to ensure that they meet at **X** at the same time.

◆ Riders turn close together at **X** to present a crisp appearance.

INCREASING DIFFICULTY

◆ Ride the centerline shoulder-in, haunches-in, or passage (a very collected, cadenced, and elevated trot).

◆ Increase the speed.

VARIATION

◆ **HOOKED FISHHOOKS**

1 Line 1 starts at **A**, facing **F**, and line 2 starts at **C**, facing **H**.

2 Lines ride forward along the rail in open formation.

3 At **B** and **E**, horses arc toward **X**.

4 At **X**, partners pass on the right (left hands together).

5 Partners turn behind each other and continue down the quarter lines toward where they came from.

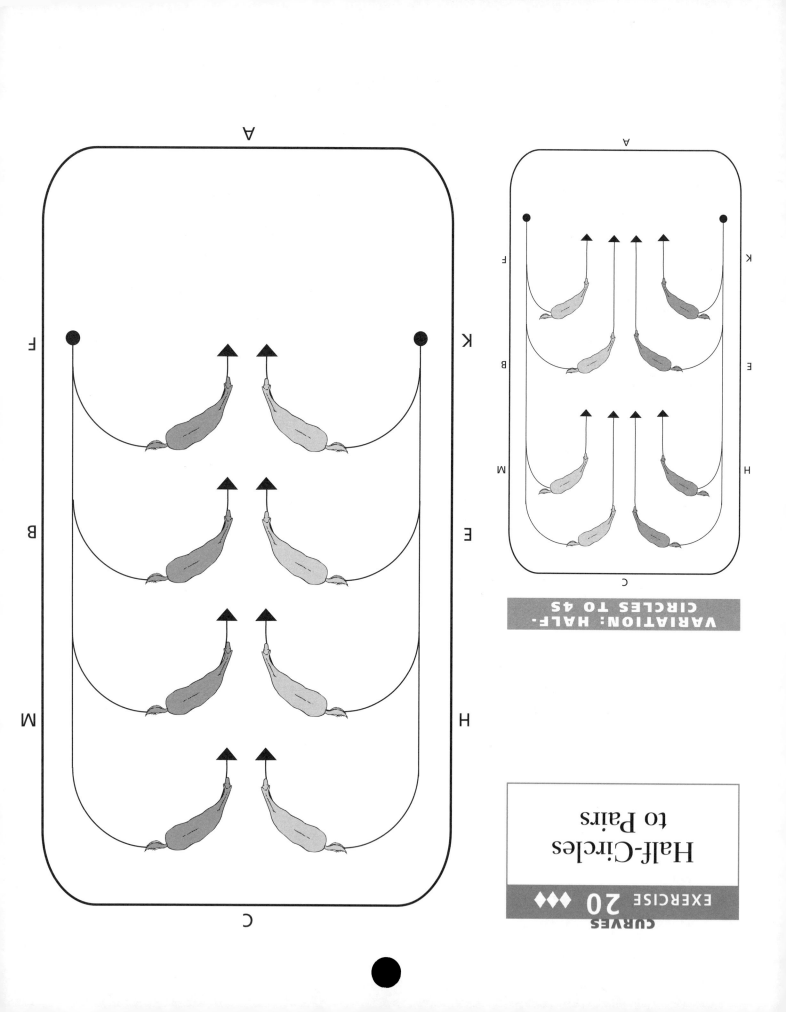

Half-Circles
to Pairs

VARIATION: HALF-
CIRCLES TO 4S

20. Half-Circles to Pairs

STARTING POINT

● Form two closed-formation lines at **K** and **F**, facing **E** and **B**.

HOW DO I RIDE THIS?

1 When all riders are centered along the rail, the caller signals.

2 Riders ride a counterclockwise half-circle to the centerline.

3 Partners pair up from the opposite line and ride in pairs down the centerline toward **A**.

KEEP IN MIND

◆ Partners watch each other.
◆ Riders look at **A** while turning.
◆ Be a BRATT (see page 23).

VARIATION

◆ Ride two, three, or four abreast down both rails. Turn to the centerline and ride four, six, or eight abreast.

pro tip

When turning down the centerline in pairs, look where you need to ride your line. The rider who is on the left side turns and rides just slightly left of the centerline as the rider on the right side turns and rides slightly right of centerline. Ride your line with your eyes and you will go there.

— **Stephanie Dobiss**
Keystone Dressage and Combined Training
Association of Central Pennsylvania

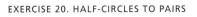

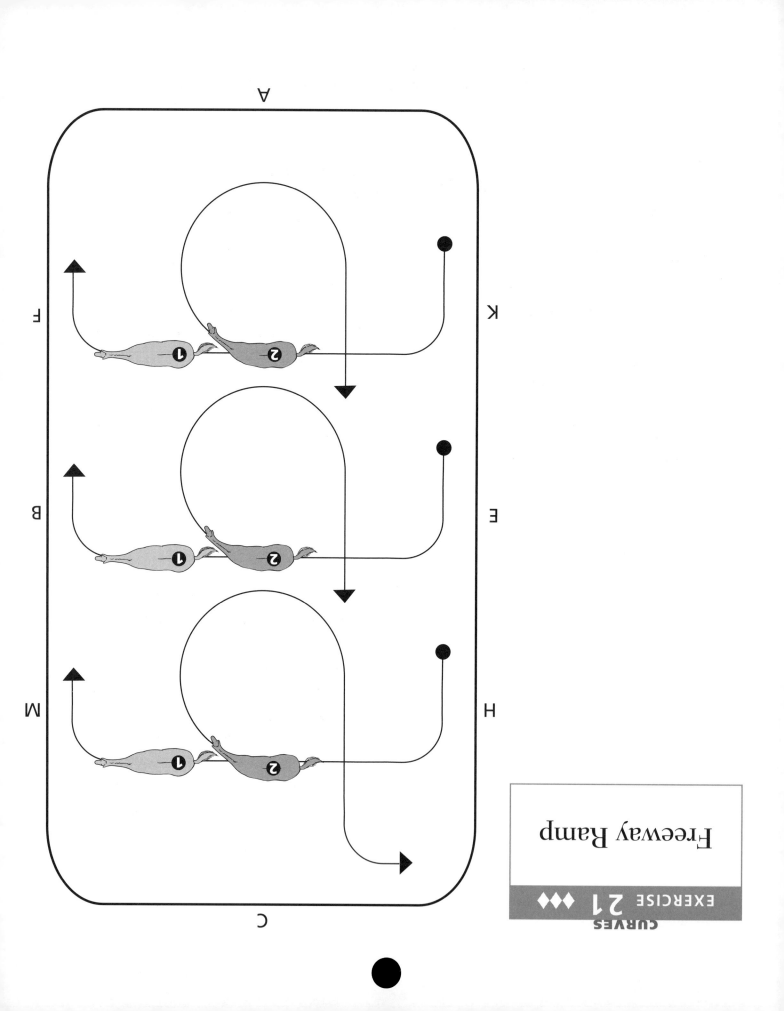

Freeway Ramp

21. Freeway Ramp

STARTING POINT

● Form a single-file, closed-formation line at **K** facing **H** and count off by twos.

HOW DO I RIDE THIS?

1 The caller gives a signal.

2 Each set of riders (1 and 2) makes an abreast turn right in single file.

3 All riders proceed straight across the arena.

4 At the centerline, number 2s circle right simultaneously.

5 Number 2s form a single-file line and continue up the quarterline toward **C**.

6 At the **M-B-F** rail, 1s turn right. At **C**, 2s turn left.

KEEP IN MIND

◆ The caller is the last rider. He gives the signal when he sees that the line is centered on the rail.
◆ Number 2s, who are circling away from number 1s, put their left legs behind the girth/cinch to encourage their horses to turn. This persuades the horses not to be herd-bound.
◆ Partners watch each other while riding toward the centerline.

INCREASING DIFFICULTY

◆ Approach this in shoulder-in or haunches-in.
◆ Instead of forming a circle, ride a spin or a pirouette.
◆ Have 1s bear flags and halt on the centerline while 2s circle around them.

VARIATIONS

◆ Ride this in reverse to form a single line at the end.
◆ Change the direction in which the riders turn at the end to set them up for their next exercise.

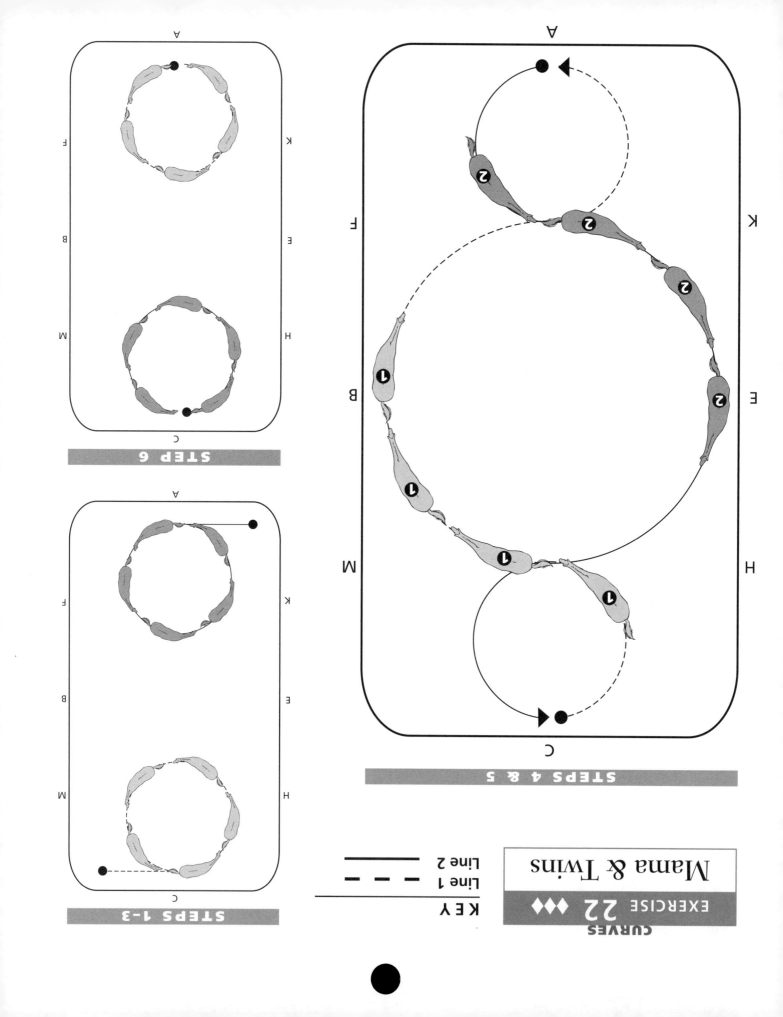

22. Mama & Twins

STARTING POINT

● Form line 1 along the rail at **C**, facing **H**.
● Form line 2 along the rail at **A**, facing **F**.

HOW DO I RIDE THIS?

1 Pass **A** or **C**.

2 Ride a small circle just big enough for the back of the line to meet the front of the line.

3 Travel one and a half revolutions.

4 Cross the centerline. Make a large half-circle to **B** or **E**.

5 Continue to the centerline.

6 Turn and make a small circle toward **A** or **C**.

KEEP IN MIND

◆ Pairs watch their partners at the other end of the arena to ensure that both are at the same point in the exercise at the same time.
◆ Riders' heads are facing forward, watching where they are going.
◆ Half-circles in each pair are the same size.

VARIATIONS

◆ Place a rider with a flag in each circle, or place just one in the middle.
◆ Have someone perform a spin or a pirouette in each circle, or someone performs just one in the middle.

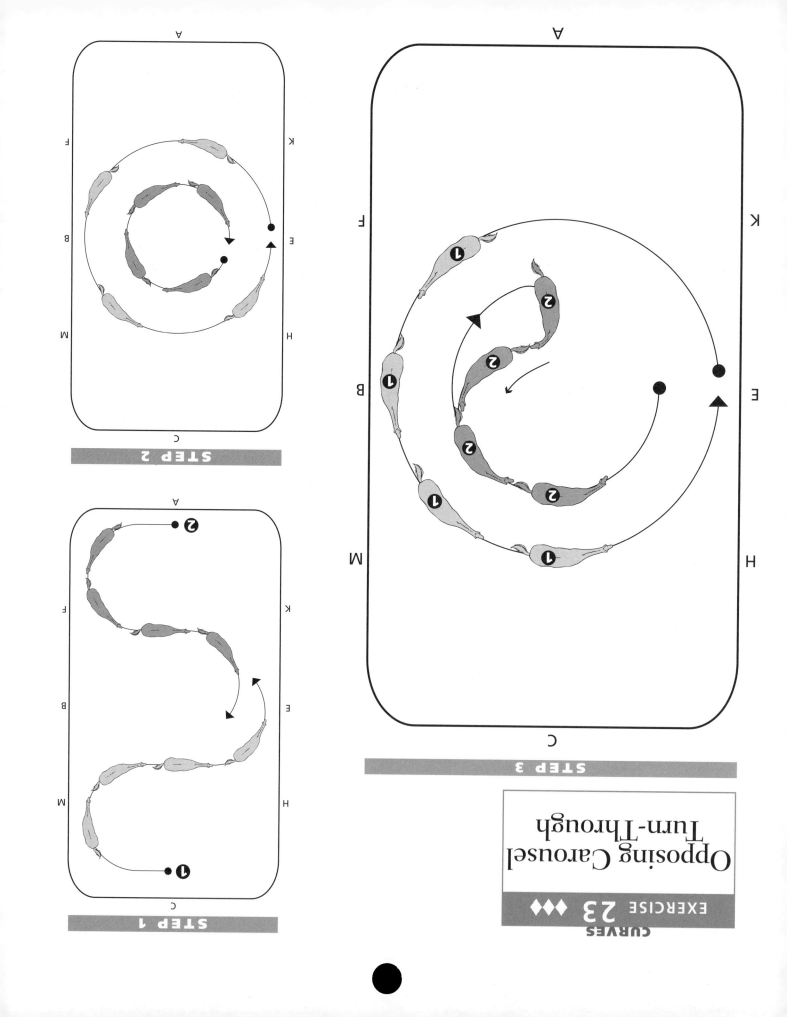

STEP 2

STEP 1

STEP 3

CURVES
EXERCISE 23 ◆◆◆
Opposing Carousel
Turn-Through

23. Opposing Carousel Turn-Through

STARTING POINT

- Form line 1 at **C**, facing **M**.
- Form line 2 at **A**, facing **F**.

HOW DO I RIDE THIS?

STEP 1: THE WRAP

1 Move forward to **M** or **F**.

2 Pass the letter and turn toward **E**, as if doing a serpentine (see Exercise 38).

3 At **E**, pass riders in the other line left hand to left hand.

STEP 2: OPPOSING CAROUSEL

Line 1 circles counterclockwise between **E** and **B**. Line 2 circles clockwise inside line 1's circle.

STEP 3: CAROUSEL TO PAIRS

1 After one revolution, line 2 turns toward the center of the circle and reverses just in time to pair up with partners from the outer circle.

2 Exit the carousel in pairs.

KEEP IN MIND

- When approaching the other line head-on, riders stay to the right (left hand to left hand).
- Practice helps to get the timing correct for the reverse.

VARIATION

- After one or two revolutions on the opposing carousel, skip the reverse. Have one line return to the wall at the same time as the other line and continue straight along the fence as two single-file lines going in opposite directions.

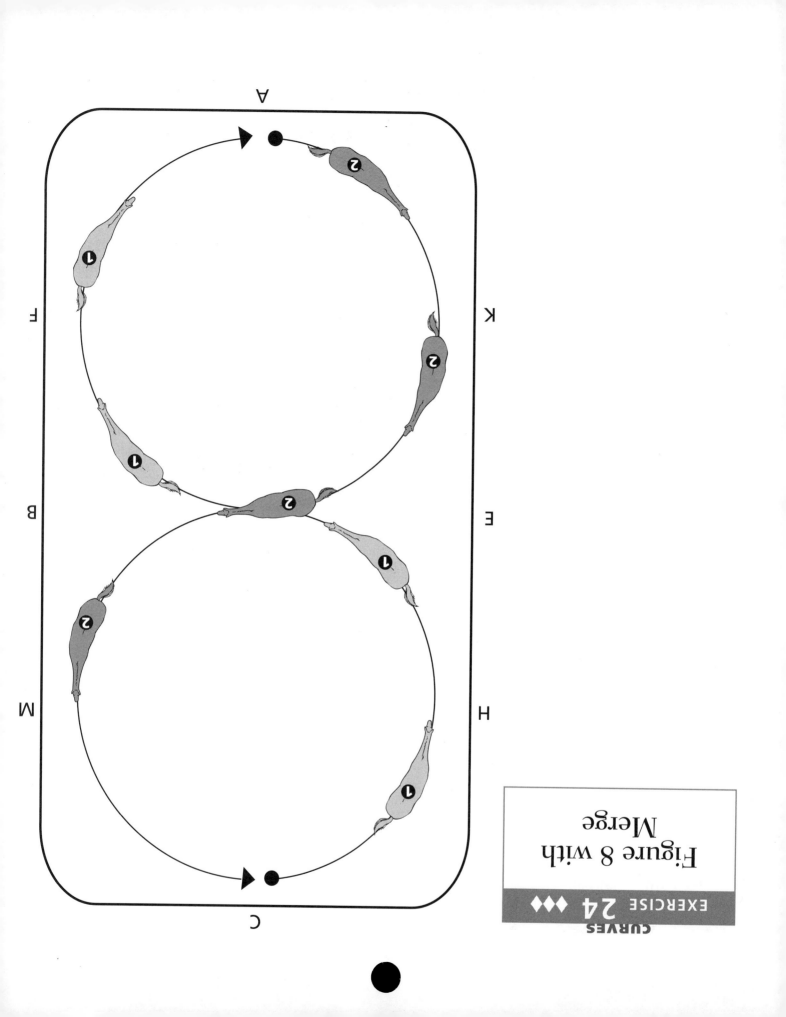

24. Figure 8 with Merge

STARTING POINT

- Form line 1 at **C**, facing **H**, in open formation.
- Form line 2 at **A**, facing **K**, in open formation.

HOW DO I RIDE THIS?

1 Riders in line 1 move forward counterclockwise to make a half-circle from **C** to **X**. Riders in line 2 make a clockwise half-circle from **A** to **X**.

2 At **X**, lines cross, alternating riders from lines 1 and 2.

3 Riders split away from each other to continue on the figure 8. Riders in line 1 make a half-circle from **X** to **A**. Riders in line 2 make a half-circle from **X** to **C**.

4 Riders repeat this pattern on the next side to complete the figure 8.

5 Each time the team arrives at **X**, riders merge and split again into their original lines.

KEEP IN MIND

- Teams predetermine which one will cross **X** first.
- Riders watch the other line and rate their horses so lines can merge as if by magic.

INCREASING DIFFICULTY

- Increase speed.

VARIATION

- Ride figure 8 in pairs.

pro tip

Practices should be mandatory. How much you practice will be reflected in your performance.

— The All-American Cowgirl Chicks
Fort Worth, Texas

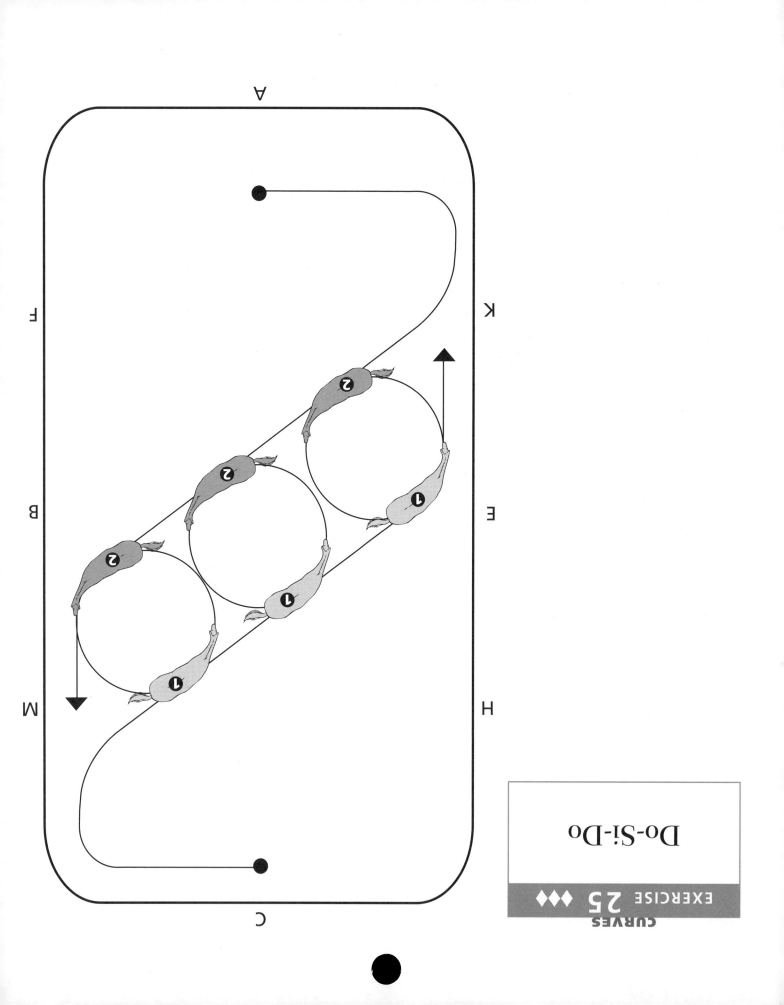

25. Do-Si-Do

STARTING POINT

● Form line 1 at **C**, facing **M**, in open formation.
● Form line 2 at **A**, facing **K**, in open formation.

HOW DO I RIDE THIS?

1 Ride past **M** and **K**.

2 Head across the diagonal. Pass the other riders left hand to left hand. Leave 3 to 5 meters (10 to 16.5 feet) between lines.

3 When you are parallel to your partner, make a small circle counter-clockwise. Partners stay directly across from each other on the circle.

4 After returning to your original position, continue across the diagonal.

KEEP IN MIND

◆ Riders watch horse-and-rider teams ahead and behind to be sure they all turn at the same rate.
◆ Circles are all the same size.
◆ Partners watch each other and stay even across the circle.

VARIATION

◆ Perform on the centerline or from **E** to **B**.

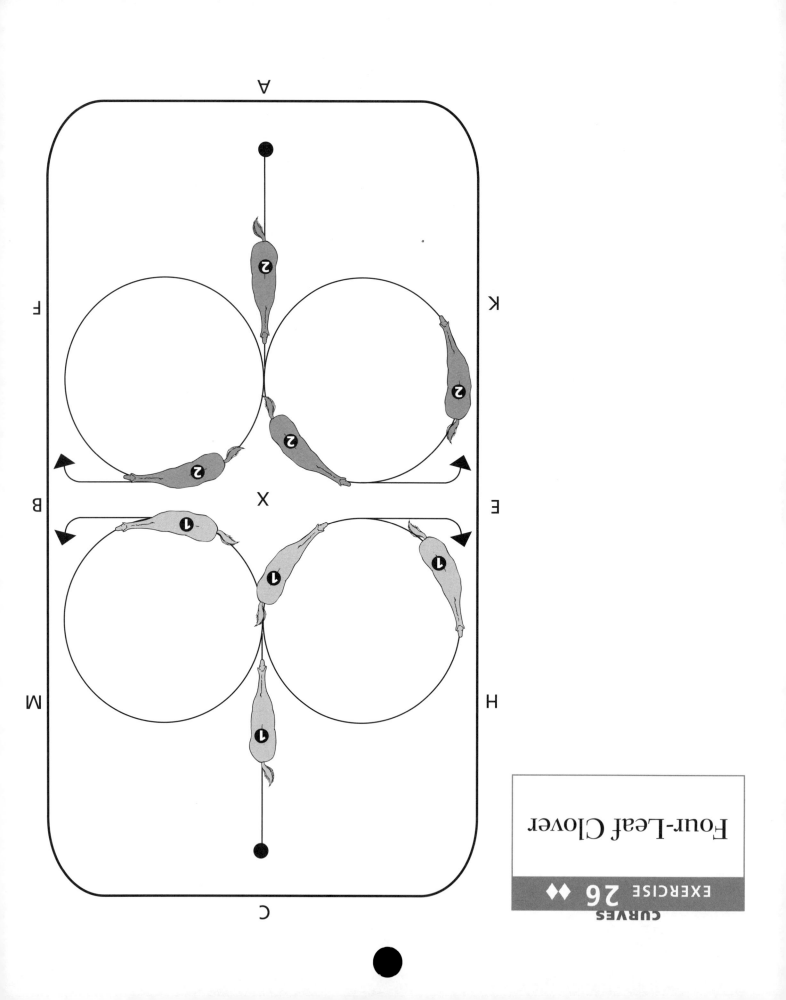

26. Four-Leaf Clover

STARTING POINT

- Form line 1 at **C**, facing **X**, in closed formation.
- Form line 2 at **A**, facing **X**, in closed formation.

HOW DO I RIDE THIS?

1 Proceed down centerline toward **X**.

2 At **X**, the first riders from each line turn as a pair toward **E**. The second riders from each line turn as a pair toward **B**.

3 Continue this pattern until everyone has turned.

4 At **E** and **B**, pairs split and each horse rides its own circle.

5 Upon reaching the centerline, briefly merge into your original line.

6 At **X**, turn toward the same letter as before.

7 At **E** and **B**, split and follow the fence line.

KEEP IN MIND

- Staring straight at **A** or **C** helps the rider to ride a straight centerline.
- Riders watch as their partners approach **X** from the opposite direction to pair themselves on their opposing circles.
- Partners watch each other to help reach the corners of the circle at the same time.
- When returning to **X**, riders leave enough space to allow others to merge into the original line.

INCREASING DIFFICULTY

- Increase the speed.

VARIATION

- Have a rider carrying a flag stand in the center of each circle before the pattern begins.

SUGGESTED EXERCISES TO LEAD OR
FOLLOW THIS ONE

◆ Exercise 31: Spin-Off Carousel
◆ Exercise 76: Meet & Greet

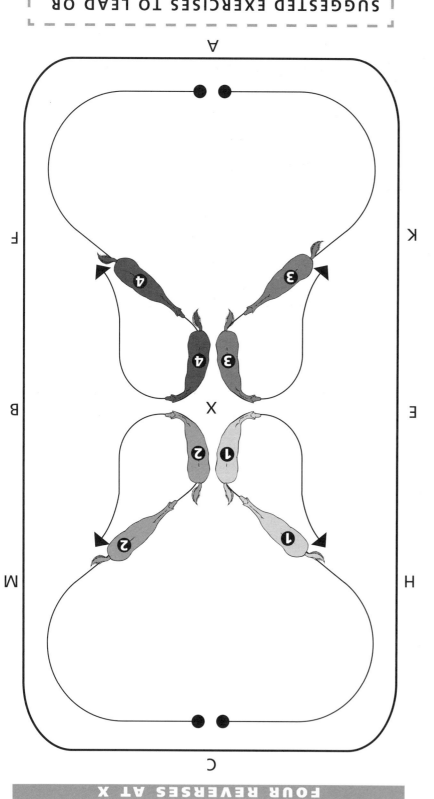

FOUR REVERSES AT X

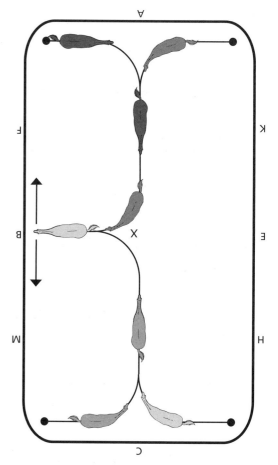

TURNING FOUR LINES INTO ONE

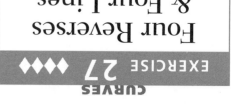

CURVES

EXERCISE 27 ◆◆◆◆

Four Reverses
& Four Lines
into One

27. Four Reverses & Four Lines into One

STARTING POINT

- Form line 1 at **C**, facing **H**, in closed formation.
- Form line 2 at **C**, facing **M**, in closed formation.
- Form line 3 at **A**, facing **K**, in closed formation.
- Form line 4 at **A**, facing **F**, in closed formation.

HOW DO I RIDE THIS?

FOUR REVERSES AT X

1 Move around the corner and pass the letter nearest you.

2 Turn toward **X**.

3 Meet up with your partner (lines 1 and 2 and lines 3 and 4 form partners) at **X**.

4 Immediately turn away from your partner and pair up with the rider from the other end of the arena who has turned in the same direction.

5 Split from your new partner and return to the same track from which you just came, heading in the reverse direction.

TURNING FOUR LINES INTO ONE

1 Move back to the corner from which you came, in open formation.

2 Turn down the centerline, merging every other horse.

3 Place yourselves back into open formation.

4 At **X**, turn toward **B** and merge every other horse into a single-file line. At **B**, continue along the fence (your team may go either right or left).

- - - - - - - - - - - - - - - - - -

KEEP IN MIND

- The riders focus on the exact path that they are riding.
- Riders are BRATTs (see page 23).
- The reverses are uniform in shape and size.

- - - - - - - - - - - - - - - - - -

VARIATION

- Perform this in pairs.

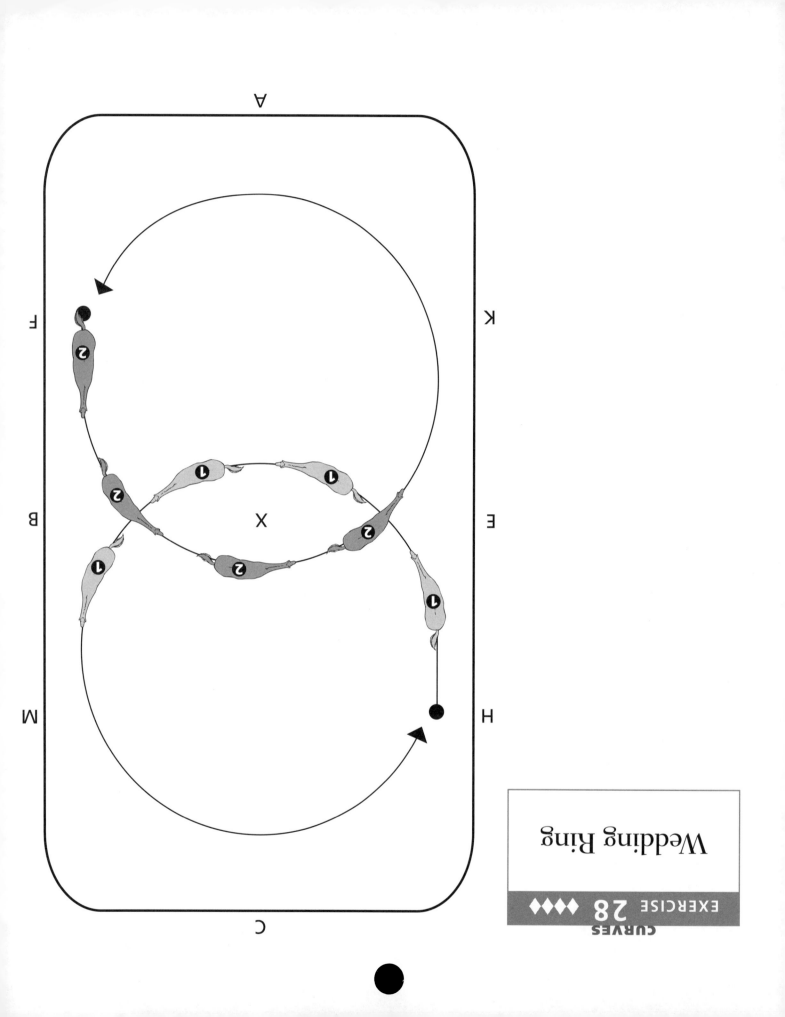

CURVES
EXERCISE 28 ◆◆◆◆

Wedding Ring

28. Wedding Ring

STARTING POINT

● Form line 1 at **H**, facing **E**, in open formation.
● Form line 2 at **F**, facing **B**, in open formation.

HOW DO I RIDE THIS?

1 Ride two large circles that intersect near **X**.

2 Allow two horses at a time to cross one side of the opposing circle before crossing the other side.

pro tip

Practice the things that you don't think are seen by an audience, such as mounting and dismounting, because there is always someone watching. Everyone should do the movement the same way.

— **Sergeant Mayo**
Royal Canadian Mounted Police
Ontario, Canada

KEEP IN MIND

◆ With a small group, the first riders meet at the first intersection point so that everyone can thread through the opposing line.

INCREASING DIFFICULTY

◆ Increase the speed.
◆ Use smaller spacing.

VARIATION

◆ Ride this in pairs, threes, or fours.

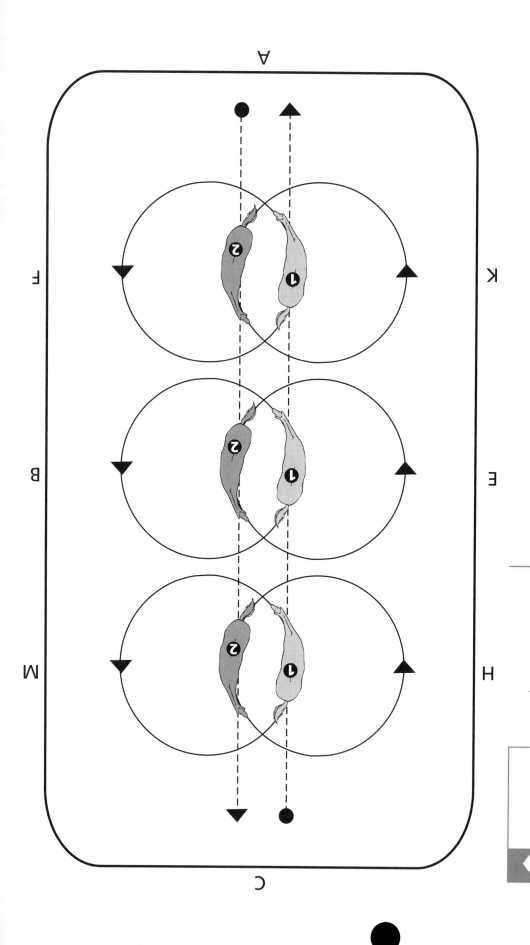

Swing Your Partner

This exercise is considered difficult because of the tightness of the circle. Try Exercise 15: Synchronized Circle Pairs on the Diagonal before you attempt this one.

29. Swing Your Partner

STARTING POINT

● Form line 1 at **C**, facing **A**, in open formation.
● Form line 2 at **A**, facing **C**, in open formation.

HOW DO I RIDE THIS?

1 Move ahead, staying to the right of the centerline.

2 When you are beside your partner, left hand to left hand and nose to tail, circle left. Your horse's nose should turn toward your partner's horse's tail. Pass behind your partner.

3 Continue on a small circle left until you are back where you started.

4 Continue down the centerline in two single-file lines, as before.

KEEP IN MIND

◆ Be a BRATT (see page 23).
◆ Pace yourself to synchronize with your partner, the pair in front, and the pair behind, at each quarter-point of the circle.
◆ Ride an accurate 10-meter (33-foot) circle or smaller. Imagine turning around a barrel as in barrel racing.
◆ The circle is big enough for riders to comfortably turn and avoid crashes.
◆ Watch where you are going.
◆ This closeness makes some horses uncomfortable. Watch for aggressive behavior and curb it.

VARIATIONS

◆ Do only half of a circle and go in the opposite direction from which you came.
◆ Do the circles from **E** to **B**, on the diagonal, or along the quarter line. (Leave ample room wherever you perform the exercise.)

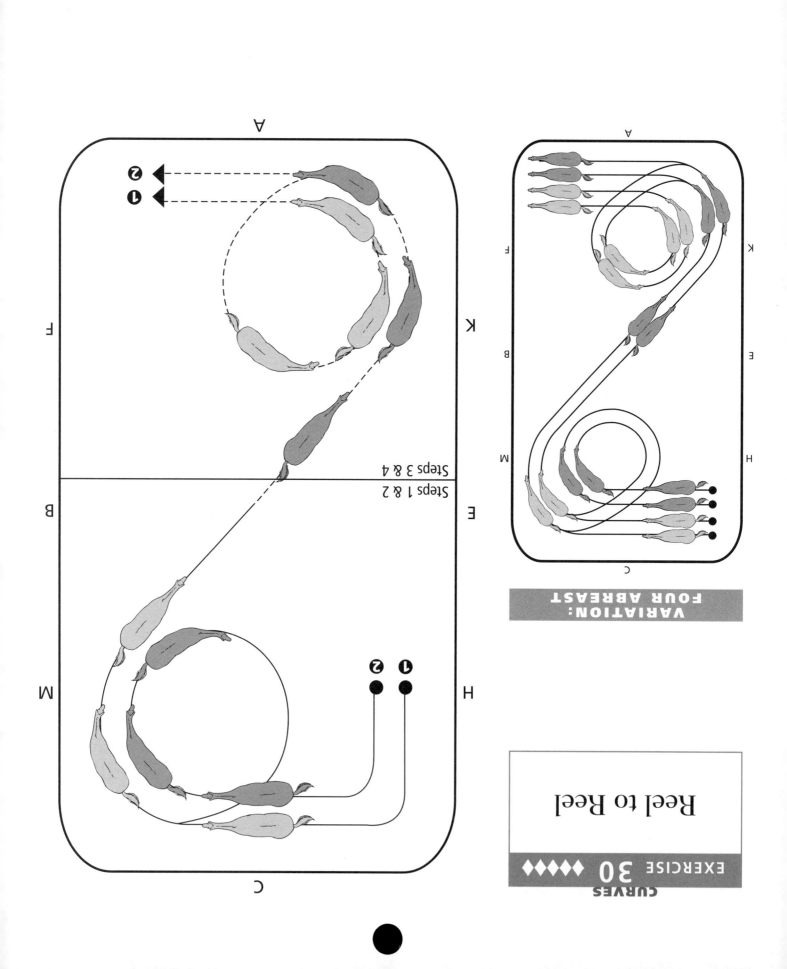

CURVES
EXERCISE 30 ◆◆◆◆◆

Reel to Reel

VARIATION: FOUR ABREAST

Steps 1 & 2
Steps 3 & 4

30. Reel to Reel

STARTING POINT

● Form line 1 by rail at **H**, facing **C**, in closed formation.

● Form line 2 on the inside track at **H**, facing **C**, in closed formation.

Lines 1 and 2 form pairs.

HOW DO I RIDE THIS?

1 Riders ride ahead as pairs.

2 At **M**, line 1 rides across the diagonal. Line 2 circles and enters into the line behind line 1.

3 At **K**, line 1 circles and pairs up with partners from line 2. Line 2 continues riding along the rail toward **A**.

4 Riders continue along the rail as pairs.

KEEP IN MIND

◆ In the corners, the outside horse speeds up while the inside horse slows.

◆ Pacing is important.

◆ Watch your partner's body for positioning.

INCREASING DIFFICULTY

◆ Increase the speed.

◆ Ride three or four abreast.

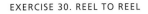

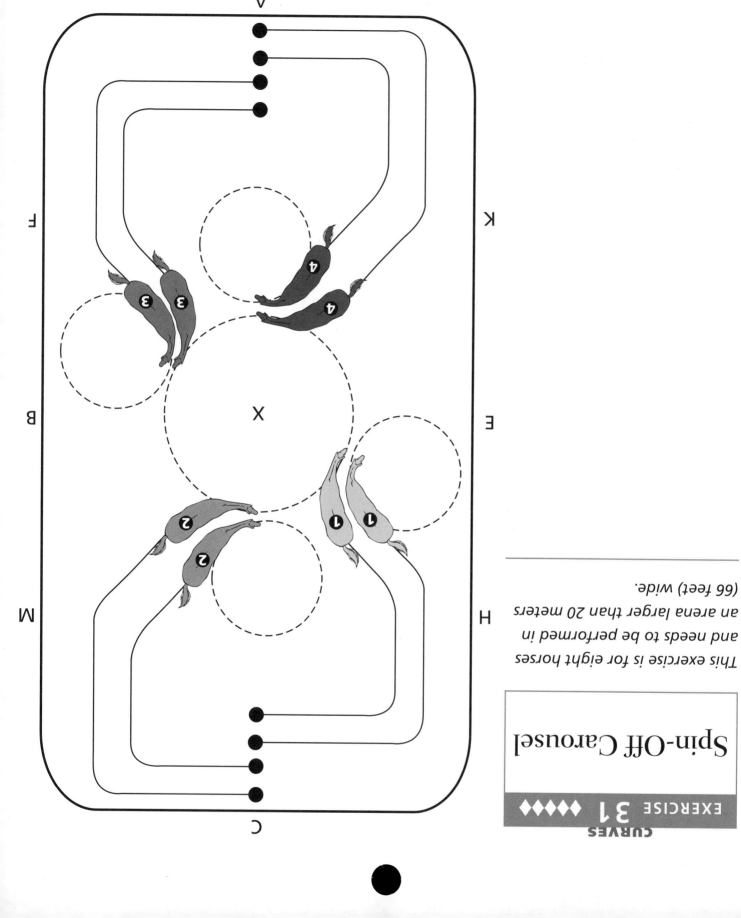

Spin-Off Carousel

This exercise is for eight horses and needs to be performed in an arena larger than 20 meters (66 feet) wide.

31. Spin-Off Carousel

STARTING POINT

- Form pair 1 at **C**, facing **H**.
- Form pair 2 at **C**, facing **M**.
- Form pair 3 at **A**, facing **F**.
- Form pair 4 at **A**, facing **K**.

HOW DO I RIDE THIS?

1 Proceed straight ahead and through the corner as if you are going to cross on the diagonal.

2 At the quarter line, riders on the left of each pair form a small circle around **X**. Riders on the right of each pair circle right.

3 The center circle turns one revolution. Riders on the right circle back to pair up with their partners on the center circle.

KEEP IN MIND

- Be a BRATT (see page 23).
- Riders circling away look at their partner as soon as they begin to turn back toward the center circle to gauge their distance and speed.
- Keep turns uniform so that circles remain round.

VARIATIONS

- In step 3, when riders pair back up, ride the small circle to the right as pairs.
- Have riders who spin off to the right do pirouettes or spins instead of circles.

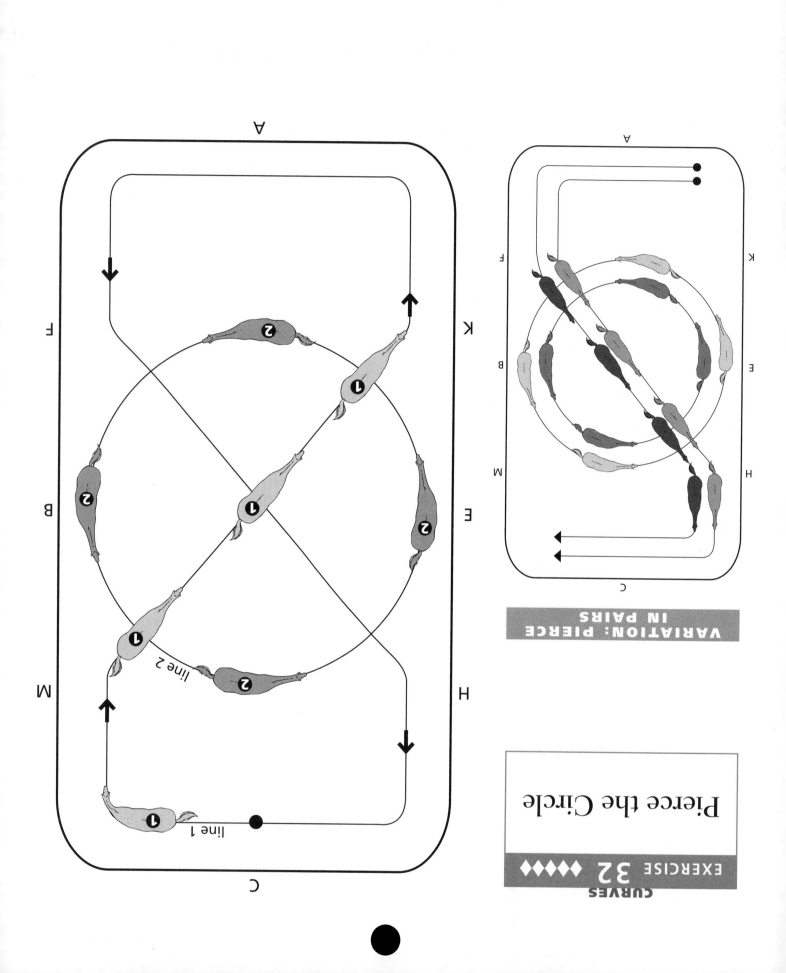

Pierce the Circle

VARIATION: PIERCE
IN PAIRS

32. Pierce the Circle

STARTING POINT

● Form line 1 at **C**, facing **M**, in open formation.
● Form a large circle with line 2 between **E** and **B**, in open formation.

HOW DO I RIDE THIS?

1 Line 2 rides the circle. Line 1 rides to **M** and across the diagonal, moving through the circle.

2 Line 2 continues to circle.

3 Line 1 rides along the rail, past **A**. At **F**, line 1 turns and rides across the diagonal, piercing the circle again.

KEEP IN MIND

◆ If you have a lot of riders crossing the school on the diagonal, they may also need to Thread the Needle at **X**. (See Exercise 83.)

VARIATIONS

◆ Line 1 rides down the centerline to pierce the circle.
◆ Pairs can pierce the circle together.
◆ Riders go three or four abreast through the circle, passing side by side through every other horse on the circle.

pro tip

A single smile is greater than words, for it reaches out to give a warm touch.

— **Tom Maier**
Founder, Riata Ranch Cowboy Girls
Exeter, California

EXERCISE 33 ◆◆◆◆◆

Carousel Switch-Up

Review Exercise 23: Opposing Carousel Turn-Through before doing this exercise.

STEP 1

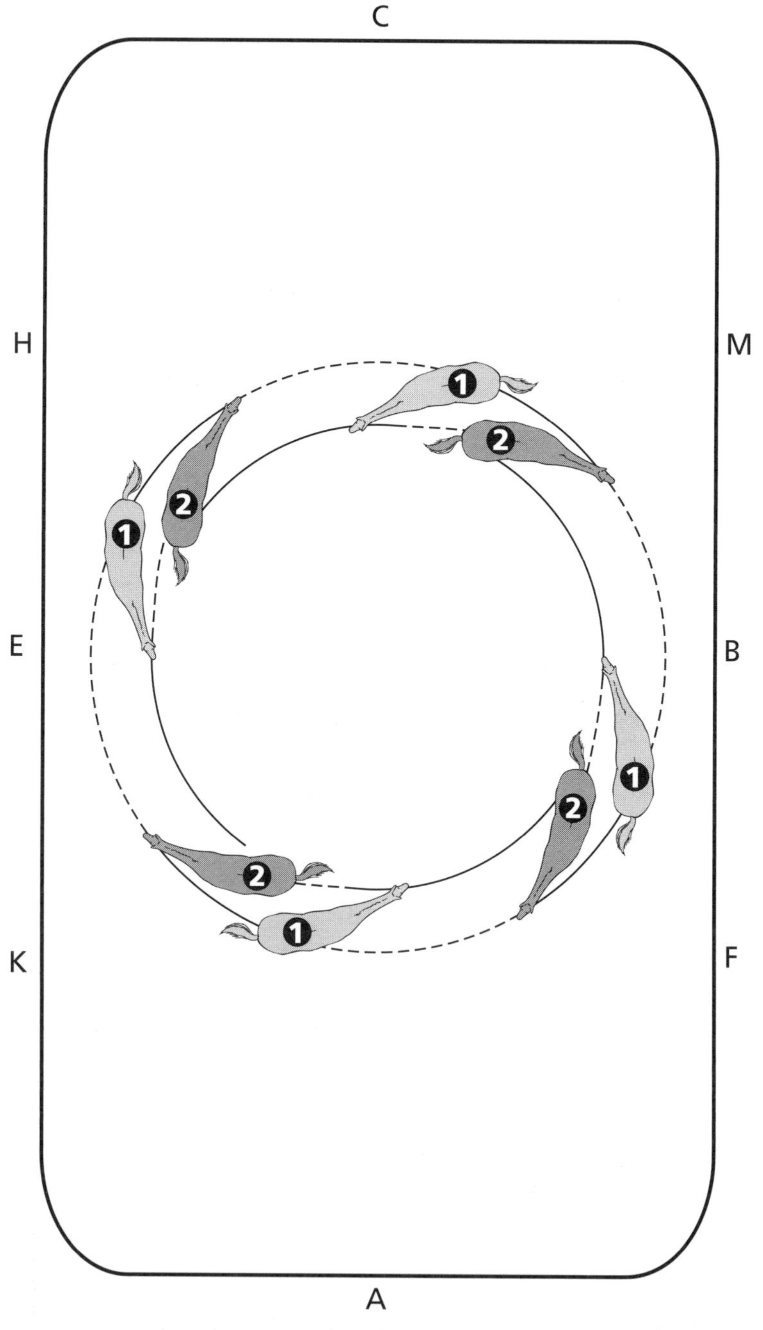

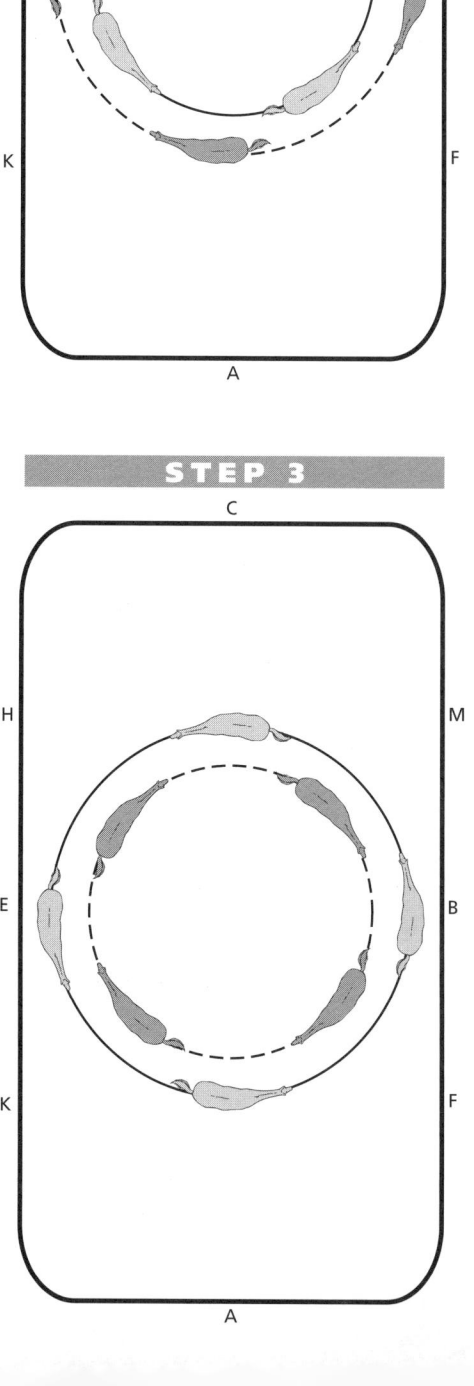

STEP 2

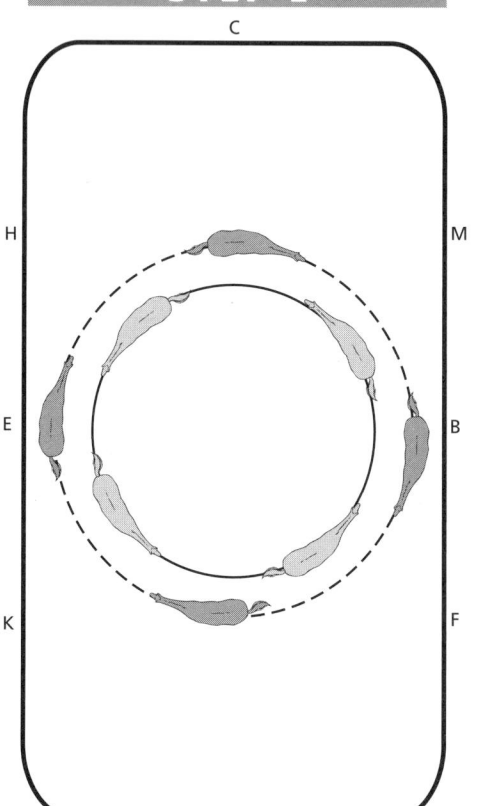

STEP 3

33. Carousel Switch-Up

STARTING POINT

● Line 1 circles counterclockwise between **E** and **B**, in open formation.

● Line 2 circles clockwise inside line 1's circle, in open formation.

HOW DO I RIDE THIS?

1 When the caller signals, turn toward your partner on the other circle and pass with left hands together.

2 Continue to travel on the new circle in the same direction that you were traveling before.

3 After several revolutions, pass your partner again and return to your original circle.

KEEP IN MIND

◆ Riders maintain a consistent circle size.

◆ Riders maintain a steady pace.

INCREASING DIFFICULTY

◆ Perform this exercise several times. Do at least one full revolution before passing your partner. This will look more impressive.

VARIATION

◆ If you have a very large group, riders can ride in pairs around the circles. Turn them inside out together just as you would for one rider, but be sure to leave more space in the lines.

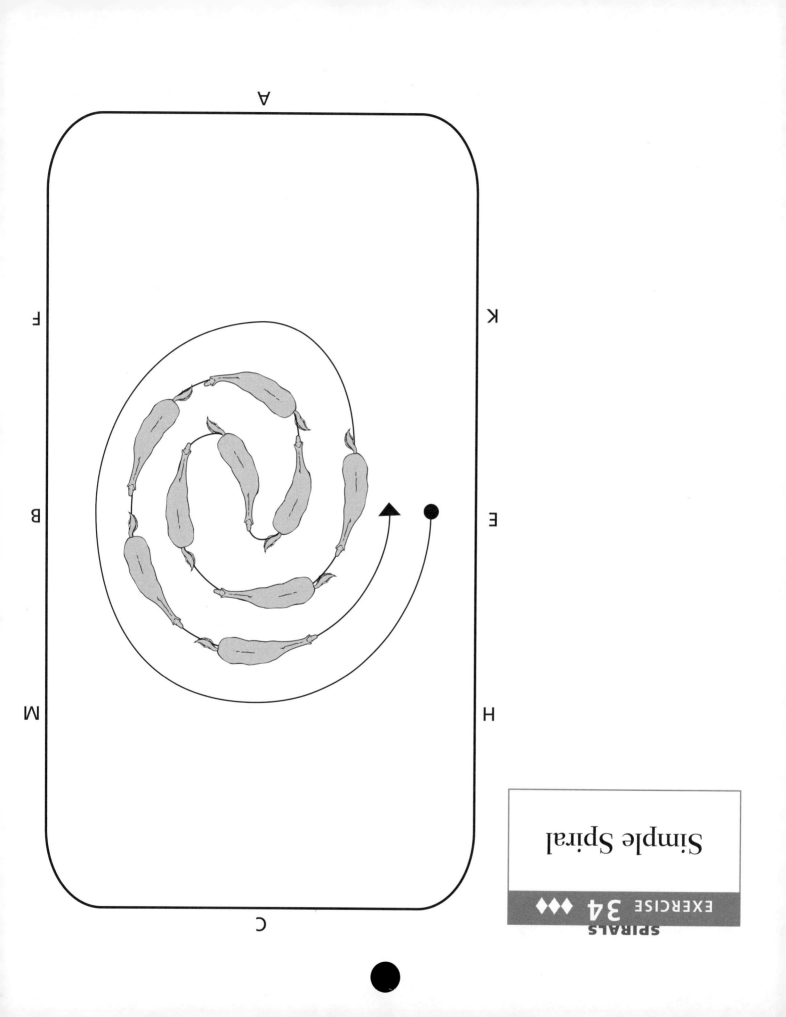

A

F

K

B

E

M

H

C

34. Simple Spiral

STARTING POINT

● Form a single-file, closed-formation line at **E**, facing **H**.

HOW DO I RIDE THIS?

1 At **E**, make a large circle to **B**.

2 Each time the line makes a complete revolution, spiral in to make a smaller circle.

3 When the circle is about 10 meters (33 feet) in diameter, the leader crosses through the center and changes direction.

4 Follow the leader through the turn and spiral out.

5 The spiral is complete when the circle has returned to its full size.

6 Ride straight ahead at **E**.

KEEP IN MIND
◆ The space between horses stays even and small.
◆ Riders keep moving.
◆ Greater speed calls for more room for the reverse.

INCREASING DIFFICULTY
◆ Increase the speed.
◆ Leg yield in and out on the spiral.
◆ Ride an 8-meter (26-foot) reverse.

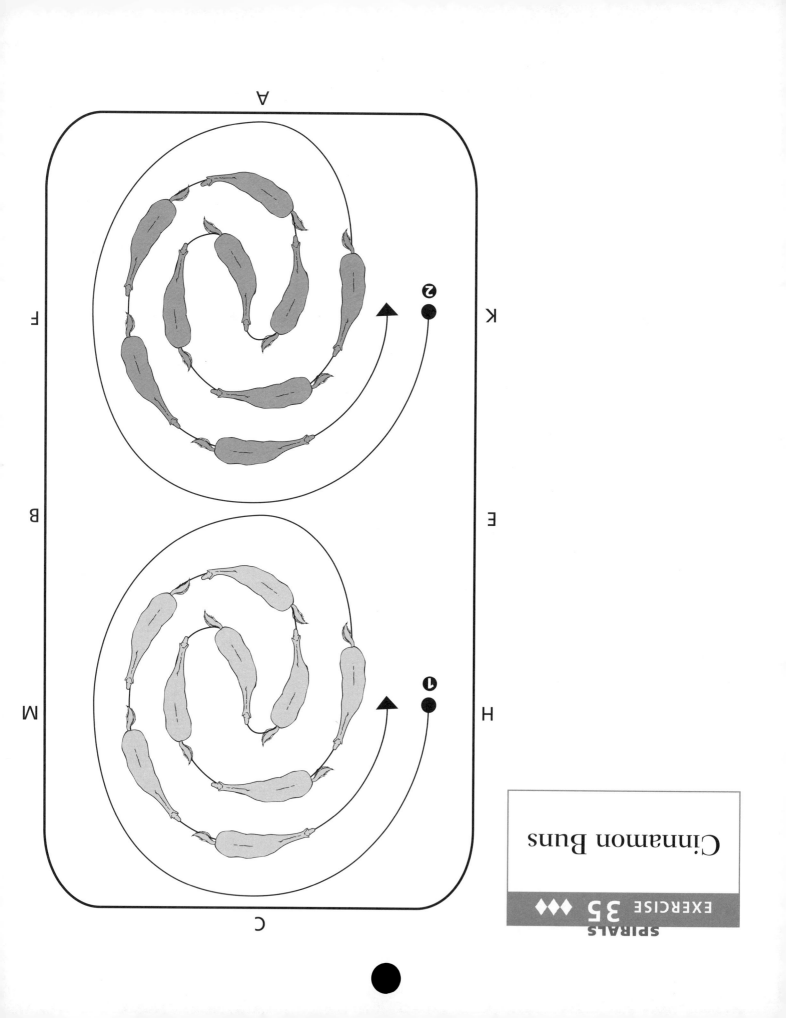

35. Cinnamon Buns

STARTING POINT

● Form line 1 at **H**, facing **C**, in closed formation.
● Form line 2 at **K**, facing **E**, in closed formation.

HOW DO I RIDE THIS?

1 Riders in line 1 ride a large circle between **H** and **M**. Riders in line 2 ride a large circle between **K** and **F**.

2 Each line does a Simple Spiral. (See Exercise 34.)

3 When the lines have returned to **H** and **K**, line 1 will follow line 2, in single file.

KEEP IN MIND

◆ Riders watch their partner in the other line to help arrive at the same place on the spiral at the same time.

INCREASING DIFFICULTY

◆ Increase the speed.

VARIATION

◆ This can be performed at a walk, trot/jog, or canter/lope. The canter/lope requires a flying lead change at **X**.

pro tip

Always have a disaster plan. A rider might need to leave the ring or everyone may need to stop. More-advanced riders can usually get it together and continue, but you should do what is safest for the entire team.

— Friesians of Majesty
Townshend, Vermont

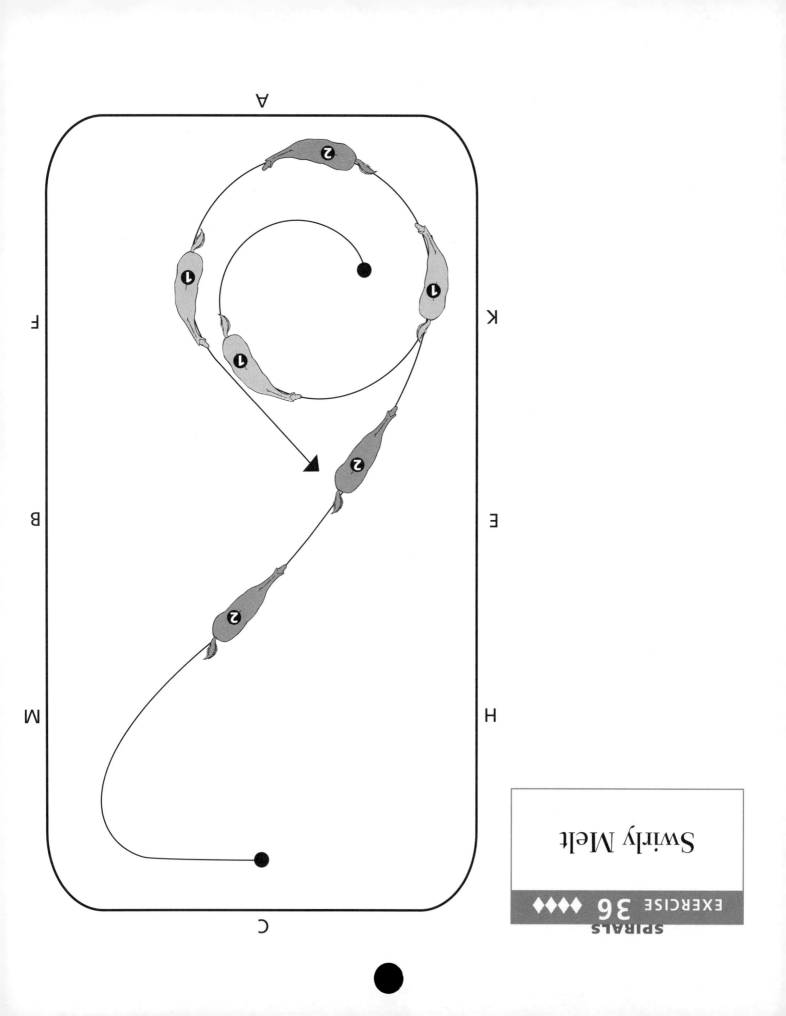

A

F

K

B

E

M

H

C

36. Swirly Melt

STARTING POINT

● Form line 1 on the quarter line at **K**, facing **A**, in open formation.

● Form line 2 at **C**, facing **M**, in open formation.

HOW DO I RIDE THIS?

1 Riders in line 1 ride a circle that reaches past the centerline and back to **K**. Riders in line 2 move past **M** and cross the diagonal to **K**.

2 At **K**, the two lines merge (alternating every other horse).

3 The new single-file line rides to the outside of the original circle and heads across the diagonal to **H**.

KEEP IN MIND

◆ The width of the circle at **K** depends on the size of the group.

◆ The outside circle stays close to the inside circle.

INCREASING DIFFICULTY

◆ If your group is large, the merged line may have to thread through line 2 at **X**. (See Exercise 83.)

VARIATION

◆ Ride this in pairs.

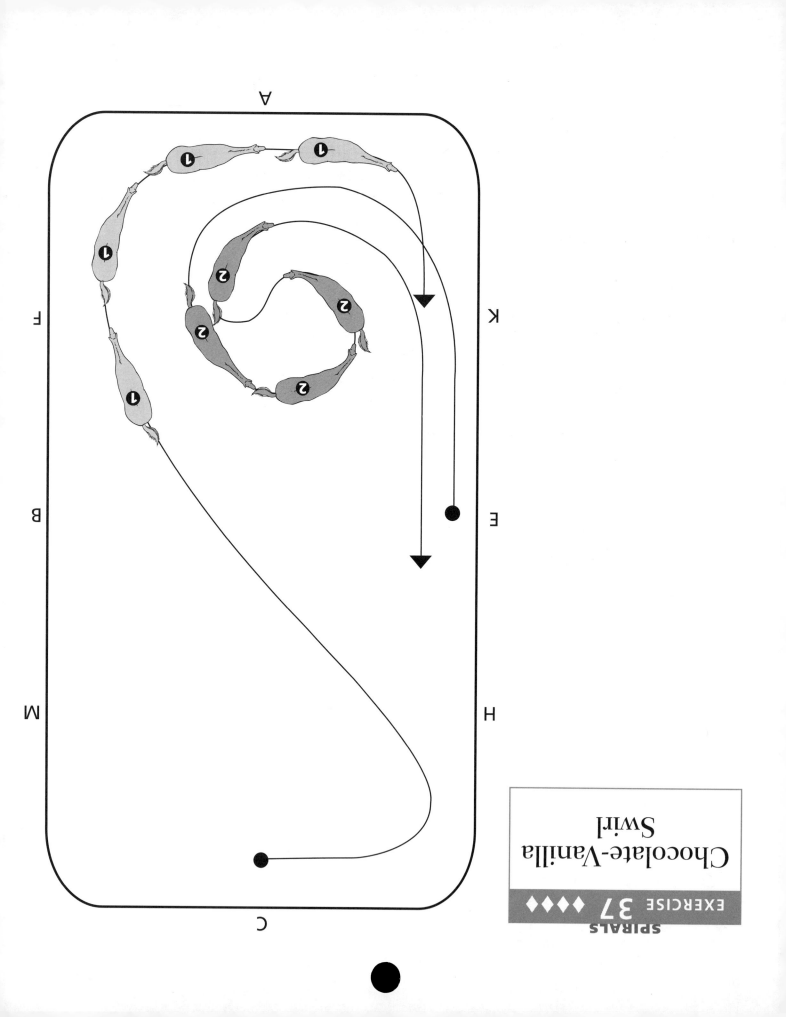

A

K

E

H

B

M

C

F

SPIRALS

EXERCISE 37 ◆◆◆◆

Chocolate-Vanilla
Swirl

37. Chocolate-Vanilla Swirl

STARTING POINT

● Form line 1 at **C**, facing **H**, in closed formation.
● Form line 2 at **E**, facing **K**, in closed formation.

HOW DO I RIDE THIS?

1 Line 1 rides a rounded Z (see Exercise 3) from **C** to **H**, **F**, **A**, and **K**. Line 2 rides to **K** and does a simple spiral (see Exercise 34) far enough off the rail to allow line 1 to pass to the outside along the rail.

2 At **E**, line 2 continues in a single-file line to **H**.

3 At **K**, line 1 follows line 2 in a single-file line.

KEEP IN MIND

◆ Riders watch the other line so they arrive at the rail in time to form a single-file line.
◆ Be a BRATT (see page 23).
◆ If riding at a canter, riders need to do a flying lead change in the middle of the spiral and on the Z.

INCREASING DIFFICULTY/ VARIATIONS

◆ Use a leg yield across the diagonal.
◆ Use a half-pass across the diagonal.

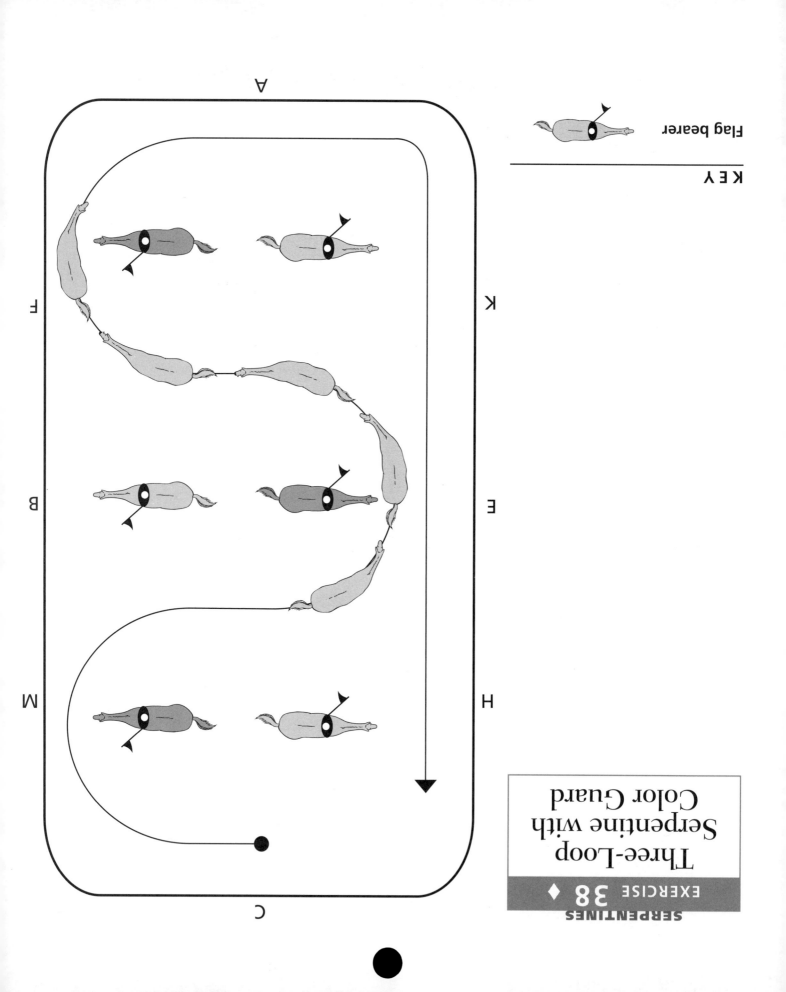

A

F

B

M

C

K

E

H

KEY

Flag bearer

SERPENTINES
EXERCISE 38 ◆
Three-Loop
Serpentine with
Color Guard

38. Three-Loop Serpentine with Color Guard

STARTING POINT

● Form a single-file line in closed formation at **C** facing **M**.

HOW DO I RIDE THIS?

1 At **C**, ride a half-circle, passing **M** and arcing toward the centerline.

2 Ride a half-circle left from the centerline past **E**.

3 Ride a half-circle right from the centerline past **F** and along the rail.

4 Continue straight along the rail.

5 End at **A** or ride a straight line down the fence line to **C** and perform the exercise again.

KEEP IN MIND

◆ The rider looks around the corners.

◆ At each letter, the horse is parallel to the fence.

◆ The rider's body passes the letter before making the turn.

◆ The rider uses aids (legs, seat, and reins) to prevent his horse from cutting corners to keep up with the horse ahead.

◆ Practice perfects the accuracy of the figure and the spacing between horses.

◆ The rider uses correct body position and aids to bend his horse into corners.

INCREASING DIFFICULTY

◆ Increase the speed.

◆ At a canter, do simple or flying lead changes or counter-canter.

VARIATION

◆ Before the exercise begins, position flag bearers in the loops, as shown in the illustration. If you have only three flag bearers, position them close to each loop (darker horses in diagram).

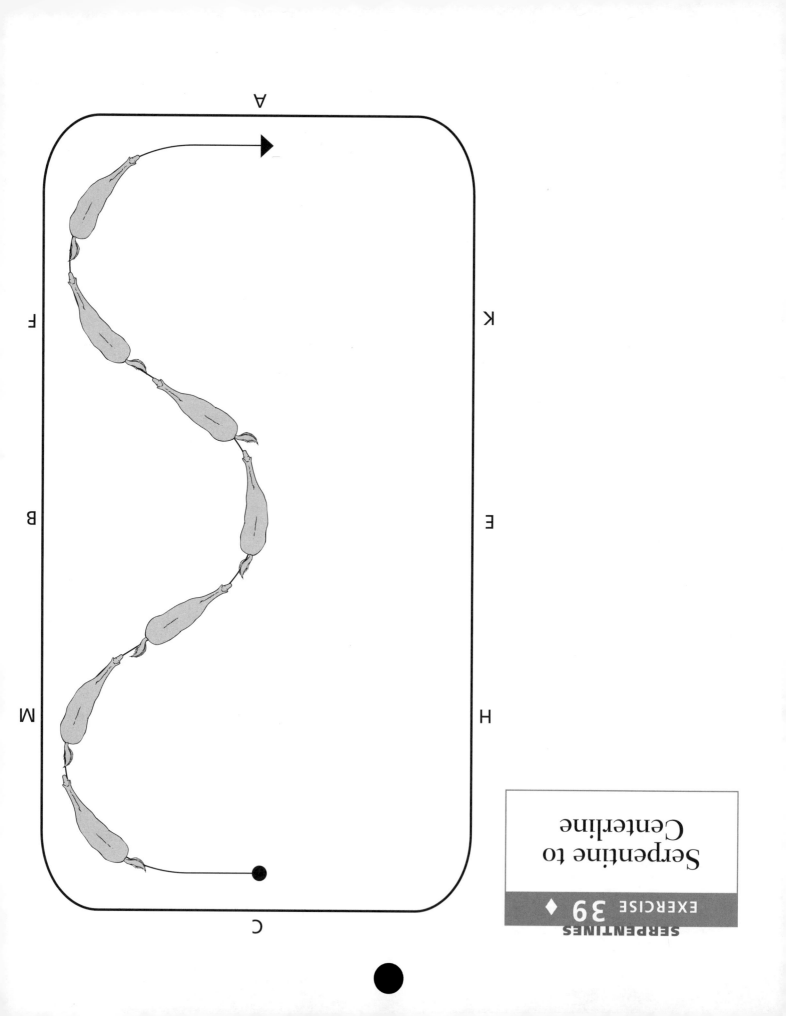

39. Serpentine to Centerline

STARTING POINT

● Form a single-file line in closed formation at **C** facing **M**.

HOW DO I RIDE THIS?

1 Ride from **C** to **M**.

2 Arc to **X**.

3 Arc to **F**.

4 Follow the rail.

KEEP IN MIND

KEEP IN MIND

◆ Riders determine the location of **X** by looking at the centerline and plotting where it intersects a line from **E** to **B**.

INCREASING DIFFICULTY

◆ Ride counter-canter on some of the loops.

VARIATION

◆ Ride the exercise again on the other side.

pro tip

Consider where your audience will be and design your drill with this in mind. Some moves look better from above and some look better from the ground.

— **Friesians of Majesty**
Townshend, Vermont

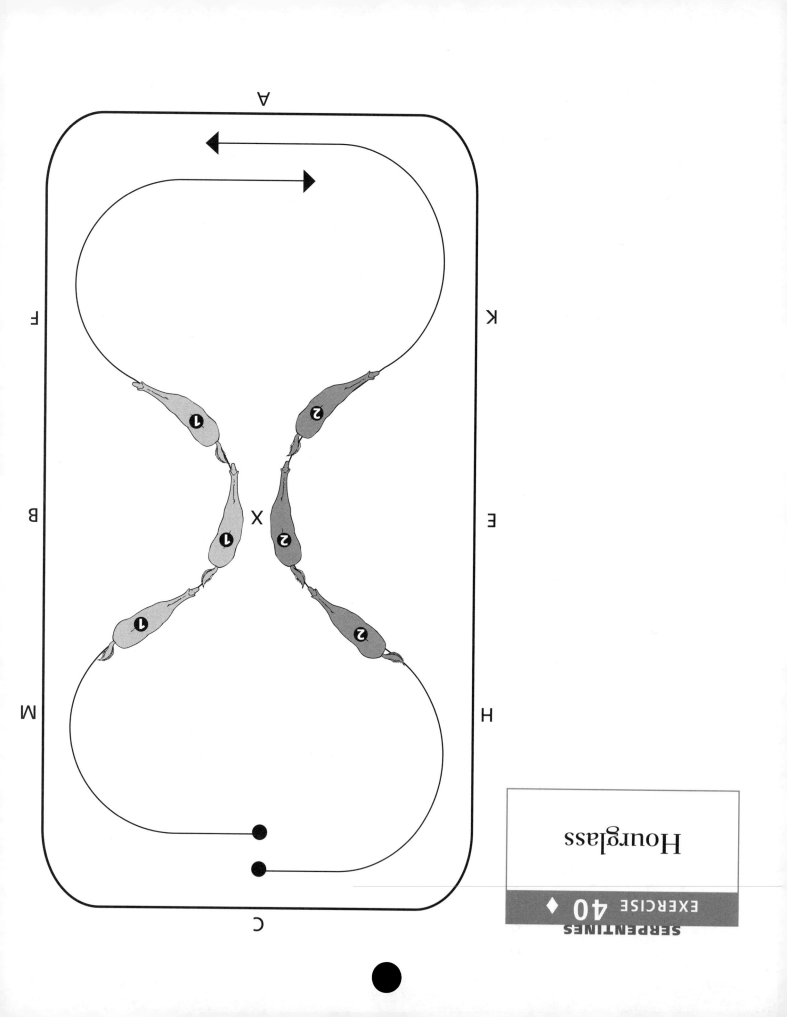

40. Hourglass

STARTING POINT

● Form line 1 at **C**, facing **M**, in closed formation.

● Form line 2 at **C**, facing **H**, in closed formation.

HOW DO I RIDE THIS?

1 Proceed along the rail and do a Serpentine to Centerline, as in Exercise 39.

2 At **X**, meet up with your partner from the other line for a few strides and then continue with the serpentine.

KEEP IN MIND

◆ Riders look down their side of the centerline.

◆ Riders watch their partners out of the corners of their eyes.

◆ Be a BRATT (see page 23).

VARIATION

◆ Have your lines intersect at **X**, as in the Wedding Ring, in Exercise 28.

pro tip

Maintaining a steady pace is probably the biggest key to success in drill movements.

— **Sergeant Mayo**
Royal Canadian Mounted Police
Ontario, Canada

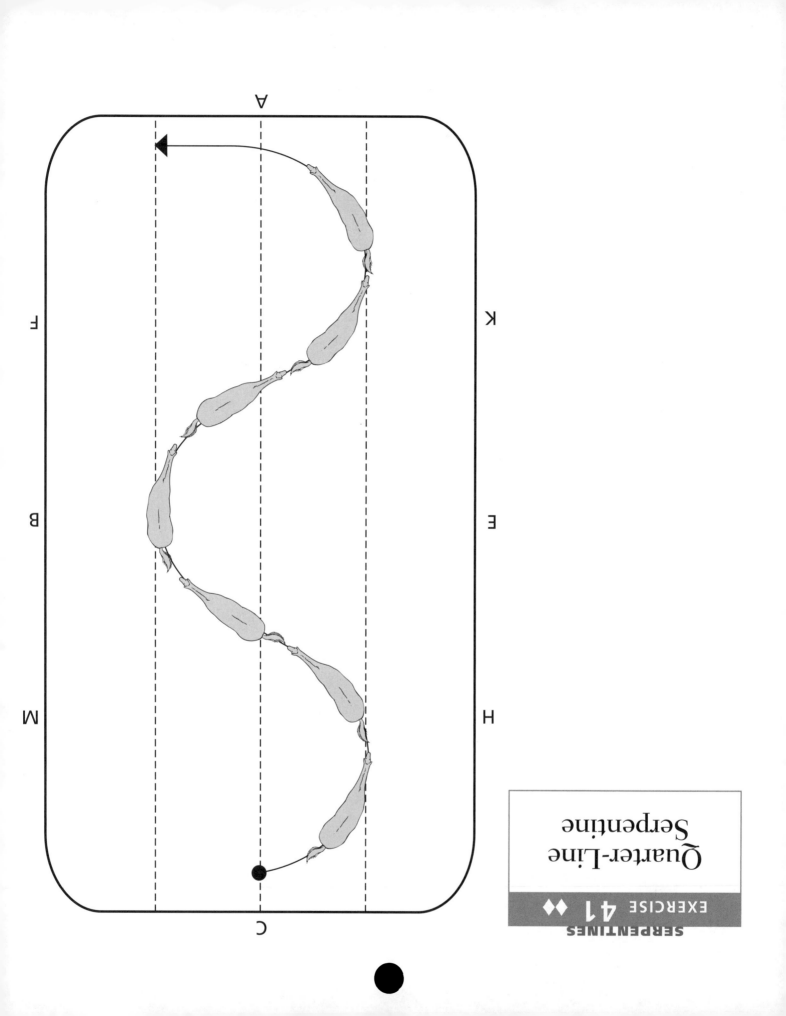

41. Quarter-Line Serpentine

STARTING POINT

● Form a single-file line in closed formation at **C** facing **H**.

HOW DO I RIDE THIS?

1 At **C**, ride a half-circle to the quarter line near **H**, then arc toward the centerline.

2 From the centerline, ride a half-circle right to the quarter line near **B**, arcing again toward the centerline.

3 Ride a half-circle from the centerline to the quarter line near **K** and along the rail.

4 Continue straight along the rail at **A**.

5 End at **A** or ride a straight line down the fence to the starting point and do it again.

KEEP IN MIND

◆ Riders determine the quarter lines by looking down the arena toward **A** and finding a point halfway between **A** and the corner; that's the focal point where the bending line straightens and arcs back again to the centerline.

◆ It is helpful to mark the quarter lines at the rail with cones or colored tape.

◆ Your horse will want to turn early. Keep him on the track and bending around the curves.

INCREASING DIFFICULTY

◆ Increase the speed.

◆ Use a leg yield into the loops.

◆ Ride counter-canter to true canter.

◆ Do flying lead changes.

VARIATION

◆ End your quarter-line serpentine facing whichever way works best for your next exercise. Add or subtract loops to change the direction that you face at the end.

EXERCISE 42 ◆◆◆

Double
Serpentine

VARIATION: EIGHT RIDERS

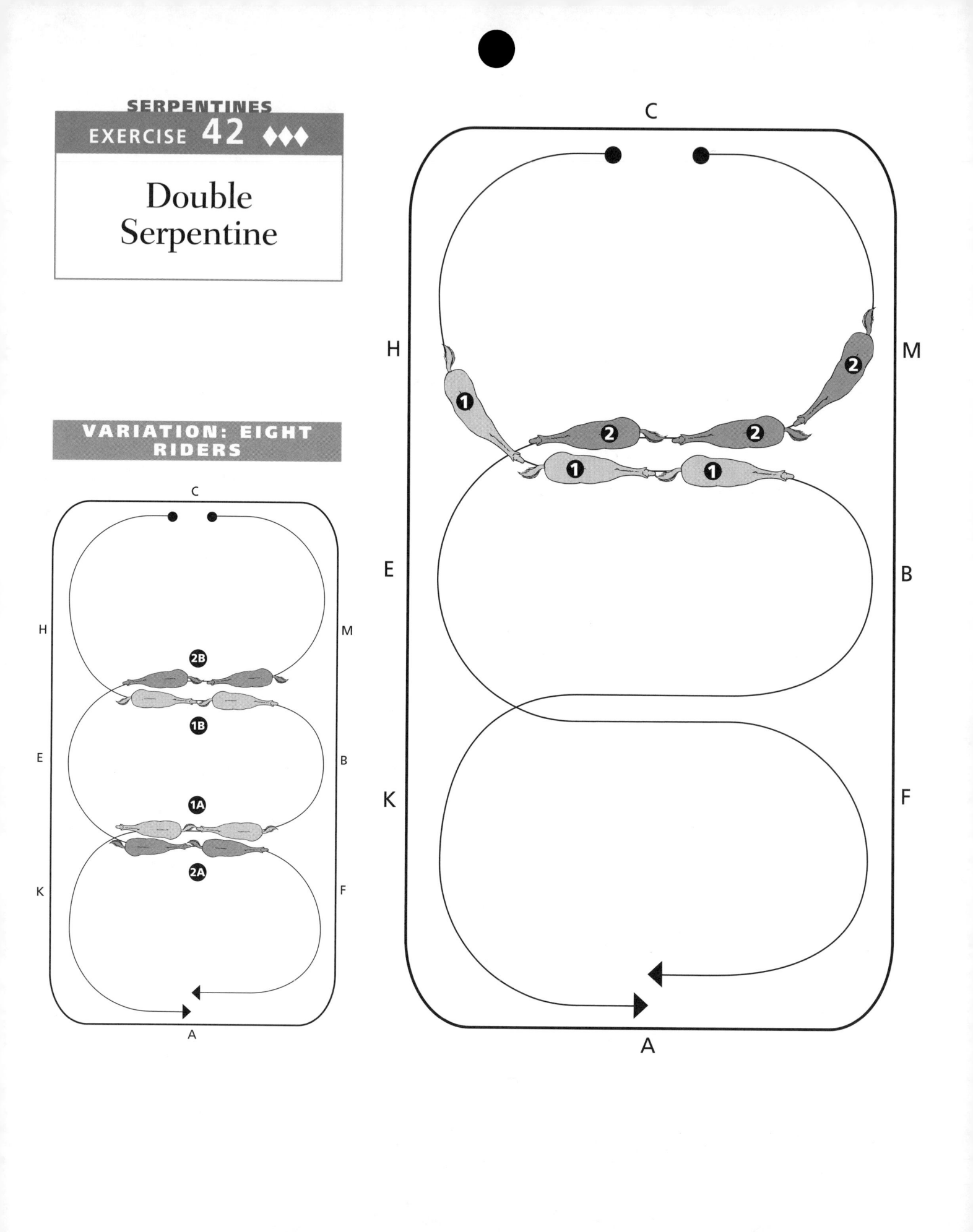

42. Double Serpentine

STARTING POINT

● Form line 1 at **C**, facing **H**, in closed formation.
● Form line 2 at **C**, facing **M**, in closed formation.

HOW DO I RIDE THIS?

1 Riders in line 1 ride a half-circle past **H**. Riders in line 2 ride a half-circle past **M**.

2 Pass your partner left hand to left hand on the centerline.

3 Riders in line 1 ride a half-circle right from the centerline past **B**. Riders in line 2 ride a half-circle left from the centerline past **E**.

4 Pass your partner again left hand to left hand on the centerline.

5 Riders in line 1 ride a half-circle left from the centerline past **K** and along the rail. Riders in line 2 ride a half-circle right from the centerline past **F** and along the rail.

6 Pass your partner left hand to left hand on the centerline at **A**.

7 Continue straight along the rail.

KEEP IN MIND
◆ The size of the arena determines the number of riders who can pass each other at one time.

INCREASING DIFFICULTY
◆ Ride this in pairs.

VARIATION
◆ If there are more than six riders, divide your lines into two subgroups. Space groups A and B so that they pass each other on different loops.

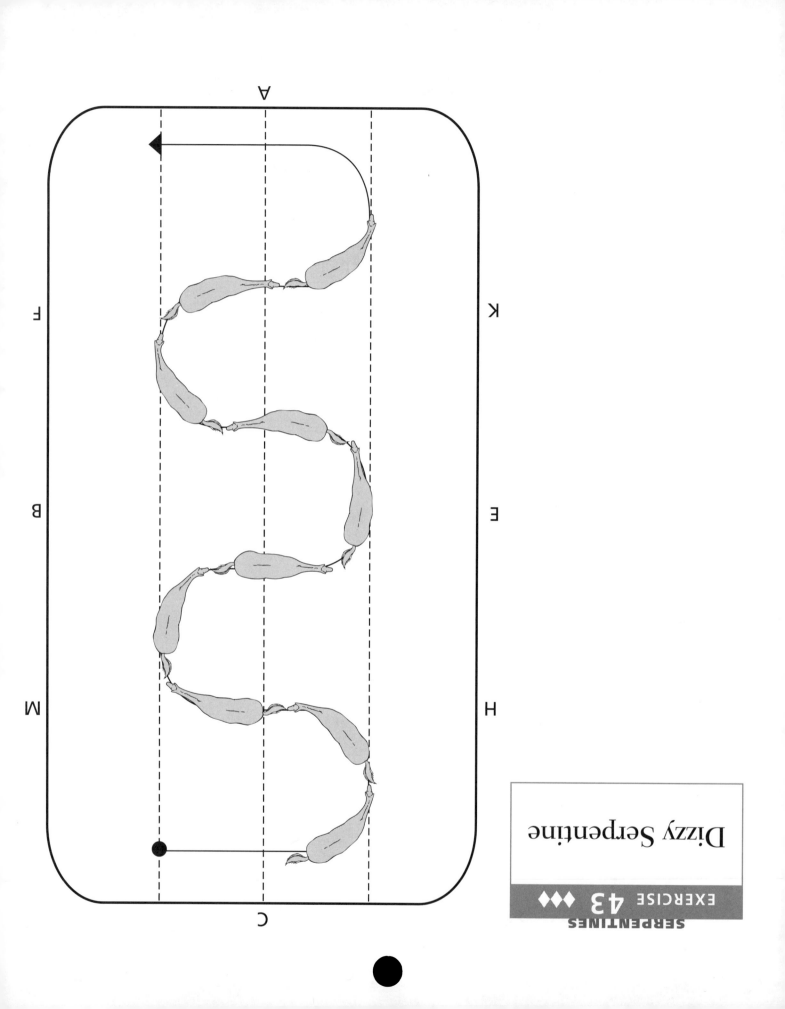

43. Dizzy Serpentine

STARTING POINT

● Form a single-file line in closed formation, facing **H**, at the quarter line between **C** and **M**.

HOW DO I RIDE THIS?

1 Pass **C** and make a loop to the quarter line.

2 Arc to the next quarter line and make another loop.

3 Continue making loops at the quarter lines all the way down the arena.

KEEP IN MIND

◆ A horse may want to turn early, but riders stay on the track and bend around the curves.

◆ Riders make as many loops on the serpentine as are appropriate for the arena size and the horses' speed.

◆ The Dizzy Serpentine ends facing in the direction that works best for your next exercise.

INCREASING DIFFICULTY

◆ Make more loops.

◆ Increase the speed.

VARIATIONS

◆ Do the Dizzy Serpentine from the long side to the centerline.

◆ Use the whole arena for the exercise.

 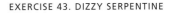

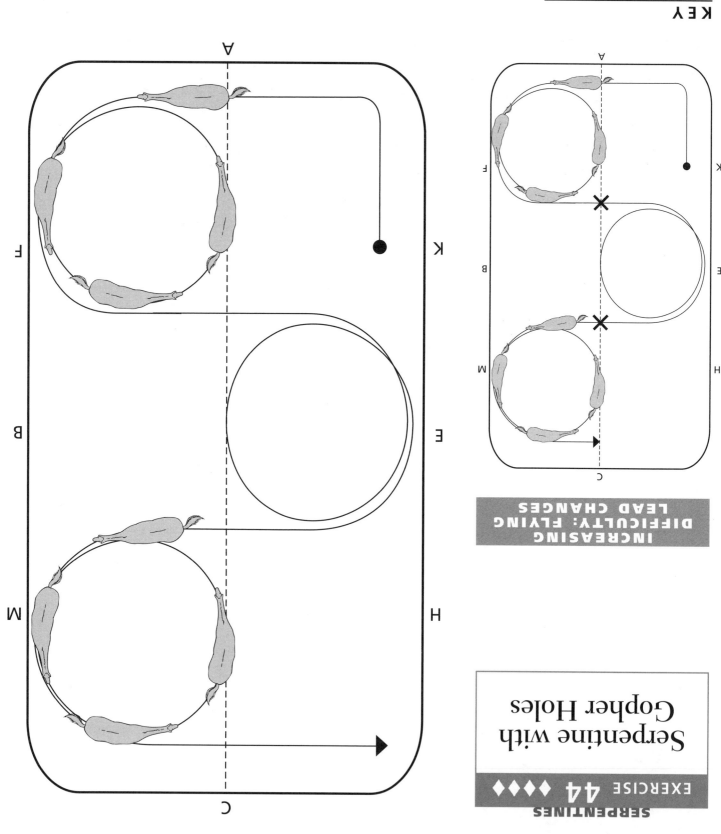

SERPENTINES

EXERCISE 44 ◆◆◆◆

Serpentine with Gopher Holes

INCREASING DIFFICULTY: FLYING LEAD CHANGES

KEY

✗ Flying lead change

44. Serpentine with Gopher Holes

STARTING POINT

● Form a single-file line in closed formation at **K** facing **A**.

HOW DO I RIDE THIS?

1 Ride to **F**.

2 At **F**, ride a circle to the centerline and back to **F**. Continue riding to **E**.

3 At **E**, ride a circle to the centerline and back to **E**. Continue riding to **M**.

4 At **M**, ride a circle to the centerline and back to **M**. Continue riding to **C**.

5 Continue straight along the rail at **C**.

KEEP IN MIND

◆ Be a BRATT (see page 23).

◆ All groups begin the circle at the same time.

◆ Riders pass the quarter lines and centerline of the arena at the same time in all the circles.

INCREASING DIFFICULTY

◆ Use a leg yield to the outside of the circle to make the circle rounder. Before you reach the centerline to continue with the next circle, straighten your horse.

◆ Do flying lead changes on the centerline.

◆ Ride the middle loop in counter-canter.

◆ Ride the first and last loops in counter-canter.

VARIATIONS

◆ If you have more than six people in the drill, divide your group into three sections. Have the groups space themselves out so that the second and third groups do not enter the circles until the group before them has finished that circle.

◆ Position a member with a flag in the center of each circle before the exercise begins.

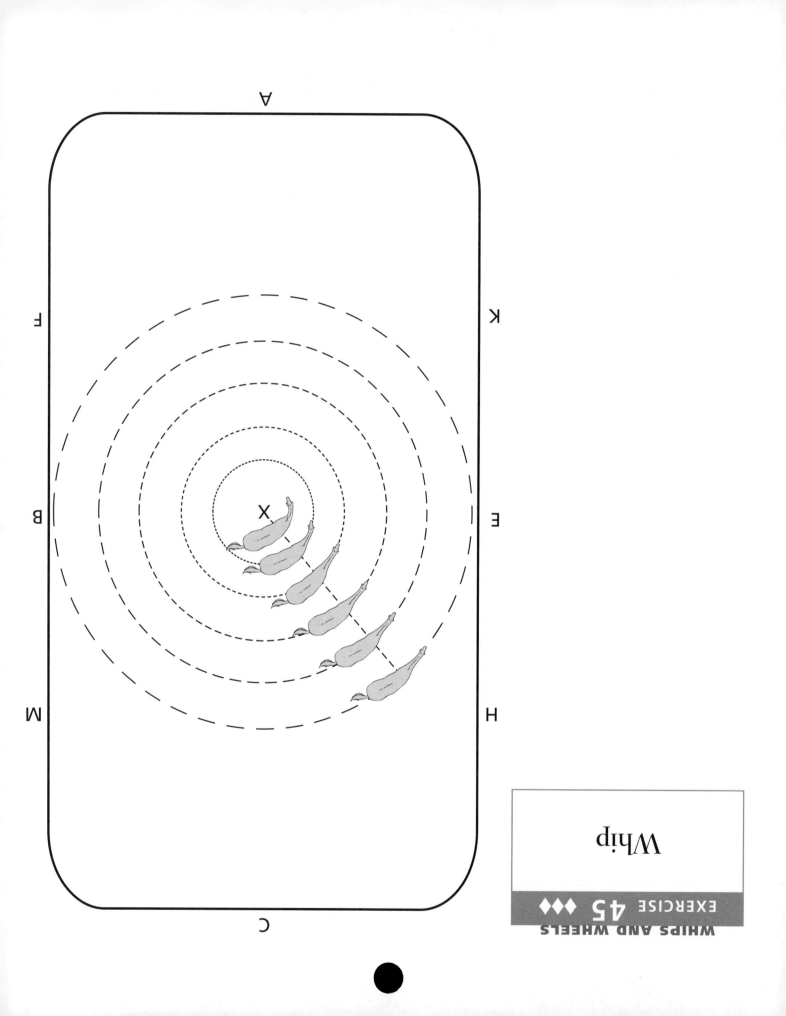

45. Whip

STARTING POINT

● Form an abreast line between **E** and **X**. Riders should be in closed formation, about 1 meter (3 feet) apart.

HOW DO I RIDE THIS?

1 Pivot the line of riders in a large circle around the rider at **X**.

2 Remain abreast in line for the entire circle.

pro tip

If you don't wish to give commands for each step, teach the riders to count to themselves quietly. For example, the command could be "Team Mount," and the riders would say to themselves "pick up the reins, *two*, *three*; foot in the stirrup, *two*, *three*; get in the saddle, *two*, *three*; sit down quietly and wait, *two*, *three*." The audience hears no counting out loud, but the team works as one to produce a very sharp-looking movement.

— **Sergeant Mayo**
Royal Canadian Mounted Police
Ontario, Canada

KEEP IN MIND

◆ The rider at **X** stays at **X** and makes a very tiny circle at a walk.
◆ Riders watch partners on both sides and keep their bodies even.
◆ Outside riders move faster (trot, jog/canter, or lope) than inside riders.
◆ Be a BRATT (see page 23).

VARIATIONS

◆ Have the inside rider do a turn on the forehand, walk pirouette, or pivot.
◆ Stagger the horses.
◆ Have the center horse ride a small circle instead of pivoting.

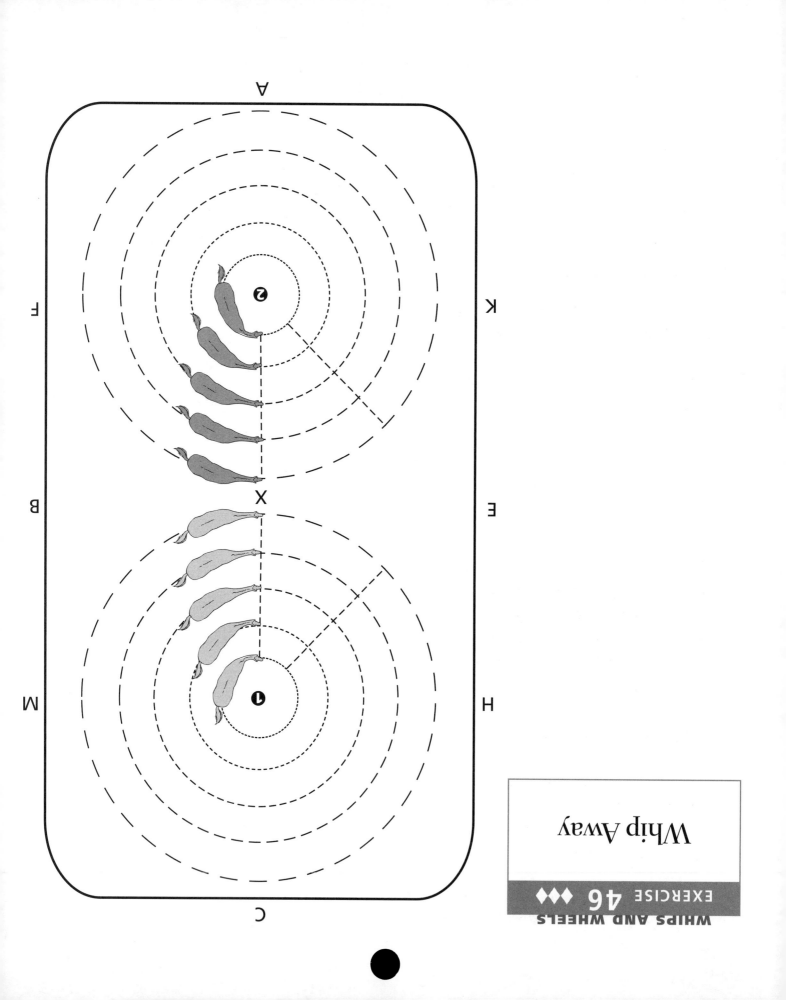

46. Whip Away

STARTING POINT

● Form line 1 with riders abreast on the center-line between **X** and **C**, facing the **H-E-K** rail.

● Form line 2 with riders abreast on the center-line between **X** and **A**, facing the **H-E-K** rail. Both lines should be in closed formation and closer to **X** than to **A** or **C**.

HOW DO I RIDE THIS?

1 Riders in line 1 pivot around the rider closest to **C**. Riders in line 2 pivot around the rider closest to **A**.

2 Riders connect again at **X** to form one long line with riders abreast.

KEEP IN MIND

◆ Watching the riders on either side helps to keep the line straight.

◆ Watching the other line helps to get back to **X** at the same time.

VARIATIONS

◆ Line 1 faces the **B** wall. Line 2 faces the **E** wall.

◆ Both lines travel clockwise. Line 2 pivots around horse at **X**.

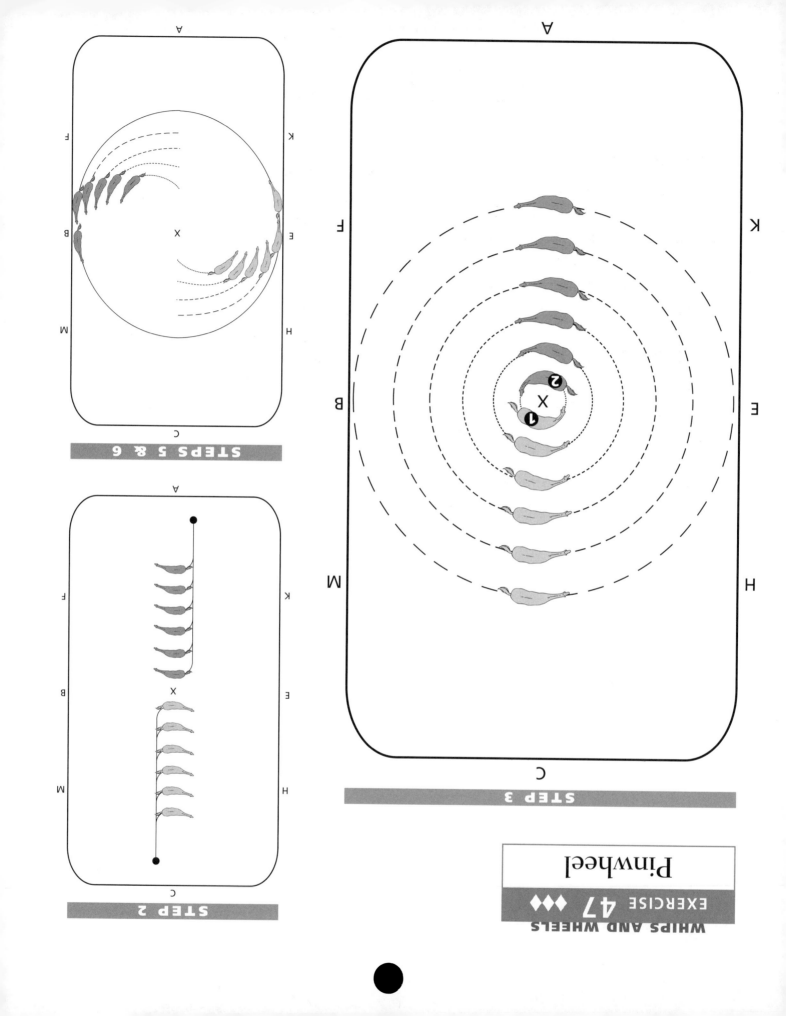

STEPS 5 & 6

STEP 2

STEP 3

Pinwheel

EXERCISE 47 ◆◆◆

WHIPS AND WHEELS

47. Pinwheel

STARTING POINT

● Form line 1 at **C**, slightly to the left of the centerline, and proceed to **X** in single file and closed formation.

● Form line 2 at **A**, slightly to the right of the centerline, and proceed to **X** in single file and closed formation.

HOW DO I RIDE THIS?

1 When the two lines meet at **X**, halt.

2 On the caller's signal, line 1 turns toward **H-E** and line 2 turns toward **F-B**.

3 Everyone rides forward on a circle, pivoting from **X**.

4 Complete one or two circles.

5 To disembark, riders on the outside of the pinwheel move forward, ahead of the riders to their left.

6 The next rider moves forward ahead of the rider to his left. Continue in this manner until everyone is in a single-file circle.

KEEP IN MIND

◆ The outside riders trot, jog/canter, or lope while the inside riders walk.

◆ The two riders at **X** turn their horses' noses toward their partners' tails to make a very tight turn.

◆ Watching the riders on both sides helps to keep the line straight.

◆ Riders keep their heads up and face straight ahead.

VARIATIONS

◆ Ride abreast from opposing sides of the arena to line up on the centerline.

◆ When disembarking, ride abreast lines straight ahead to the rail.

◆ Stagger the lines to give a pinwheel shape as you move out to disembark.

◆ Ride out of the pinwheel the same way you came in.

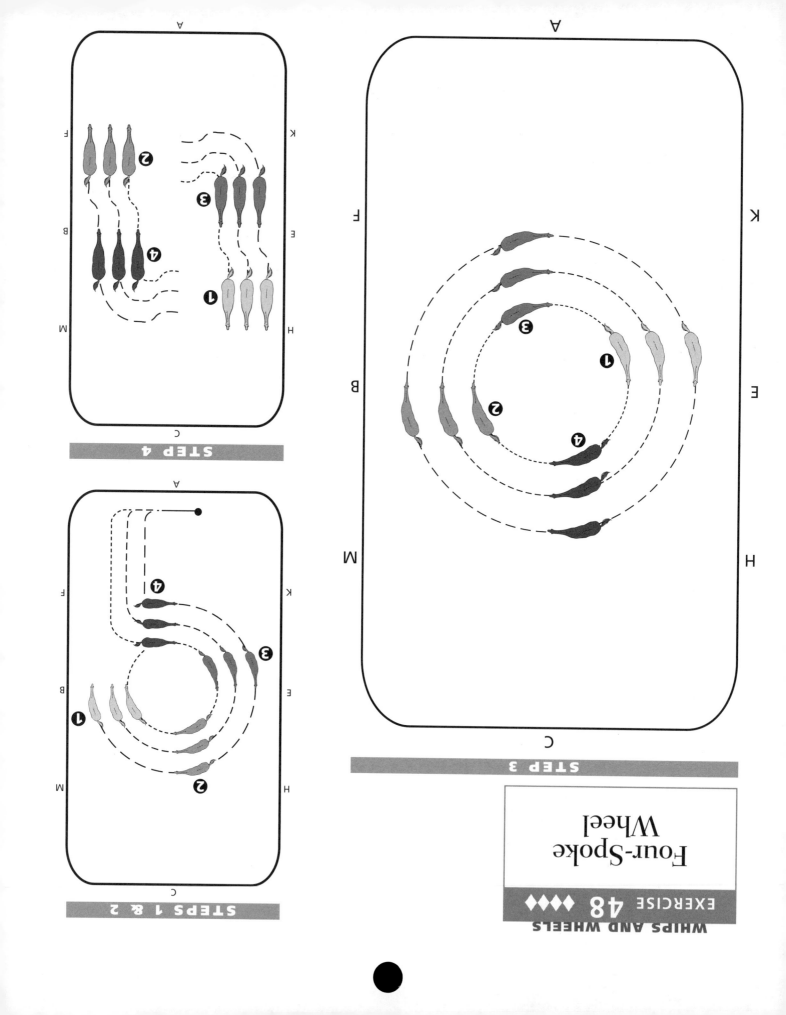

STEP 4

STEPS 1 & 2

STEP 3

WHIPS AND WHEELS

EXERCISE 48 ◆◆◆◆

Four-Spoke Wheel

48. Four-Spoke Wheel

STARTING POINT

● Form a single-file line in closed formation at **A** facing **F**.

HOW DO I RIDE THIS?

1 After passing **A**, turn left in four abreast columns on the quarter line.

2 After passing the **K-F** line, turn left again.

3 Circle clockwise in abreast formation between **E** and **B**. Spread out your abreast columns so they are evenly spaced on the circle.

4 Disembark when all horses are on the centerline or the **E-B** line. The caller signals and abreast columns ride ahead, turn right at the rail, and follow the rail.

KEEP IN MIND

◆ Watching your partner helps to keep abreast lines straight.
◆ Watching the rest of the team helps to keep riders across from or at right angles to the other lines.
◆ Be a BRATT (see page 23).
◆ You can get into and out of this by forming columns. (See Exercise 62: Abreast Columns).

INCREASING DIFFICULTY

◆ Increase the speed.
◆ Increase or decrease the size of the circle with each revolution.

VARIATION

◆ Perform this at either end of the arena.

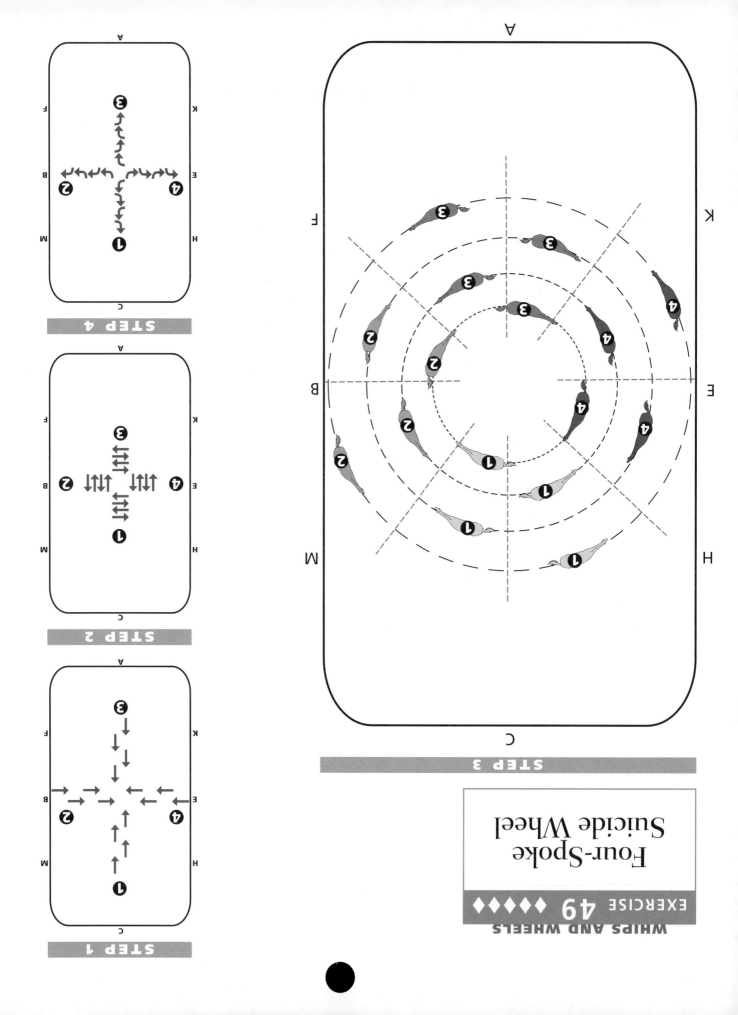

STEP 1

STEP 2

STEP 4

STEP 3

Four-Spoke
Suicide Wheel

◆◆◆◆◆ EXERCISE 49

WHIPS AND WHEELS

49. Four-Spoke Suicide Wheel

STARTING POINT

● Form four staggered lines of pairs at **C**, **B**, **A**, and **E**.

HOW DO I RIDE THIS?

1 All staggered lines move toward **X** until they are about 8 meters (26 feet) from **X**.

2 When the caller signals, turn 90 degrees, forming an abreast line with every other horse facing counterclockwise.

3 Make a full circle.

4 To disembark, halt where you started. Turn away from **X** and ride to the appropriate letter in a single-file line.

KEEP IN MIND

◆ To keep lines straight and at right angles, riders watch others that are turning in the same direction.
◆ Riders watch others traveling in the opposite direction and rate their horses to pass through the other lines on the centerline and on the line between **E** and **B**.
◆ Riders ride their own lines.
◆ Riders leave room for oncoming riders to pass through their line.

INCREASING DIFFICULTY

◆ Increase the speed.
◆ Vary the speed with each rotation, such as slow-fast-slow.

Wheel to Thread-the-Needle

This exercise must be performed in an arena that is at least 30 meters (100 feet) wide.

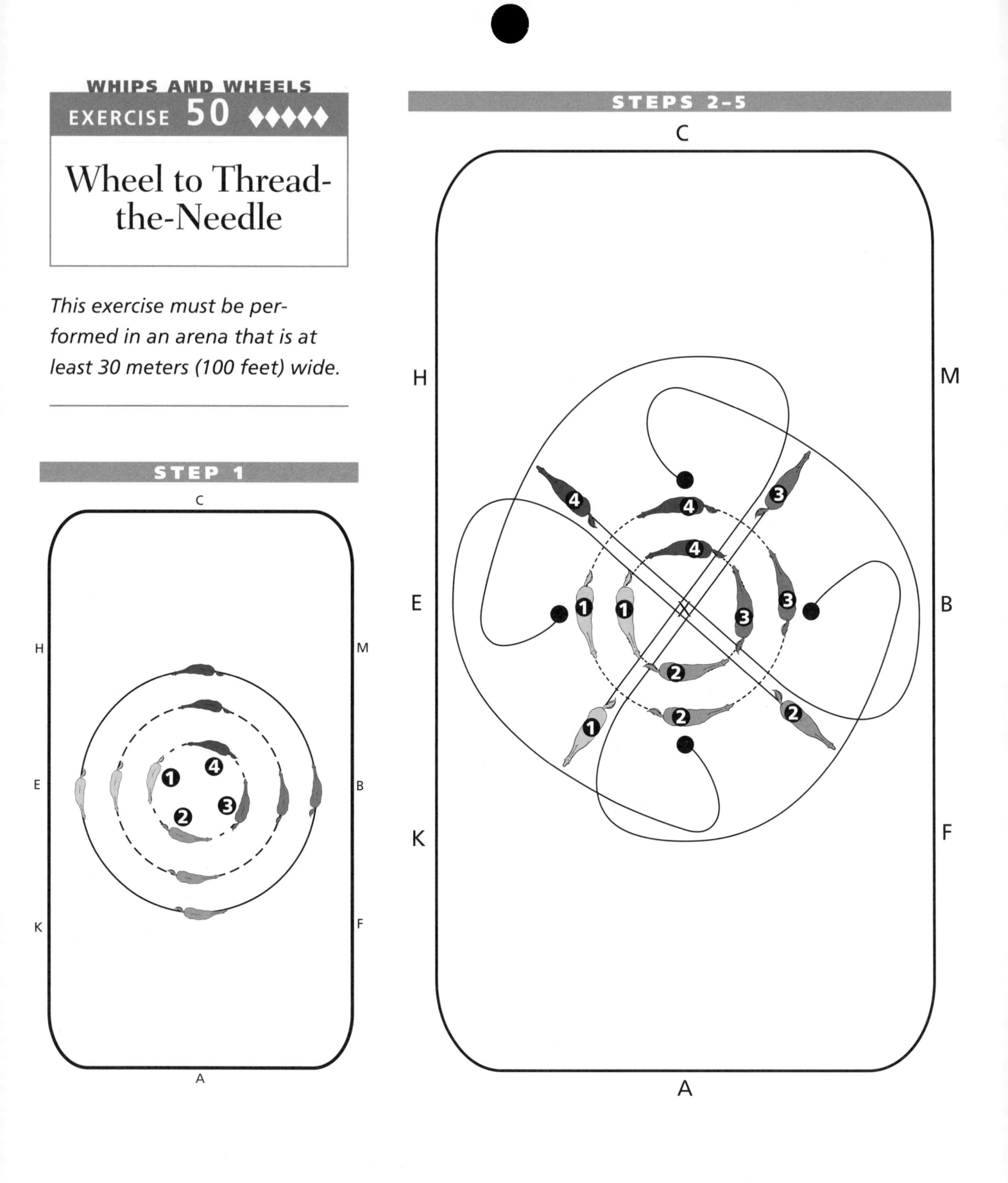

STEP 1

STEPS 2–5

50. Wheel to Thread-the-Needle

STARTING POINT

● Form line 1 at **E** facing **K**.
● Form line 2 on the centerline facing **F** and **B**.
● Form line 3 at **B** facing **M**.
● Form line 4 on the centerline facing **H** and **E**.
Riders in all lines should be abreast and in closed formation.

HOW DO I RIDE THIS?

1 Ride a complete circle. Leave enough room between the rail and the outside of the circle for horses to turn around.

2 Outside riders turn back and pass the line of abreast riders. They pass the next line of abreast riders and turn behind them toward **X**. The inside riders continue to circle throughout this exercise.

3 The outside riders in lines 1 and 3 pass through **X** at the same time.

4 The outside riders in lines 2 and 4 pass through **X** immediately after the outside riders in lines 1 and 3.

5 After crossing **X**, all outside riders exit the circle simultaneously.

KEEP IN MIND

◆ If you increase the speed, increase the space between horses.
◆ Be a BRATT (see page 23).

INCREASING DIFFICULTY/ VARIATION

◆ Have horses Thread the Needle (see exercise 83) individually at **X**.

pro tip

During the performance, try to make your signals very subtle so the crowd sees the show and wonders "How did they do all that with no one telling them what was next?"

— **Sergeant Mayo**
Royal Canadian Mounted Police
Ontario, Canada

Single-file lines are an easy way to give your team an air of stately organization.

CHAPTER THREE

LINEAR EXERCISES

FOR LINEAR EXERCISES, you must ride in a straight line and through right-angled corners. Sound easy? Think again. In order to ride a horse in a straight line, you must keep yourself straight and pay attention to a number of factors.

Straighten Yourself

Make sure that both seat bones are equally weighted in the saddle; don't favor one side over the other. To do this, imagine that you have one ruler on either side of you between your hip bone and your armpit. The rulers should measure the same distance.

Look in a mirror or have a friend watch you ride from the front, side, and back. Are your shoulders, hips, knees, and feet even? Are you tilting forward or backward? Are you leaning to one side? Are you off center? Strive to make yourself straight first, and then you can help your horse to straighten.

Straighten Your Horse

Move your horse forward without putting on the brakes or flying. Often horses move forward but they have their brakes on in preparation for stopping, causing them to become crooked.

At high speeds, horses are "flying" fast and can lose their balance around corners. If your horse is flying fast, exhale, sit deeper into the saddle, and squeeze your fingers. It is also helpful to bend your horse through the corners. This will help him to regain his balance, prompting him to slow down because he is not scrambling to stay upright.

Use the position of your body to direct your horse's movement. Point your chest and hip bones in the direction you want to ride. By shifting your weight, you help the horse to go where you want him to while staying balanced. If the horse moves too far to the inside, bend him back into the correct position with your inside leg and seat.

pro tip

Remember your audience. If you are entertaining a crowd who doesn't understand good rider form and advanced horse training, you can get away with putting in less experienced horses or riders.

— **Friesians of Majesty**
Townshend, Vermont

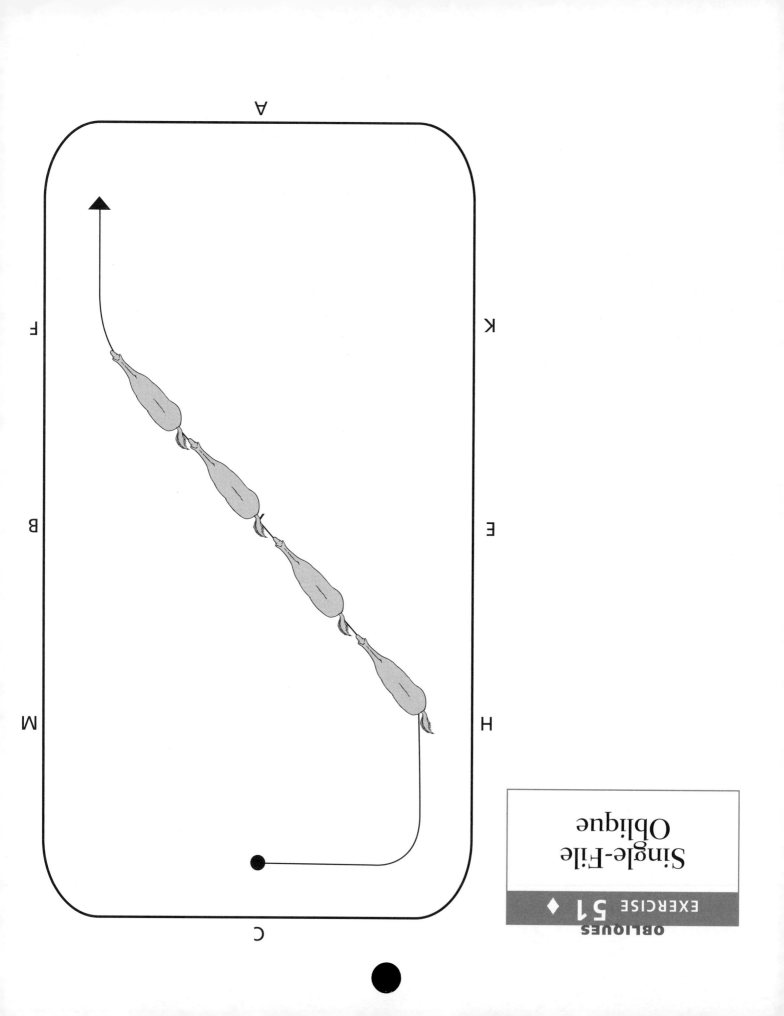

A

F

K

B

E

M

H

C

Single-File
Oblique

OBLIQUES
EXERCISE 51 ♦

51. Single-File Oblique

STARTING POINT

● At **C**, form a single-file line in closed formation facing **H**.

HOW DO I RIDE THIS?

1 Proceed to **H**. After your body has passed **H**, turn and ride across the diagonal.

2 When you get to the other long side, turn right.

KEEP IN MIND

◆ Riders keep lines very straight across the diagonal.
◆ It takes practice not to turn too early, before or after the diagonal.

INCREASING DIFFICULTY

◆ Put a jump along the diagonal. Be sure to space your horses at least three horse-lengths apart for this.
◆ Tie balloons to the sides or bottom of the jump. Be sure to desensitize your horses to the balloons before you try this.
◆ Do a flying lead change at **X** or do a counter-canter after **X**.
◆ When crossing the diagonal, have the first horse do shoulder-in right and the second horse do shoulder-in left. Repeat this pattern down the line, alternating sides of the shoulder.
◆ Instead of doing shoulder-in, do haunches-in across the diagonal.
◆ Do a leg yield across the diagonal.

VARIATION

◆ Cross the diagonal at a different angle or in a different place.

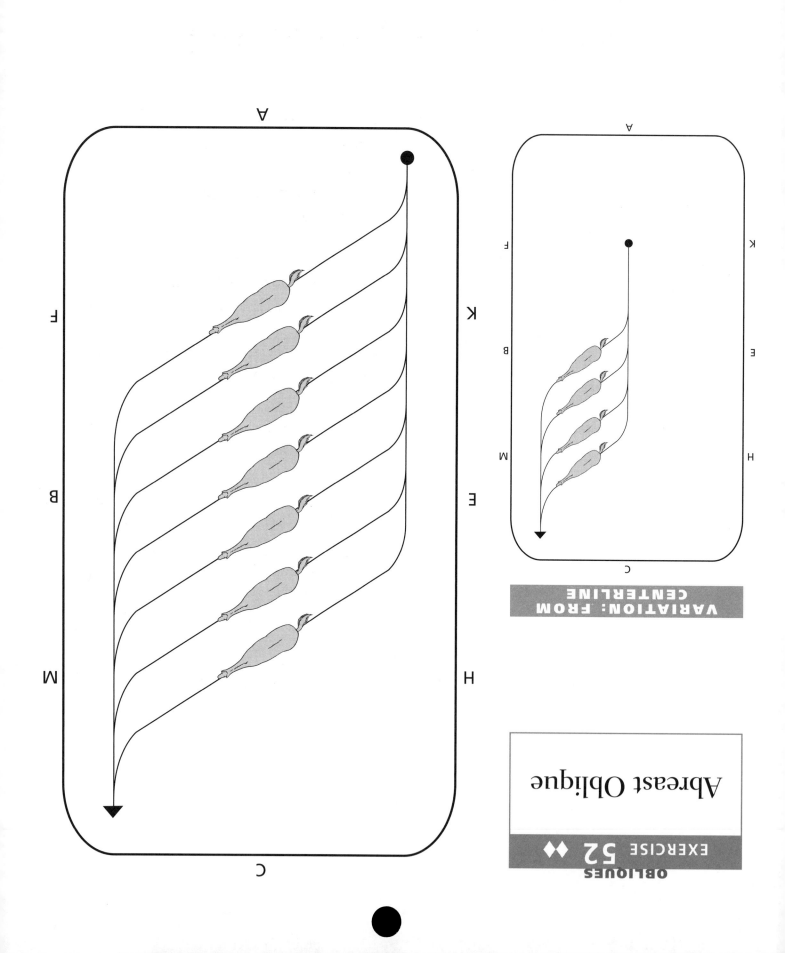

Abreast Oblique

VARIATION: FROM
CENTERLINE

52. Abreast Oblique

STARTING POINT

● Form a single-file line in closed formation at **K** facing **E**.

HOW DO I RIDE THIS?

1 Ride forward.

2 When all riders are on the long side, the caller signals.

3 Turn simultaneously with other riders and ride across the diagonal side by side.

4 At the wall, turn left and form a single-file line.

KEEP IN MIND

◆ When riding abreast, riders rate horses to stay even with the bodies of the riders on both sides.

INCREASING DIFFICULTY

◆ Increase the speed.
◆ Do flying lead changes on the centerline.
◆ Ride counter-canter after the centerline.
◆ Turn on the haunches to turn across the diagonal.
◆ Turn on the forehand when you reach the wall.
◆ Use a leg yield on the diagonal.

VARIATION

◆ Ride down the centerline and make an oblique turn toward the wall.

Reverse & Merge Back on the Diagonal

This is an interesting way to reverse your lines and bring them back together.

STEPS 1-3: REVERSE ON DIAGONAL

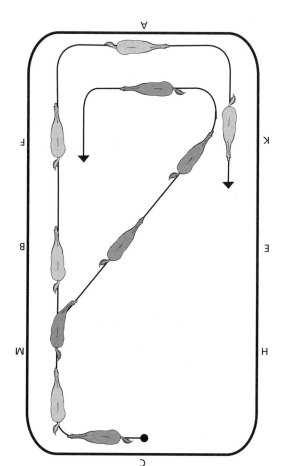

STEPS 4-6: MERGE BACK ON DIAGONAL

53. Reverse & Merge Back on the Diagonal

STARTING POINT

● Form a single-file line in closed formation at **C** facing **M**. Count off 1s and 2s.

HOW DO I RIDE THIS?

1 Move toward **M**.

2 After **M**, the number 1 horses ride straight along the fence. Number 2 horses go across the diagonal to **K**. Everyone is now in open formation.

3 Continue along the fence.

4 At **C**, the lines pass left hand to left hand.

5 Line 1 passes **M** and rides straight ahead. Line 2 passes **H** and moves across the diagonal.

6 Lines 1 and 2 merge, forming a single line at **F**.

KEEP IN MIND

◆ Riders maintain an open formation after they split.
◆ Riders watch the other line to pick out the spot to merge into the line.
◆ Leaders of the lines rate their speed so that they pass their partners left hand to left hand at **C**.

VARIATIONS

◆ Ride another exercise that requires two lines in opposing directions, such as Exercise 33: Carousel Switch-Up, before you merge.
◆ Start facing **K**, **F**, or **H**.

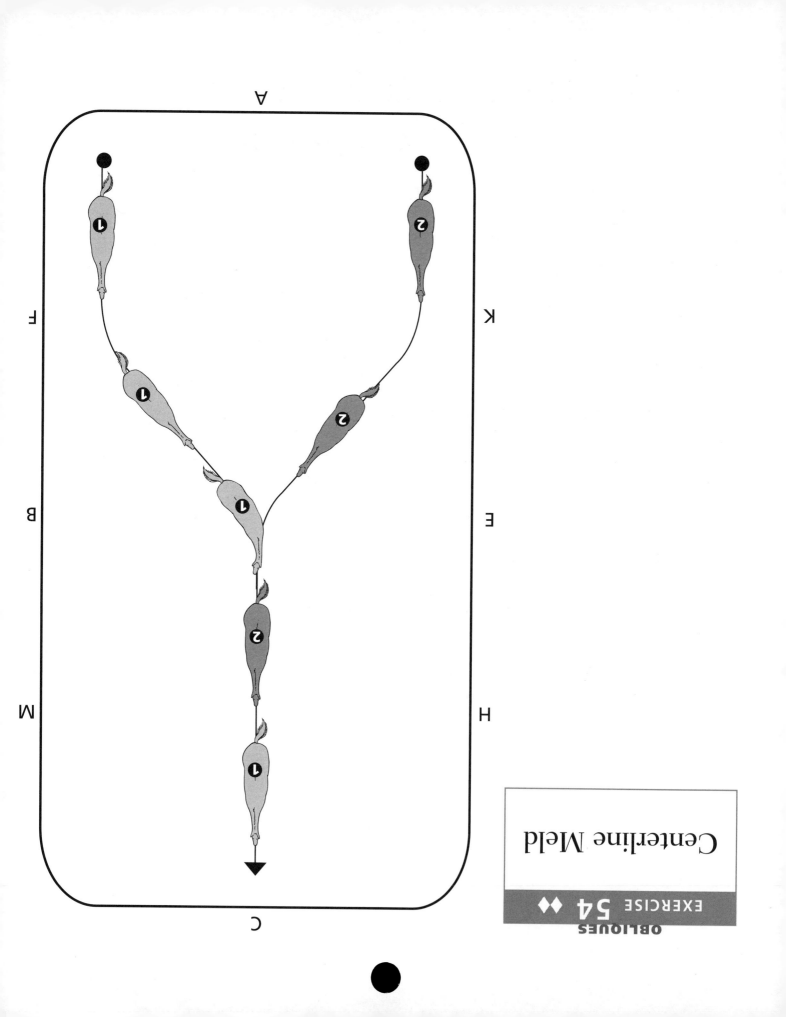

A

F

K

B

E

M

H

C

54. Centerline Meld

STARTING POINT

- Form line 1 in the corner between **A** and **F**, facing **F**, in open formation.
- Form line 2 in the corner between **A** and **K**, facing **K**, in open formation.

HOW DO I RIDE THIS?

1 Ride past **K** or **F** and turn diagonally toward **X**.

2 At **X**, every other horse merges into one line.

3 Continue as one line to **C**.

KEEP IN MIND

- Riders leave enough space ahead for the rider from the other line to merge.
- Riders watch the other line and rate their horse, so that the lines fit together seamlessly.
- Riders gauge the position of **X** by visualizing a line from **E** to **B** intersecting with a line from **A** to **C**.
- Help keep the line straight by looking straight at **X** after passing **K** or **F**, and by looking straight at **C** when at **X**.

INCREASING DIFFICULTY

- Horses can move down the centerline with haunches-in or shoulder-in. The first horse turns to the left, the second to the right, and so forth.

VARIATION

- Ride this in pairs.

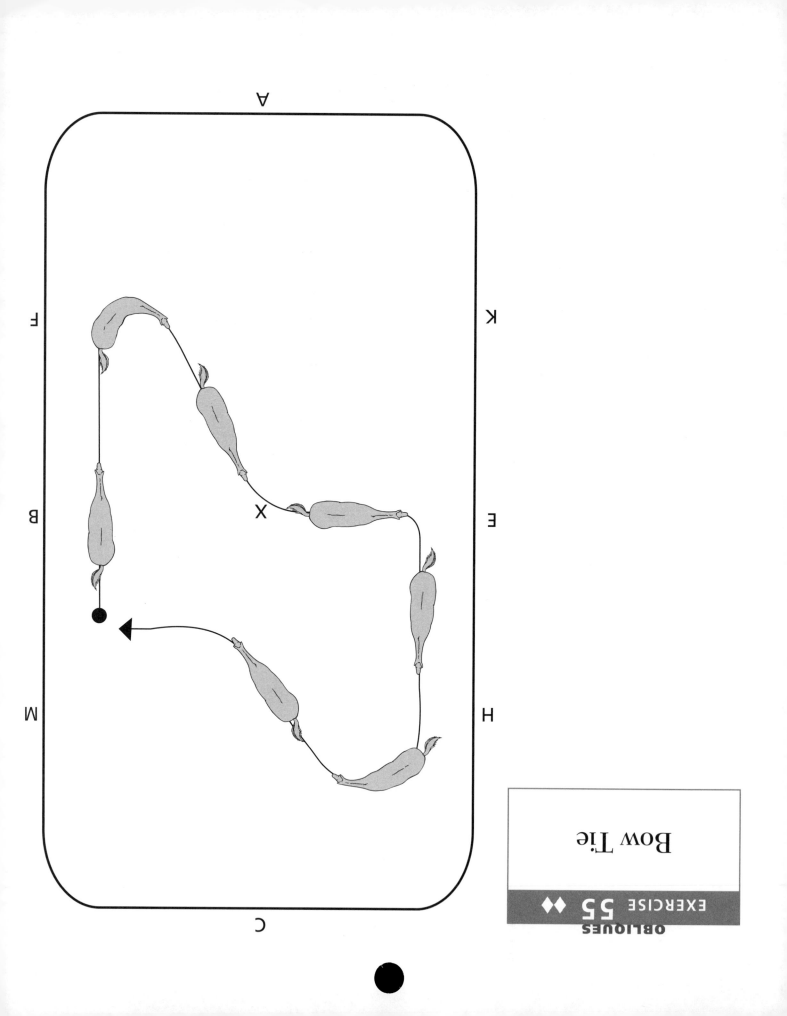

55. Bow Tie

STARTING POINT

● Form a single-file line near **B**, facing **F**, in closed formation.

HOW DO I RIDE THIS?

1 Advance to **F**.

2 At **F**, make a sharp turn and ride an oblique line to **X**.

3 At **X**, turn left toward **E**.

4 At **E**, turn right toward **H**.

5 At **H**, make a sharp right turn and ride an oblique line toward **X**.

6 Before reaching **X**, turn left toward the rail.

KEEP IN MIND

◆ Accurate lines and turns help to make this exercise look like a bow tie.
◆ Be a BRATT (see page 23).

INCREASING DIFFICULTY/ VARIATIONS

◆ At each turn, turn on the haunches or ride a one-quarter pirouette.
◆ Ride in open formation and have horses pass through each other at **X**. (See Exercise 28: Wedding Ring.)

pro tip

You need to be "on" every nano-second you're in front of that audience. Keep the energy up, don't let go.

— **Jennifer Welch**
Director, Riata Ranch Cowboy Girls
Exeter, California

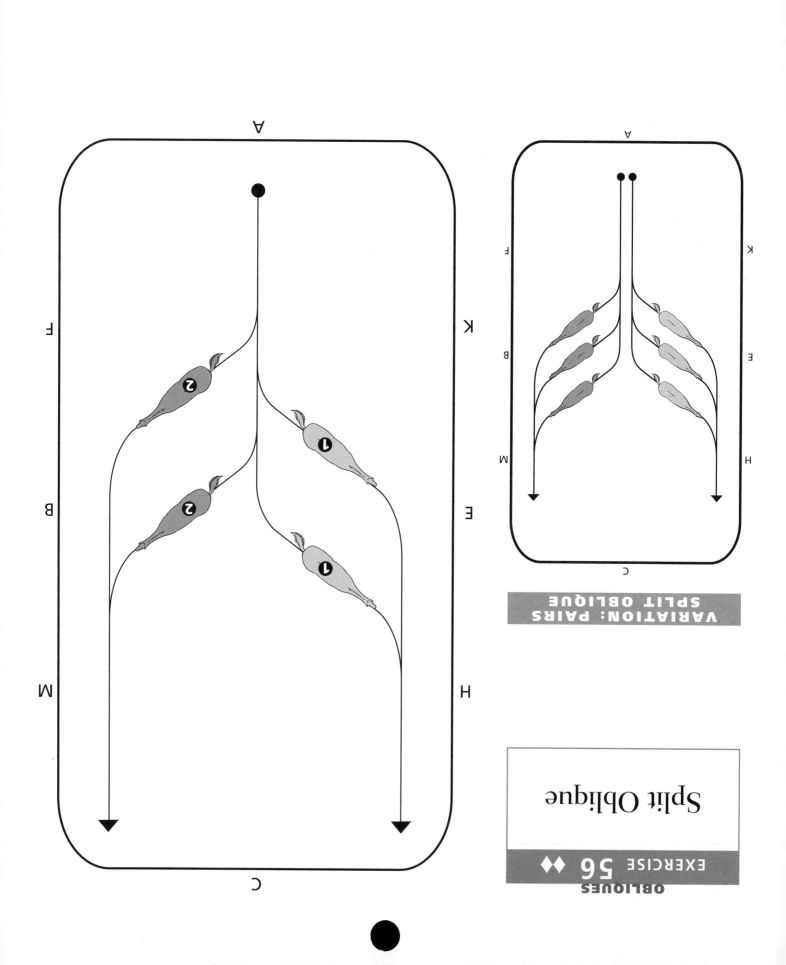

Split Oblique

OBLIQUES

EXERCISE 56 ◆◆

VARIATION: PAIRS
SPLIT OBLIQUE

56. Split Oblique

STARTING POINT

● Form a single-file line in closed formation at **A** facing **C**.

HOW DO I RIDE THIS?

1 Move down the centerline toward **C**.

2 The caller signals for all riders to split simultaneously. The first rider turns left and the second turns right. Continue alternating directions down the line.

3 Ride abreast obliquely to the fence.

4 At the fence, turn toward **C**.

KEEP IN MIND

◆ Everyone is on the centerline before the caller gives the signal to split.
◆ After the split, riders watch the bodies of the riders on both sides to keep the line straight.
◆ After the turn along the fence, riders watch partners on the other side of the arena to keep progression uniform, with partners at the same place on the fence line.

INCREASING DIFFICULTY

◆ When turning off the centerline and along the fence, do pivots, one-quarter pirouettes, or turns on the forehand or haunches.
◆ Ride down the centerline in shoulder-in or haunches-in formation.
◆ Ride the oblique line in half-pass or leg yield.
◆ Ride a side pass along the fence.

VARIATION

◆ Ride this in pairs or fours.

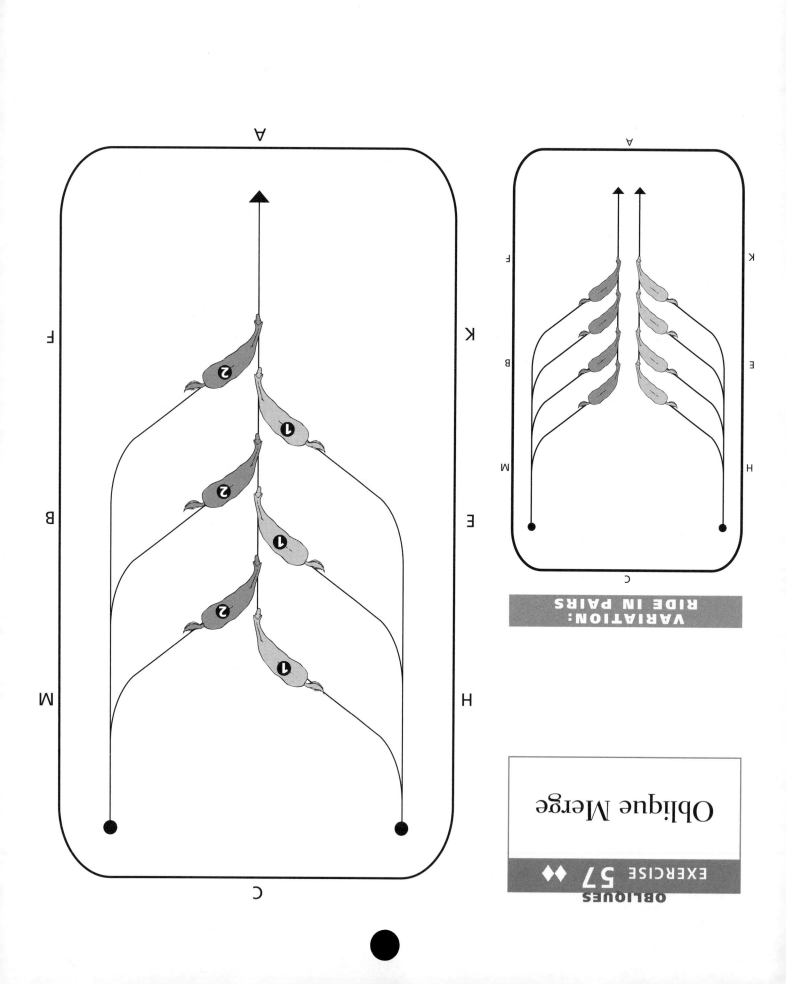

Oblique Merge

VARIATION:
RIDE IN PAIRS

57. Oblique Merge

STARTING POINT

● Form line 1 in open formation at **H** facing **E**.
● Form line 2 in open formation at **M** facing **B**.

HOW DO I RIDE THIS?

1 Ride forward.

2 When the caller gives the signal, turn and ride an oblique line toward the centerline.

3 Lines 1 and 2 merge on the center-line to form a single-file line.

KEEP IN MIND

◆ Riders know which lead rider merges first. Thereafter, every other rider falls into line.
◆ When merging on the centerline, every other rider is from line 1 or line 2.
◆ Riders are aware of their partners as they ride down the rail.

INCREASING DIFFICULTY

◆ When turning off the fence, do turns on the haunches or one-quarter pirouettes.
◆ Ride to the centerline in half-pass or leg yield.
◆ Do haunches-in or shoulder-in down the centerline.

VARIATIONS

◆ Ride this in pairs, threes, or fours.
◆ Turn toward the centerline. Meet up with your partner and ride in pairs down the centerline (see small diagram).

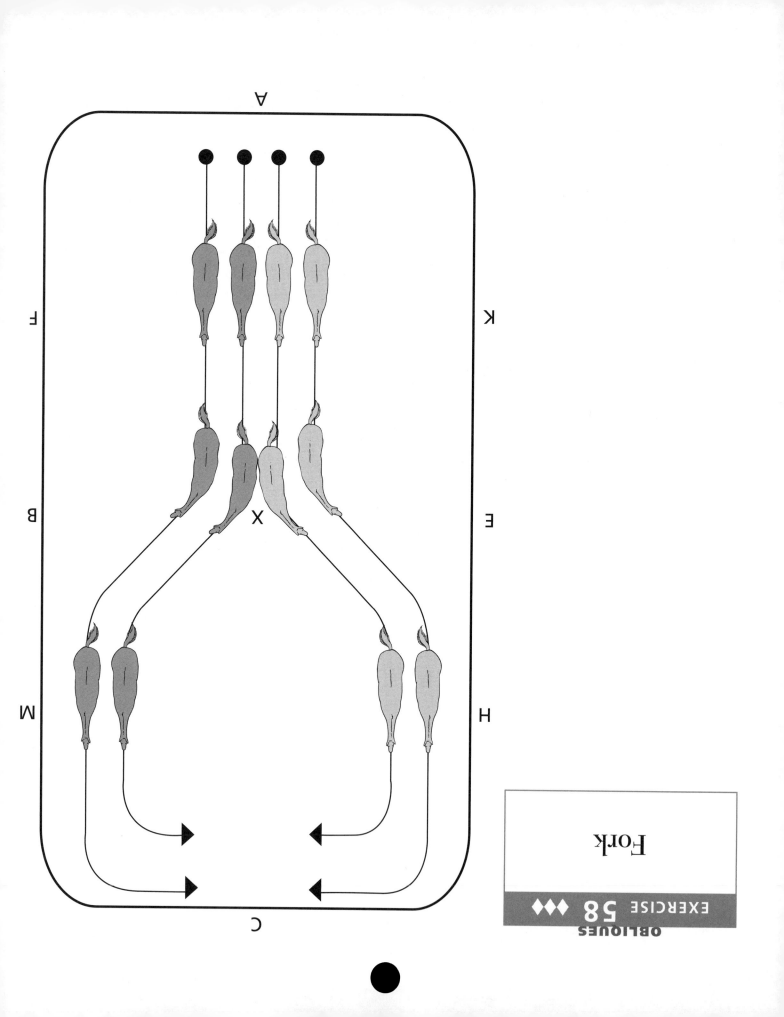

Fork

58. Fork

STARTING POINT

● Form lines of four abreast at **A** facing **C**.

HOW DO I RIDE THIS?

1 Ride down the centerline.

2 At **X**, split into pairs and ride an oblique line toward your side of the arena.

3 At the fence, turn in pairs toward **C** and ride along the fence.

◆ Outside horses move slightly ahead on the corners.

VARIATIONS

◆ After splitting, move into open formation. Merge into single-file lines when you reach the fence.

◆ All riders turn and ride the oblique four abreast to the right or left.

◆ After the split, the second row of riders can move up beside the pair in front of them to make four abreast.

pro tip

If this is your first performance, include in your drill an exercise that everyone knows well and can return to in order to regroup if necessary.

— Friesians of Majesty
Townshend, Vermont

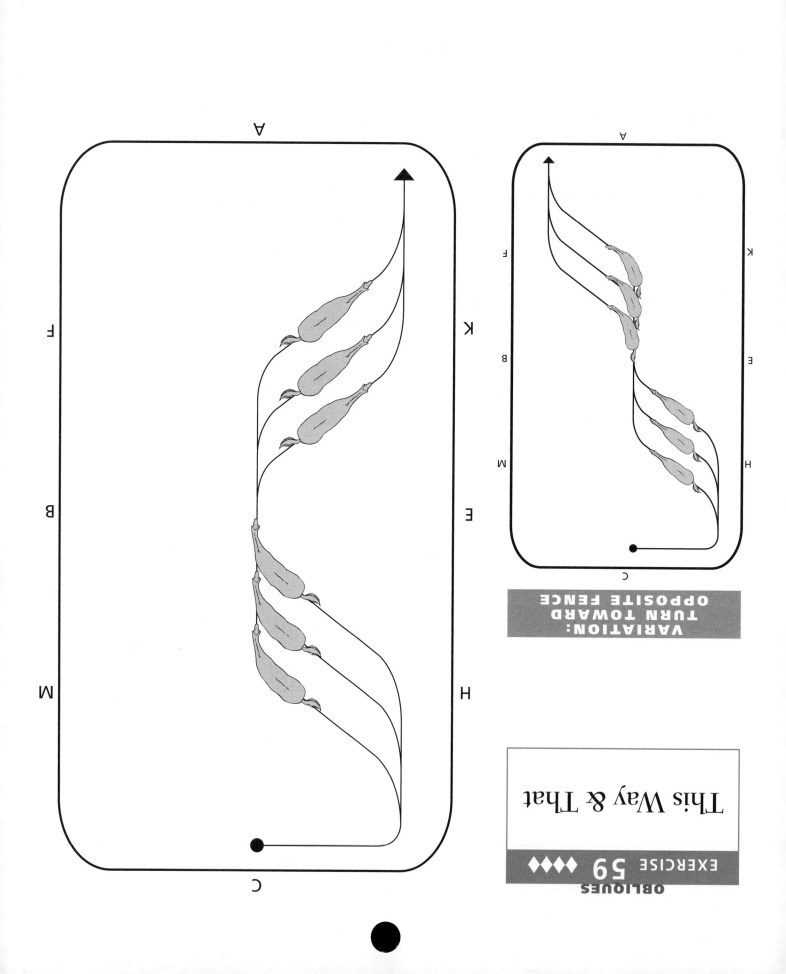

A

F

B

M

C

K

E

H

A

F

B

M

C

K

E

H

This Way & That

OBLIQUES
EXERCISE 59 ◆◆◆◆

59. This Way & That

STARTING POINT

● Form a single-file line in closed formation at **C** facing **H**.

HOW DO I RIDE THIS?

1 Ride to **H**.

2 When riders are on the long side, before **E**, the caller signals for them to simultaneously turn obliquely toward the centerline. Proceed to the centerline.

3 Move straight down the centerline for two or three strides.

4 When the caller signals, riders turn simultaneously and ride an oblique line toward **K**.

5 At **K**, turn left.

KEEP IN MIND
◆ This works best with a smaller group.

INCREASING DIFFICULTY
◆ Ride a side pass along the wall.
◆ Ride a leg yield or a half-pass on the oblique lines.

VARIATIONS
◆ After the team is centered on the centerline, make an oblique turn toward the opposite fence. (See small diagram.)
◆ For larger groups: When turning at **H**, form columns of three to five riders abreast. Have each new column ride the pattern independently and ride in open formation between columns.
◆ Repeat the exercise on the next long side. This looks especially nice with a larger team.

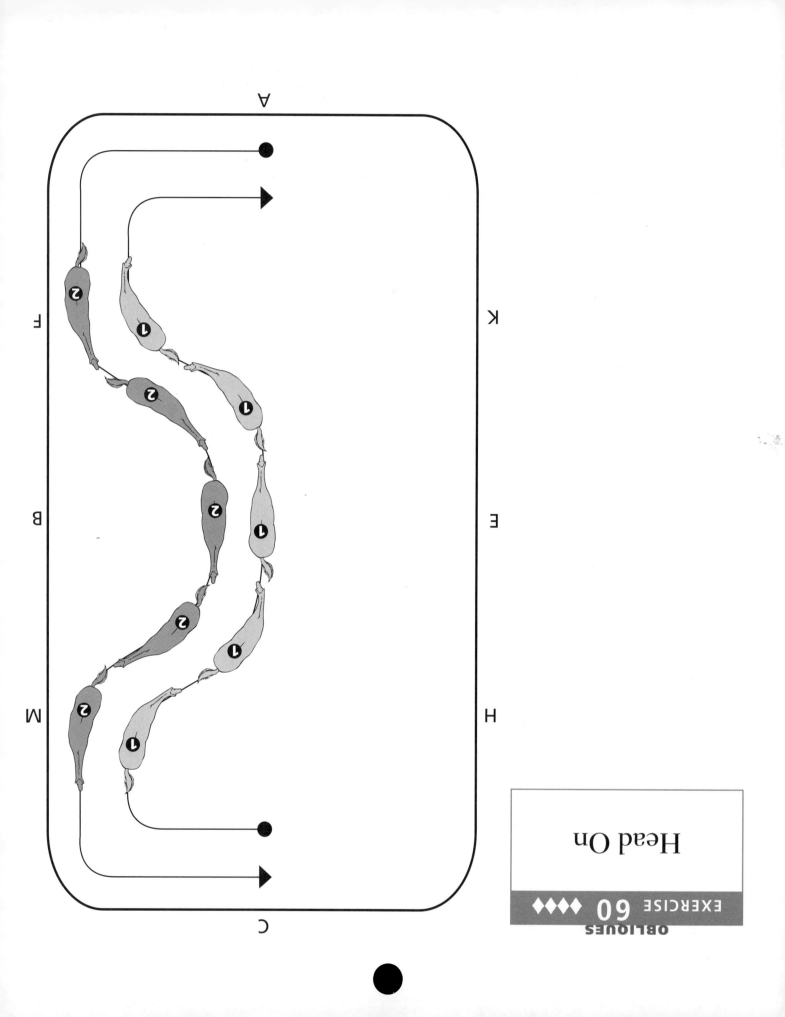

Head On

60. Head On

STARTING POINT

● Form line 1 in closed formation at **C**, facing **M** on the inside track.

● Form line 2 in closed formation at **A**, facing **F** on the outside track.

HOW DO I RIDE THIS?

1 Ride forward along the fence.

2 After **M**, line 1 turns and rides a diagonal line to the centerline. After **F**, line 2 rides a diagonal line toward the centerline.

3 Both lines ride along or near the centerline in opposite directions.

4 Both lines turn diagonally toward the rail (line 1 turns toward **F** and line 2 turns toward **M**) and ride along the fence.

KEEP IN MIND

◆ Riders stay to the right (left hand to left hand) as they pass the other line.

◆ This is an exercise with oblique lines. The lines are straight; they don't bend, as in a serpentine.

INCREASING DIFFICULTY

◆ Add leg yield, side pass, shoulder-in, haunches-in, or half-pass.

◆ For your turns, do pirouettes, pivots, or turns on the haunches.

VARIATION

◆ Ride this in pairs.

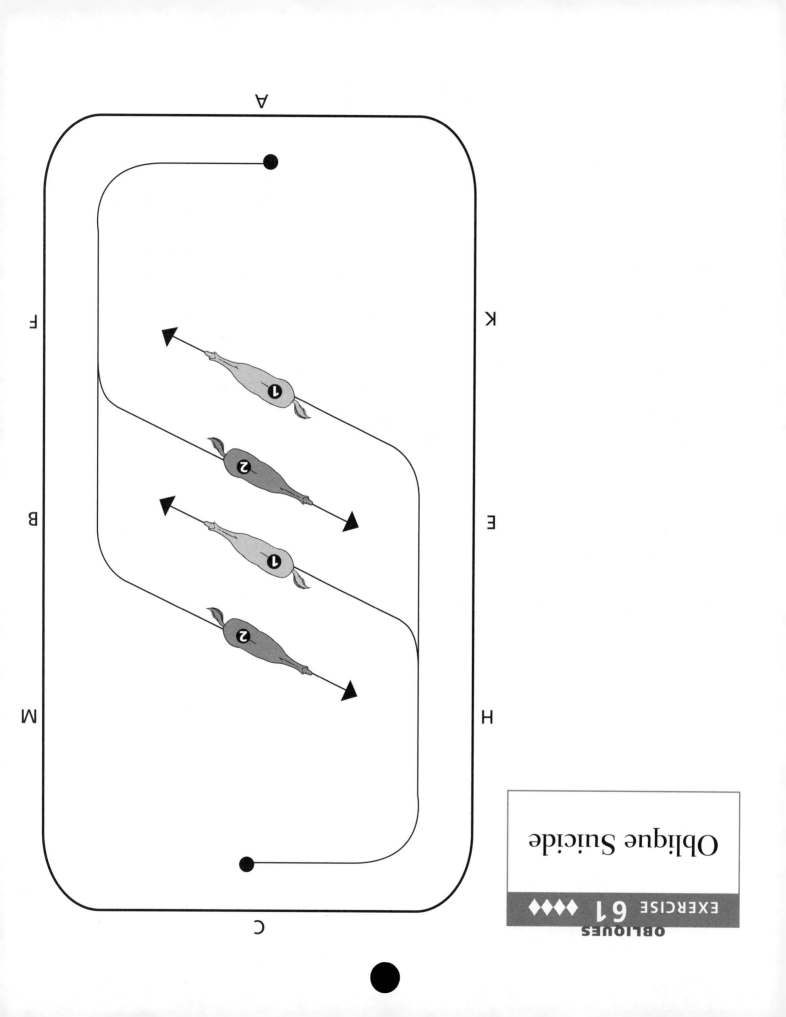

61. Oblique Suicide

STARTING POINT

● Form line 1 in closed formation at **C** facing **H**.
● Form line 2 in closed formation at **A** facing **F**.

HOW DO I RIDE THIS?

1 Riders in line 1 ride to **H-E**. Riders in line 2 ride to **F-B**.

2 At the caller's signal, riders turn and cross the diagonal side by side in open formation.

3 Riders pass those in the other line when they cross the centerline.

4 When riders get to the **H-E** or **F-B** fence, they turn right and form single-file lines.

KEEP IN MIND

◆ Riders pass left hand to left hand.
◆ Spacing is kept even.
◆ Partners watch each other to keep the abreast line straight.
◆ Riders rate their horses to pass the opposing line on the centerline.

INCREASING DIFFICULTY

◆ Pass through in pairs.

VARIATION

◆ Each line turns with two or three columns of riders riding abreast. (See Exercise 62: Abreast Columns.)

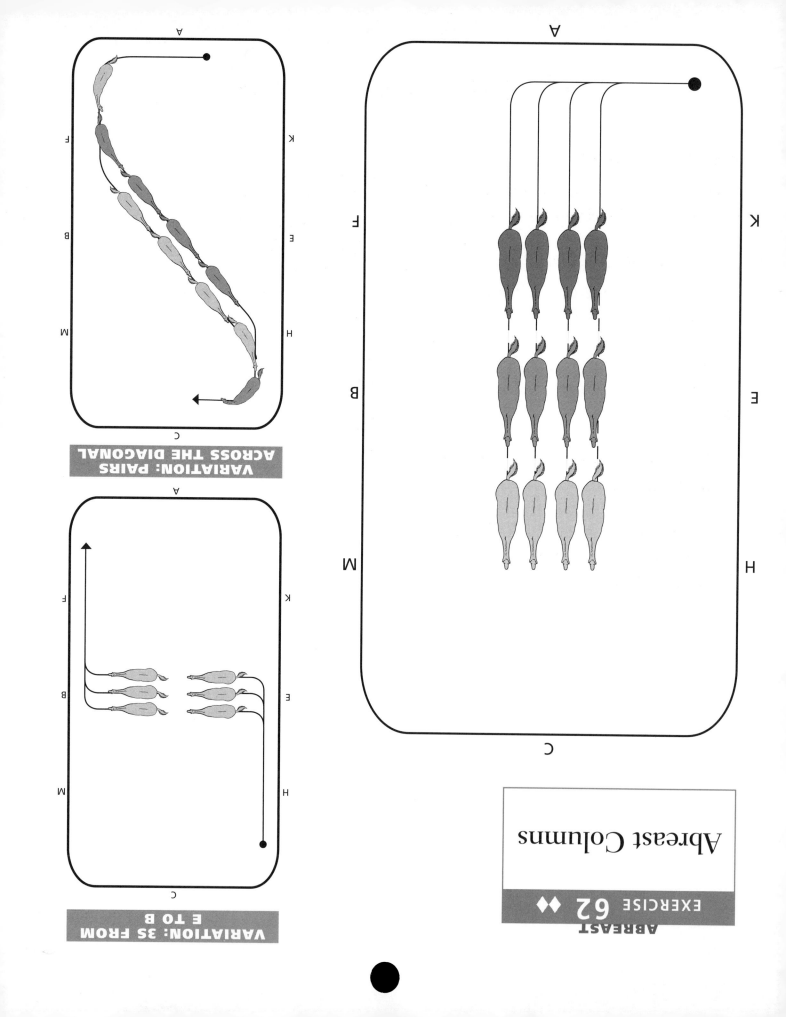

Abreast Columns

VARIATION: 3S FROM
E TO B

VARIATION: PAIRS
ACROSS THE DIAGONAL

62. Abreast Columns

STARTING POINT

● Form a single-file line in closed formation at **K** facing **A**. Divide your group into three sections.

HOW DO I RIDE THIS?

1 Move forward to **A**.

2 At **A**, the caller signals for the first group to turn. Riders turn together and travel abreast down the center of the arena.

3 The caller signals for group 2 and then for group 3 to turn at **A**.

4 All groups travel the centerline in abreast columns.

KEEP IN MIND

◆ Watching the riders on either side and rating the speed of your horse keeps columns abreast.
◆ Each group of riders maintains an equal distance from each other as they traverse the arena.

VARIATIONS

◆ Ride with a different number of riders in each column.
◆ Ride with as many columns as you wish.
◆ Ride from **E** to **B**, cross the diagonal, or ride a circle.

pro tip

The video camera is an amazing tool. Have someone videotape the drill team from the audience's point of view to determine which moves look the most dynamic. Stars look great from above, while abreast moves look better from the ground.

— **Friesians of Majesty**
Townshend, Vermont

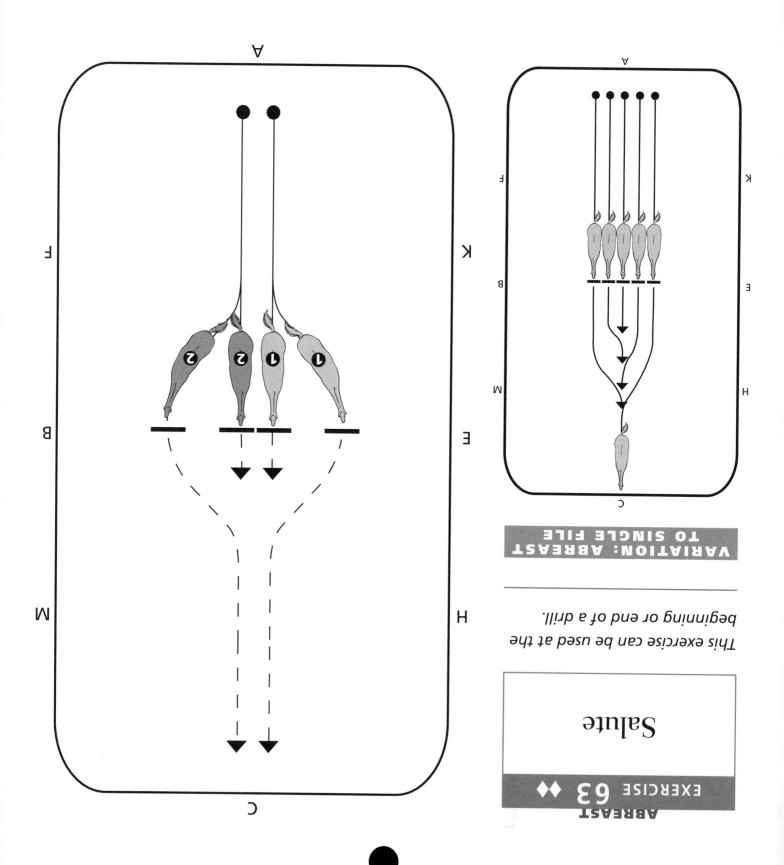

EXERCISE 63 ♦♦
ABREAST

Salute

This exercise can be used at the beginning or end of a drill.

VARIATION: ABREAST TO SINGLE FILE

63. Salute

STARTING POINT

● Form line 1 at **A**, facing **C**, on the left side of the centerline, in closed formation.
● Form line 2 at **A**, facing **C**, on the right side of the centerline, in closed formation.

HOW DO I RIDE THIS?

1 Ride down the centerline in pairs.

2 Halt at **X**. The second pair of riders fans to the outside of the first pair. Additional pairs fan to the outside of the preceding pair, making an abreast line.

3 When this is the beginning or end of the drill, salute.

4 On the caller's signal, the outside pair of riders comes together in front of the line and rides down the centerline. All other pairs follow suit.

KEEP IN MIND

◆ Knowing where partners are helps to keep bodies parallel.
◆ When riders halt, they align their bodies with the riders on either side.
◆ Riders ride their own sides of the centerline.
◆ At the start, the lead horses are at the back of the line. After the salute, they are in front.
◆ Dressage judges are seated at **C**. The riders face the judges for a salute.

INCREASING DIFFICULTY

◆ Trot or jog to halt.
◆ Canter or lope to halt.
◆ Do a sliding stop to halt.
◆ Increase the speed of the up transition.

VARIATIONS

◆ The pair in the center pulls out of the abreast line first, then riders file into line in the original order. Since some horses do better behind or in front, this may be easier.
◆ Ride abreast to single file (see small diagram).

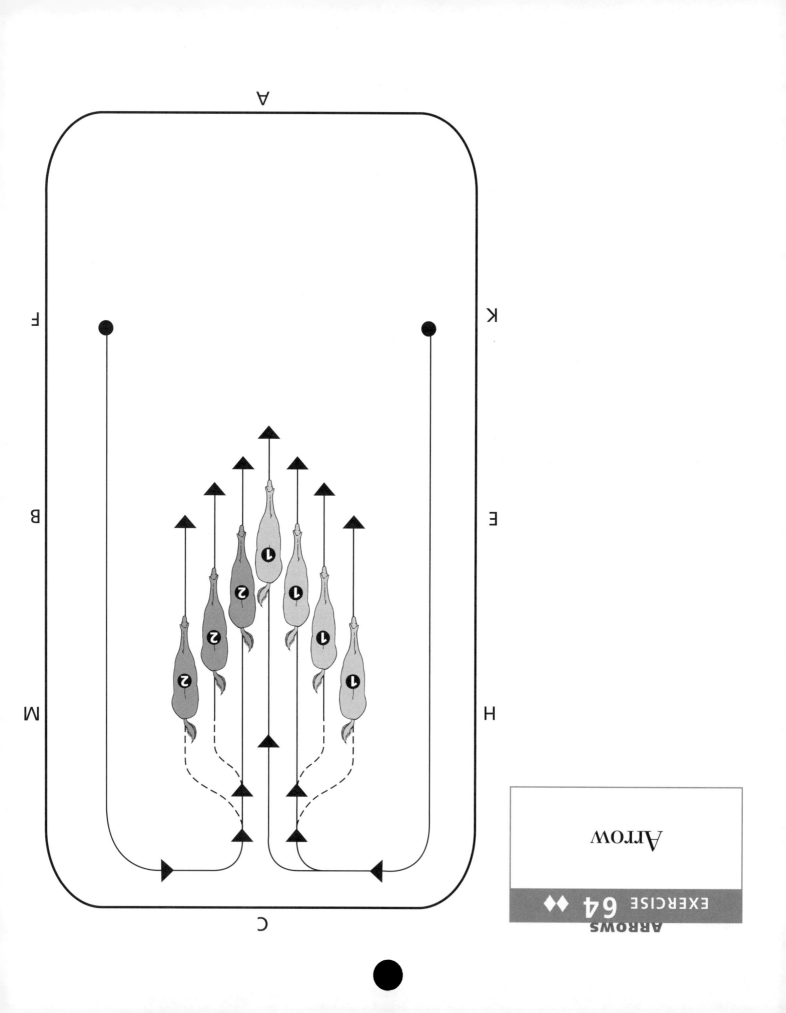

64. Arrow

STARTING POINT

● Form line 1 at **K**, facing **C**, single file in closed formation.

● Form line 2 at **F**, facing **C**, single file in closed formation.

HOW DO I RIDE THIS?

1 Ride forward to **C**. At **C**, the first rider turns down the centerline.

2 Following riders turn down the centerline and form pairs.

3 Riders fan out in the formation of an arrow.

4 Riders continue riding toward **A** in arrow formation.

KEEP IN MIND

◆ In arrow formation, the nose of the horse behind is beside the leg of the rider ahead.

INCREASING DIFFICULTY

◆ Increase the speed to add excitement.
◆ Decrease speed to impart an air of stateliness.
◆ Use a leg yield as you fan out.

VARIATION

◆ Halt in arrow formation. This makes an impressive beginning or ending to your drill and can also add suspense to the drill to come.

pro tip

One rider must be responsible for setting the pace of the movements. Be sure this rider is on one of your best, steadiest horses. Even in new areas with unusual distractions, a good leading horse will go steadily forward.

— **Sergeant Mayo**
Royal Canadian Mounted Police
Ontario, Canada

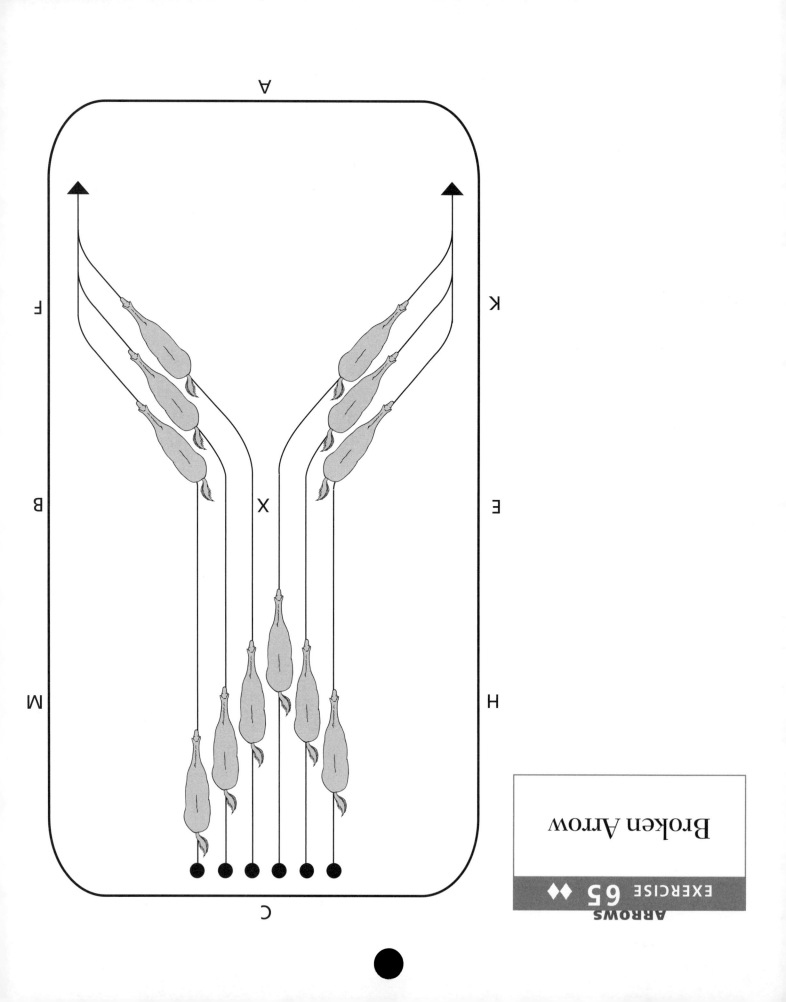

Broken Arrow

65. Broken Arrow

STARTING POINT

● Form an abreast line of an even number of riders (at least four) in closed formation at **C** facing **X**.

HOW DO I RIDE THIS?

1 Ride to **X** in arrow formation. Middle riders pull ahead.

2 Split and ride staggered and abreast diagonally to **K** and **F**.

3 Turn into single-file lines along the fence.

KEEP IN MIND

◆ In arrow formation, the nose of the horse behind is beside the leg of the rider ahead.
◆ The horses at the point of the arrow arrive at the fence first.
◆ After the split, the abreast line is staggered.

INCREASING DIFFICULTY

◆ Ride the arrow slowly. Increase the speed when you split, like the shot of the arrow.

VARIATION

◆ Split earlier or later.

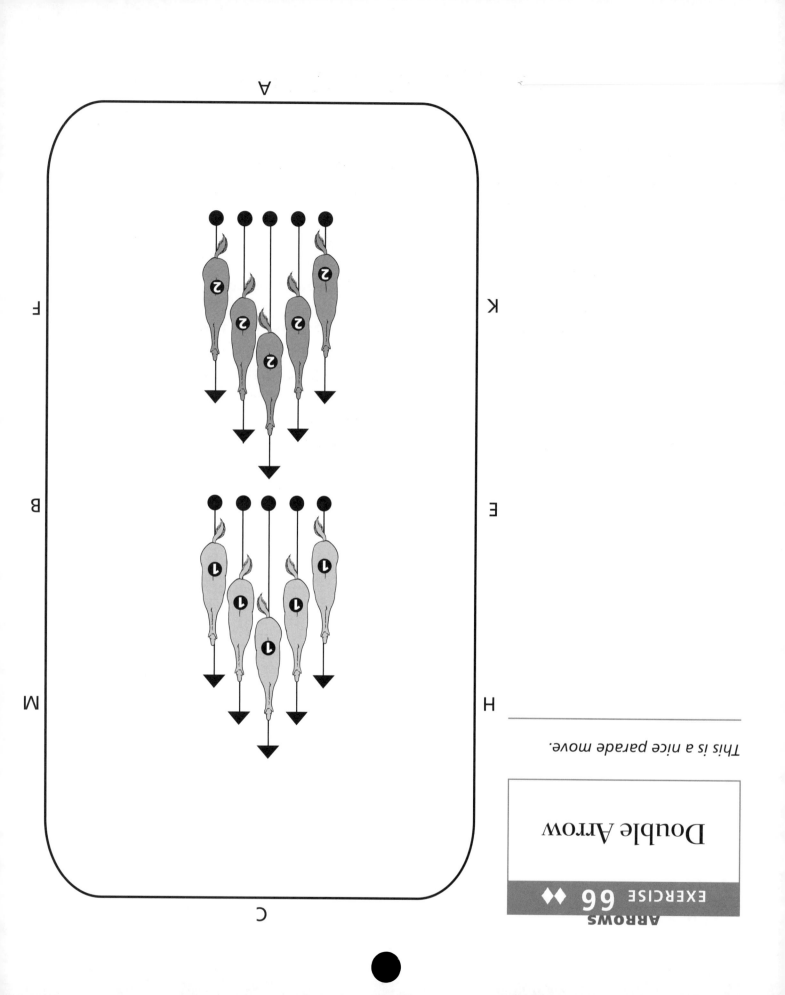

Double Arrow

This is a nice parade move.

66. Double Arrow

STARTING POINT

● Form line 1 between **E** and **B**, facing **C**, with riders abreast.

● Form line 2 between **K** and **F**, facing **C**, with riders abreast.

HOW DO I RIDE THIS?

1 Proceed down the centerline.

2 When the caller signals, inside riders pull ahead and outside riders fall back, thus forming two arrows.

3 Both arrows travel the length of the arena.

4 Before **C**, the point of the arrow slows to form an abreast line that splits at **C** (or everyone can turn right or left, depending on your needs for the next exercise).

KEEP IN MIND

◆ The two arrows form at the same time.

◆ Riders maintain the distance between arrows as they proceed down the arena.

◆ Riders rate their horses to maintain the distance between themselves and the horses ahead and behind.

◆ In arrow formation, the nose of the horse behind is beside the leg of the rider ahead.

INCREASING DIFFICULTY

◆ Go from an abreast column to an arrow, then to an abreast column, and then to a V formation (backward arrow).

VARIATIONS

◆ Form more than two arrows.

◆ Have the arrows move down the fence and turn the corner to come down the other fence line.

pro tip

Parades require you to move forward at a steady walk. Perform a simple maneuver that you can do over and over. You can walk forward and trot back to rotate riders.

— Friesians of Majesty
Townshend, Vermont

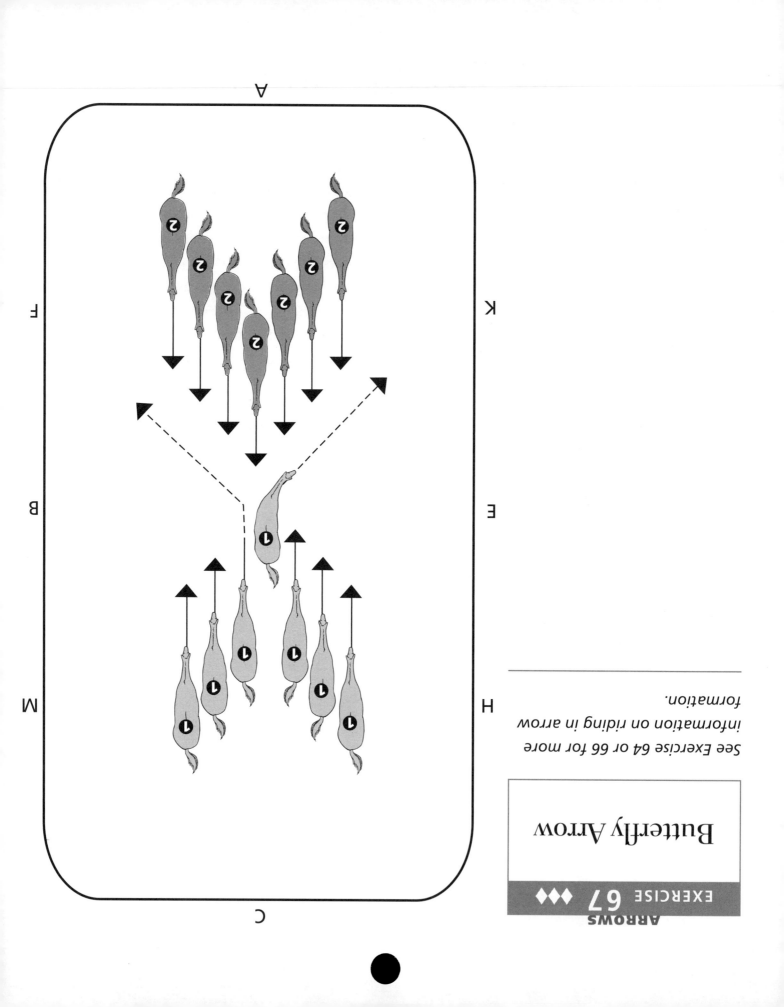

Butterfly Arrow

See Exercise 64 or 66 for more information on riding in arrow formation.

67. Butterfly Arrow

STARTING POINT

● Form arrow 1 at **C** facing **A**.
● Form arrow 2 at **A** facing **C**.

HOW DO I RIDE THIS?

1 Arrows ride toward each other.

2 Between **E** and **B**, the sides of arrow 1 split and travel along the outside of arrow 2 to the fence line.

3 Arrow 2 continues in arrow formation to **C**.

- - - - - - - - - - - - - - - -

KEEP IN MIND

◆ Riders keep moving.
◆ Arrow 1 splits when it meets arrow 2.
◆ In arrow formation, the nose of the horse behind is beside the leg of the rider ahead.

INCREASING DIFFICULTY/ VARIATIONS

◆ Increase the speed.
◆ Have riders hold streamers or flags as they move through the butterfly.

pro tip

All riders must know every position in an exercise so that they can take over and lead, or follow, if something goes wrong.

— Friesians of Majesty
Townshend, Vermont

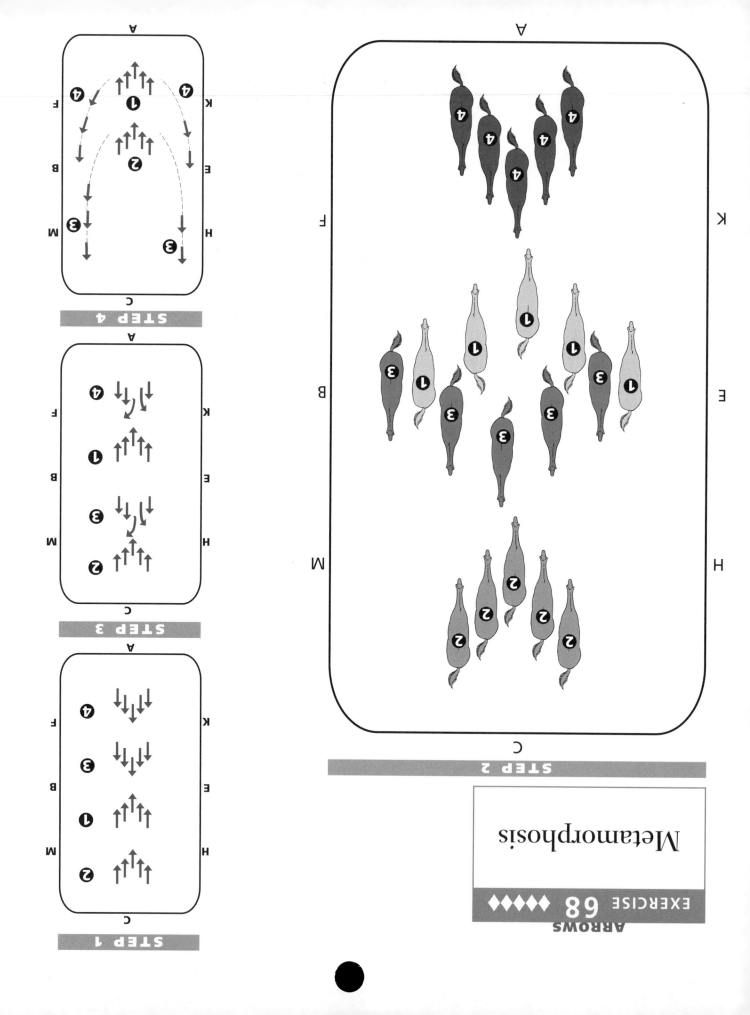

68. Metamorphosis

STARTING POINT

● Arrows 1 and 2 line up on the centerline at **C** facing **X**, in open column formation.

● Arrows 3 and 4 line up at **A** facing **X**, slightly offset to arrows 1 and 2, in open column formation.

HOW DO I RIDE THIS?

1 Ride four arrows toward each other.

2 Arrows 1 and 3 pass through each other and remain in arrow formation.

3 When arrows 1 and 4 and arrows 2 and 3 meet, arrows 1 and 2 remain in arrow formation while arrows 3 and 4 split and move along the outside of arrows 1 and 2.

4 Lines 1 and 2 remain in arrow formation until they reach **A**. Lines 3 and 4 form single-file lines along the fence and head toward **C**.

KEEP IN MIND

◆ The lines are slightly offset to enable the arrows to pass through each other.

◆ Riders on the point of the arrow pass left hand to left hand.

◆ The arrows are far enough from each other to allow the pass-through.

◆ The split should be a well-defined transition.

VARIATION

◆ Remain in arrow formation and pass through all arrows.

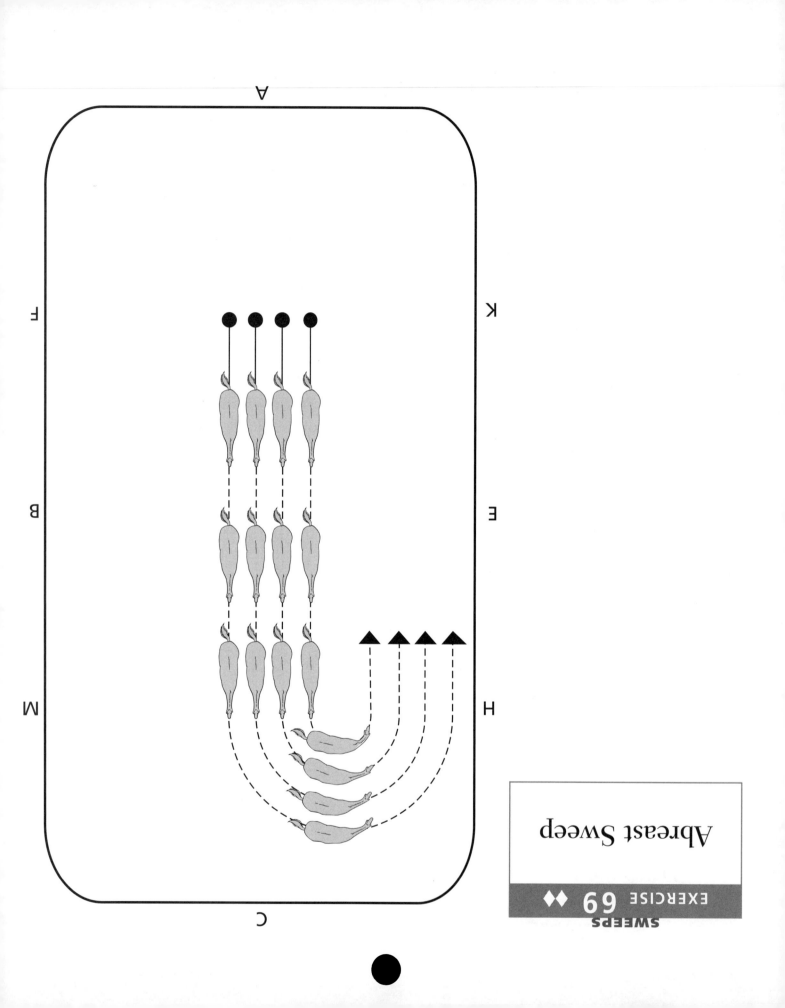

Abreast Sweep

69. Abreast Sweep

STARTING POINT

● Form abreast columns on the centerline between **K** and **F**, facing **C**, in closed formation.

HOW DO I RIDE THIS?

1 Move down the centerline.

2 Before **C**, each column makes a sweeping turn left and riders remain side by side.

3 Proceed in columns down the fence line.

KEEP IN MIND

◆ During the turn, riders leave enough room to allow the whole column of abreast horses to remain side by side. Outside horses are close to the fence.
◆ During the sweeping turn, outside horses move faster than do inside horses.

INCREASING DIFFICULTY

◆ Ride in columns along the fence. All columns turn at the same time and form one abreast line. This can move into a whip (see Exercise 45) or a wheel (see Exercise 48).

VARIATIONS

◆ Columns at the end of the line turn first, reversing the order.
◆ Columns all reverse at the same time, reversing the order.

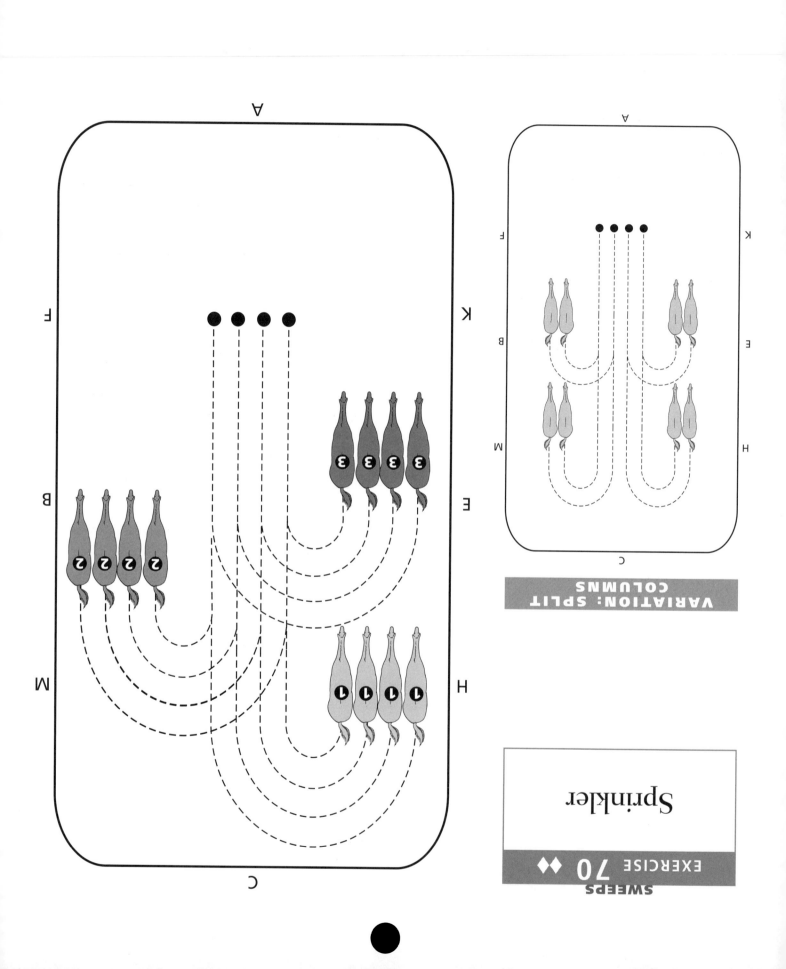

VARIATION: SPLIT
COLUMNS

70. Sprinkler

STARTING POINT

● Form abreast columns on the centerline between **K** and **F**, facing **C**, in open formation. Number the columns.

HOW DO I RIDE THIS?

1 Move down the centerline.

2 Before **C**, the caller signals.

3 All odd-numbered columns turn left and all even-numbered columns turn right. Each column makes a sweeping turn and riders remain side by side.

4 Proceed in columns down both fence lines.

KEEP IN MIND

◆ As you turn, leave enough room for the whole column of abreast horses to remain side by side. Outside horses should be close to the fence.

◆ During the sweeping turns, outside horses will have to move faster than the inside horses.

INCREASING DIFFICULTY

◆ Ride in two columns, facing **C**, along both long sides simultaneously. All columns will turn at the same time and form one column on the centerline facing **A**.

VARIATIONS

◆ Wait until your column reaches **C** before sweeping to the right or left. This will keep your team in the same order.

◆ Columns at the end of the line turn first, reversing the order.

◆ Half of the abreast column turns right and half turns left (see small diagram).

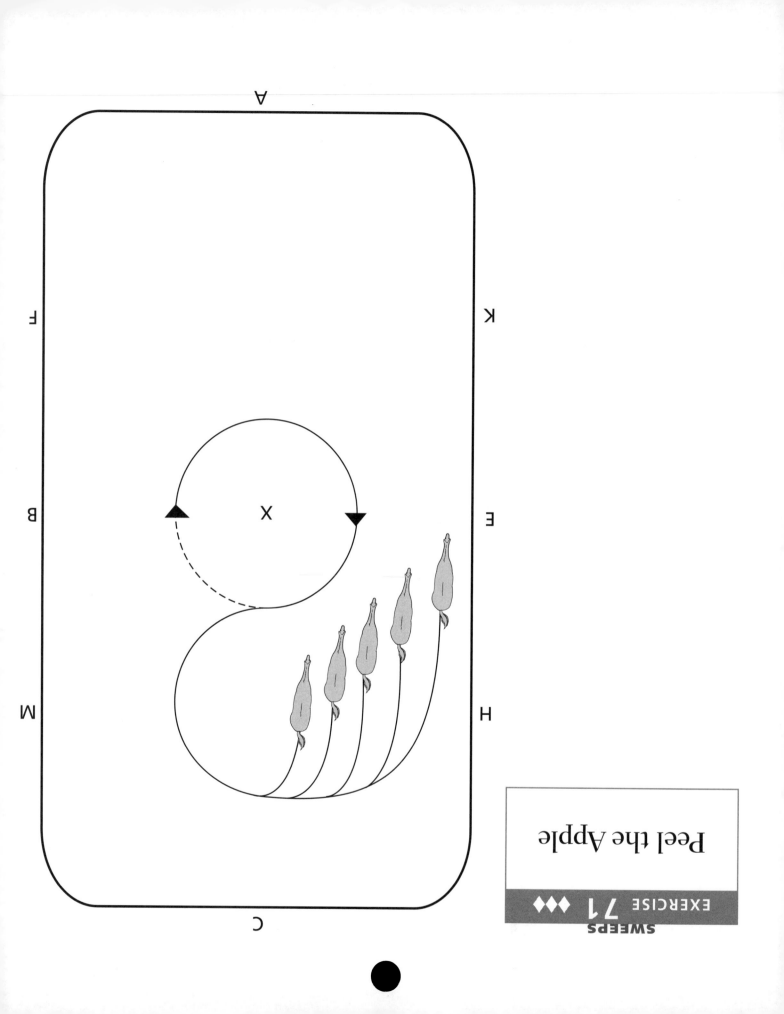

A

F   K

B   E

X

M   H

C

Peel the Apple

71. Peel the Apple

STARTING POINT

● Form a small, clockwise circle around **X** in closed formation.

HOW DO I RIDE THIS?

1 Ride the small circle clockwise.

2 Pass the centerline closest to **C**.

3 Begin turning counterclockwise toward **M**, then toward **C**.

4 Cross the centerline again, heading toward **H**.

5 Turn left with the other riders into an abreast staggered sweep.

KEEP IN MIND

◆ It is helpful to imagine you are making a small figure 8.
◆ The nose of the horse behind stays beside the shoulder of the horse ahead for the staggered look.

VARIATIONS

◆ Ride this in pairs or columns.
◆ Have a rider in the middle of the circle do a spin or a pirouette, or carry a flag.
◆ Do a spiral or a carousel before or after this exercise.
◆ Ride down the quarter line before this exercise and do a half-circle instead of the full circle if you have a large team.
◆ Form a single-file line or an abreast line following this exercise.

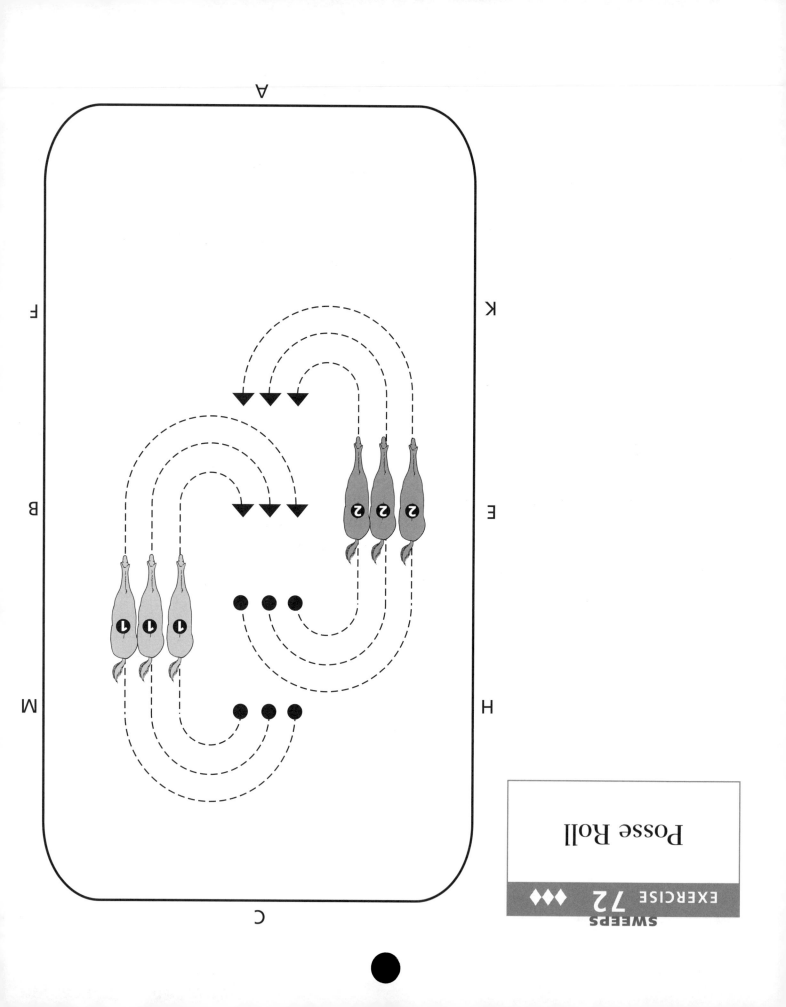

Posse Roll

72. Posse Roll

STARTING POINT

● Form two columns on the centerline, roughly between **H** and **M**, facing **C**. You should be in closed formation in each column and in open formation between columns.

HOW DO I RIDE THIS?

1 Ride down the centerline.

2 At the caller's signal, column 1 rolls to the right and column 2 rolls to the left, in abreast formation.

3 Both columns head down the rail toward **A**.

4 At the caller's signal, columns 1 and 2 turn onto the centerline, with column 2 following column 1.

5 Ride toward **C**.

KEEP IN MIND

◆ Riders watch the bodies of the other riders in the column to stay even.
◆ Riders watch the other column to help them arrive at the right place at the right time.

VARIATION

◆ Have column 1 circle behind column 2. Then have column 2 circle behind column 1.

pro tip

People believe that the more complicated the drill, the better. Not so. Do what you can well. If you successfully complete a drill, this gives a sense of accomplishment to the riders and will encourage them to try harder each time to improve and polish each performance.

— Sergeant Mayo
Royal Canadian Mounted Police
Ontario, Canada

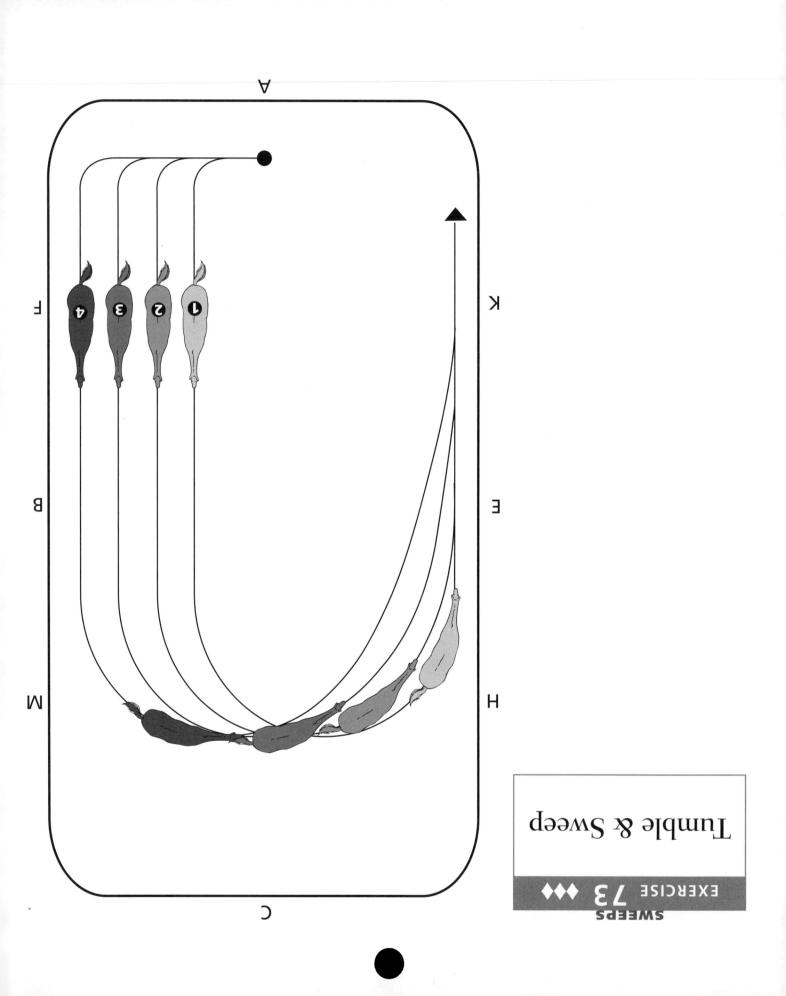

73. Tumble & Sweep

STARTING POINT

● Form a single-file line at **A** facing **F**, in closed formation.

HOW DO I RIDE THIS?

1 Ride forward.

2 At the corner before **F**, make an abreast turn to the left at the same time as the other riders.

3 Continue down the fence in abreast formation.

4 At **M**, begin a sweep to the left.

5 Rider 1 pulls ahead. Rider 2 drops behind him and moves from his right side to his left. Likewise, rider 3 moves to the left of 2 and rider 4 moves to the left of 3. The line is now in reverse order.

6 Pull forward so your horse's nose is beside the body of the rider in front of you. Now you have a staggered line.

7 Pass **H**. Spread out your line again and form a single-file line.

KEEP IN MIND

◆ It is important to be a BRATT (see page 23).
◆ If the horse to her side appears to be a possible kicker, the rider allows more space as she moves behind him.

VARIATIONS

◆ Do the sweep anywhere else in the arena.
◆ Stay in a staggered line.
◆ Move back into an abreast line.

pro tip

Always be courteous and respectful to the rodeo stock contractor and the cowboy/cowgirl contestants while warming up in the arena or behind the chutes. Remember that they pay an entry fee to be there.

— **The All-American Cowgirl Chicks**
Fort Worth, Texas

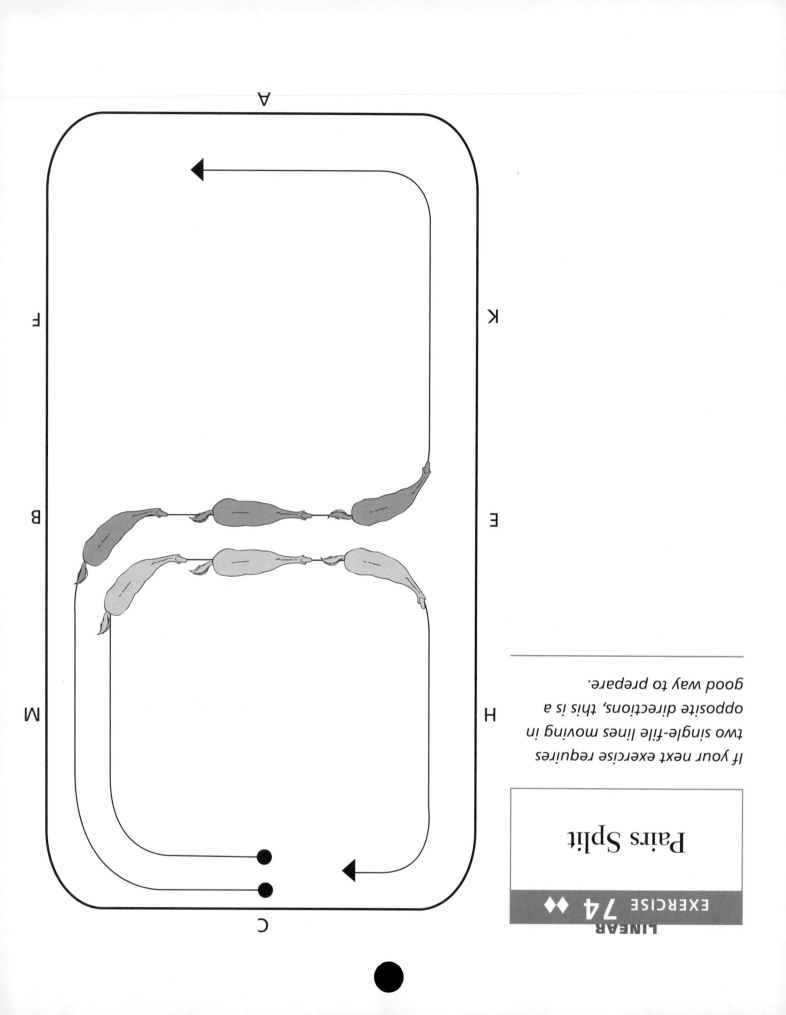

LINEAR
EXERCISE 74 ◆◆

Pairs Split

If your next exercise requires two single-file lines moving in opposite directions, this is a good way to prepare.

A

F   K

B   E

M   H

C

74. Pairs Split

STARTING POINT

● Form pairs at **C**, facing **M**.

HOW DO I RIDE THIS?

1 Proceed in pairs to **B**. At **B**, turn right toward **E**.

2 At **E**, split with your partner, with one rider going left and the other right.

3 Follow along the rail.

KEEP IN MIND

◆ The outside horse in a pair travels slightly ahead of the inside horse so that the two horses will be even after the first two turns.

VARIATIONS

◆ Make the split after riding down the centerline.
◆ Make the split after crossing the school on the diagonal.
◆ Split at **X**.

pro tip

Use markers as destination points. They will help riders from either end or side of the arena reach the same place at the same time.

— **Sergeant Mayo**
Royal Canadian Mounted Police
Ontario, Canada

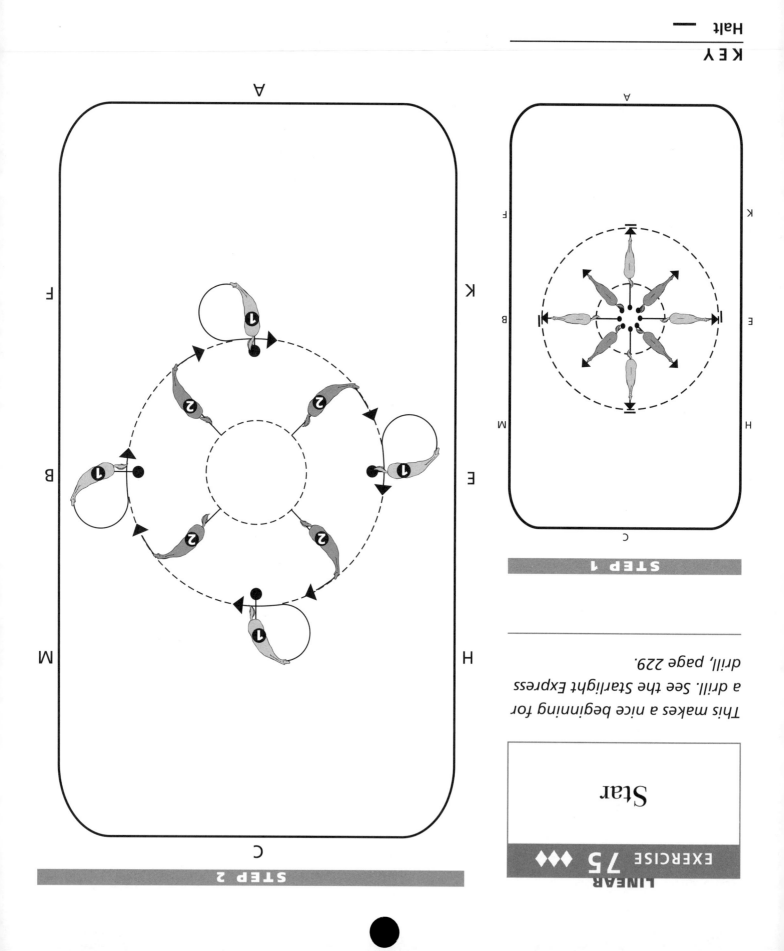

STEP 1

This makes a nice beginning for a drill. See the Starlight Express drill, page 229.

Star

LINEAR
EXERCISE 75 ◆◆◆

STEP 2

75. Star

STARTING POINT

● Form a small circle in closed formation in the center of the arena, with tails pointed toward **X**. Count off by 2s.

HOW DO I RIDE THIS?

1 At the signal, 1s move forward, form a large circle, and halt.

2 At the next signal, 1s circle left until they are facing clockwise on the large circle. Number 2s move out to the large circle and turn right on the large circle. Both 1s and 2s ride the large circle.

KEEP IN MIND

◆ Riders' movement from the smaller to the larger circle is straight, like the spokes of a wheel.
◆ Number 2s stay between the 1s as they ride their small circles.
◆ Number 1s ride a very small circle and move right into line.
◆ Everyone finishes in the same order as on the small circle.

INCREASING DIFFICULTY

◆ Instead of doing small circles, 1s can ride pirouettes, turn on the forehand, or do spins.

VARIATION

◆ Number 1s ride out to the larger circle, halt, and wait. When the caller signals, 2s ride out to the larger circle and halt. When the caller signals, all riders turn right on the large circle.

pro tip

Place your best moves at the beginning and end of your drill.

— **Friesians of Majesty**
Townshend, Vermont

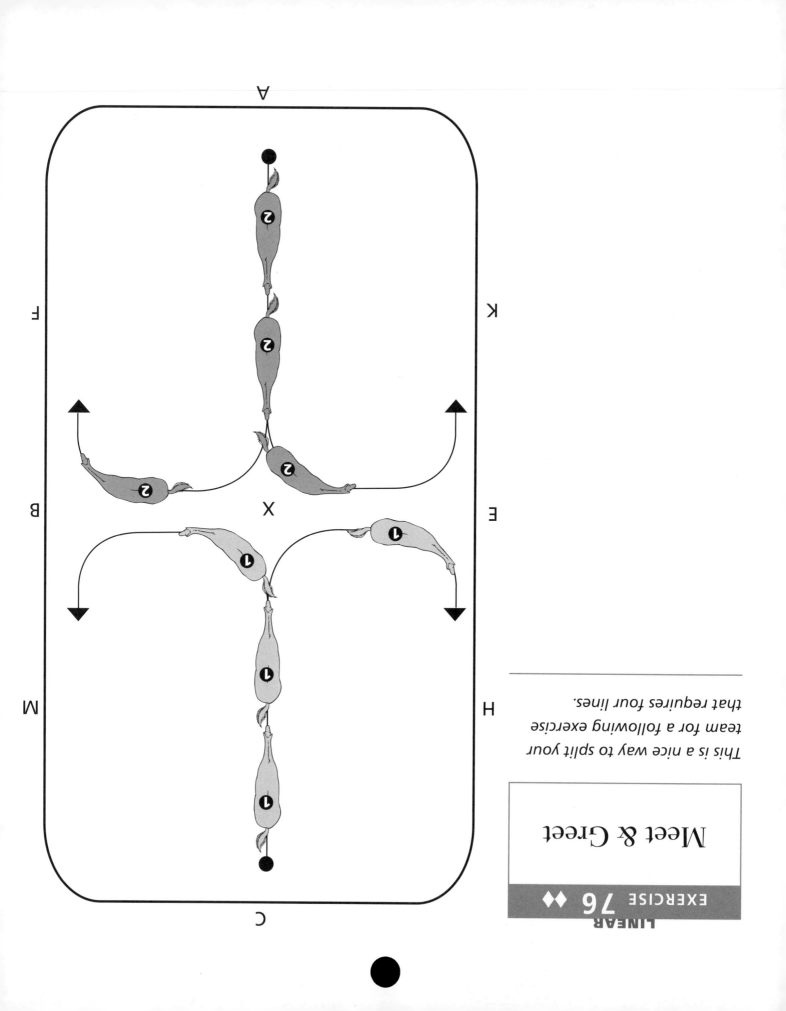

Meet & Greet

This is a nice way to split your team for a following exercise that requires four lines.

76. Meet & Greet

STARTING POINT

- Form line 1 at **C** facing **X**, in closed formation.
- Form line 2 at **A** facing **X**, in closed formation.

HOW DO I RIDE THIS?

1 Move down the centerline toward **X**.

2 At **X**, the first horses from lines 1 and 2 turn right. The second horses from each line turn left and the third horses turn right. Repeat this pattern until all horses have turned.

3 Ride in open formation.

4 Upon reaching **E** and **B**, lines from **A** turn back toward **A** and continue along the fence. The lines from **C** move along the fence toward **C**.

KEEP IN MIND

- When riding down the centerline, riders look directly at **A** or **C** and gauge their speed to reach **X** at the same time as their partner in the other line.

VARIATION

- Have both of the first horses turn toward **B** as pairs, then both of the second horses toward **E** as pairs. Every other pair turns toward **B** or **E**.

Wow your audience with a suicide move.

CHAPTER FOUR

INTERLACING

AUDIENCES LOVE TO MARVEL at the skill of horses and riders who can, as if by magic, weave their lines through each other and come out unscathed. The exercises in this chapter present a variety of weaves.

There are several types of weaves. A *true weave* is one in which one line of riders threads in and out of the other line (see Exercises 77 and 80). *Threading the needle* involves straight lines moving through each other (see Exercise 83). A *suicide* is one line of abreast horses riding head-on toward another abreast line (see Exercise 94). Weaves make a drill truly exciting!

Choosing music

Music can heighten the excitement of an already dramatic weave exercise. It can also make your drill a thing of beauty, helping to make your team appear as a cohesive body. It can bring tears to your audience's eyes.

Many types of music can work for your team. Find a theme and use the same type of music throughout the drill. Pick music that you love and can live with despite repetition, and that your horses like. Make sure that it doesn't spook them. Beyond this, think about matching the music to your horses' style or to their gait.

Consider the physical attributes and personalities of the horses in your team. Are they little, cute, or light? Select light or feminine music. If your horses are big-bodied warmbloods or draft-type horses, select powerful music. Expressive movers may be able to work with techno music. Choppy horses or those with little spring need music that doesn't have a heavy beat, such as swing. An easygoing group of horses may need music that pushes them along and makes them look lively, such as the William Tell Overture (the *Lone Ranger* music).

Consider too how the tempo relates to your horses' gait. For trot music, think of your posting rhythm: up, down, up, down, 1, 2, 1, 2. For canter music, count 1, 2, 3, 4; 1, 2, 3, 4. The numbers of beats per minute usually fall into the ranges in the chart below. Although the canter/lope is a three-beat gait, the period of suspension accounts for an additional beat. Most music with ¾ time, such as a waltz, is too slow for horses' gaits. Green horses or smaller breeds can have canters of up to 107 BPM.

TYPES OF MUSIC

Wallpaper or background music. This type of music does not influence choreography. It's the simplest use of music.

Interpretative music. This type of music influences the choreography. Transitions in the music and the choreography are simultaneous, as in ballet.

Combo music. Parts of this music are interpretative and parts are just wallpaper music.

TYPE OF GAIT	BEATS PER MINUTE	MUSICAL TIME
Walk (4-beat gait)	48–60	4/4
Trot/jog (2-beat gait)	69–84	2/4 or 4/4
Canter/lope (3-beat gait, plus a period of suspension)	90–110	4/4

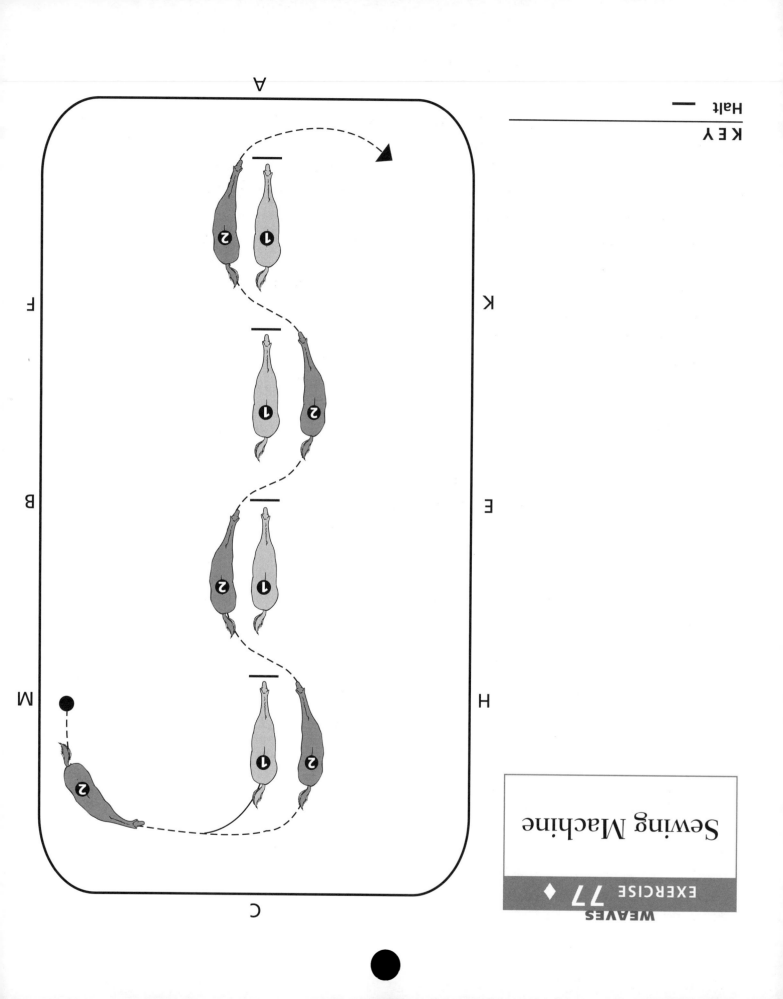

Sewing Machine

WEAVES
EXERCISE 77 ◆

KEY
Halt ▬

77. Sewing Machine

STARTING POINT

● Form a single-file line at **M** facing **C**, in open formation. The first four riders in line are number 1s; the rest are 2s.

HOW DO I RIDE THIS?

1 Move forward to **C**.

2 Number 1s ride down the centerline and halt in open formation.

3 Number 2s weave in and out between the 1s.

4 At **A**, 2s turn right. After all of the 2s have turned, the 1s follow.

KEEP IN MIND

◆ The line of number 1s is very straight.
◆ Riders keep spacing even.

INCREASING DIFFICULTY

◆ Number 2s use a leg yield or side pass through the line.
◆ Number 1s do spins or pirouettes on the centerline.

VARIATIONS

◆ Number 2s ride in closed formation.
◆ Number 2s make wider loops.

pro tip

As we all know, good riding is the most difficult and important aspect of drill team, but the music has a huge impact on the audience. Make it fun so the crowd gets into the performance.

— **Sergeant Mayo**
Royal Canadian Mounted Police
Ontario, Canada

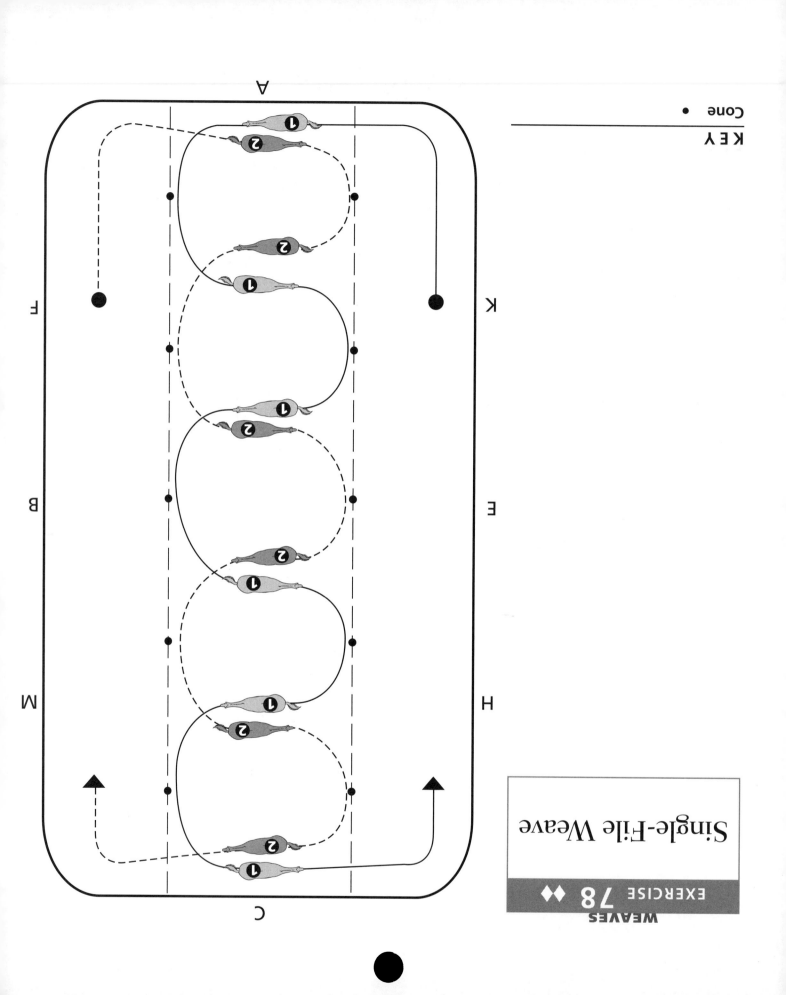

Single-File Weave

WEAVES
EXERCISE 78 ◆◆

KEY
Cone ●

78. Single-File Weave

STARTING POINT

- Form line 1 at **K** facing **A**, in open formation.
- Form line 2 at **F** facing **A**, in open formation.

HOW DO I RIDE THIS?

1 Partners from lines 1 and 2 pass each other on the centerline left hand to left hand.

2 Each rider makes a half-circle and passes her partner again on the centerline.

3 Partners continue to ride half-circles, progressing down the arena until they reach **C**.

4 At **C**, riders ride along the fence.

KEEP IN MIND

- The half-circles are uniform. Cones on the quarter line can serve as guides.
- Riders maintain spacing and open formation throughout the exercise.

INCREASING DIFFICULTY

- Increase your speed.
- When in open formation, ride with smaller spaces between horses.

VARIATION

- Ride a greater or fewer number of half-circles.

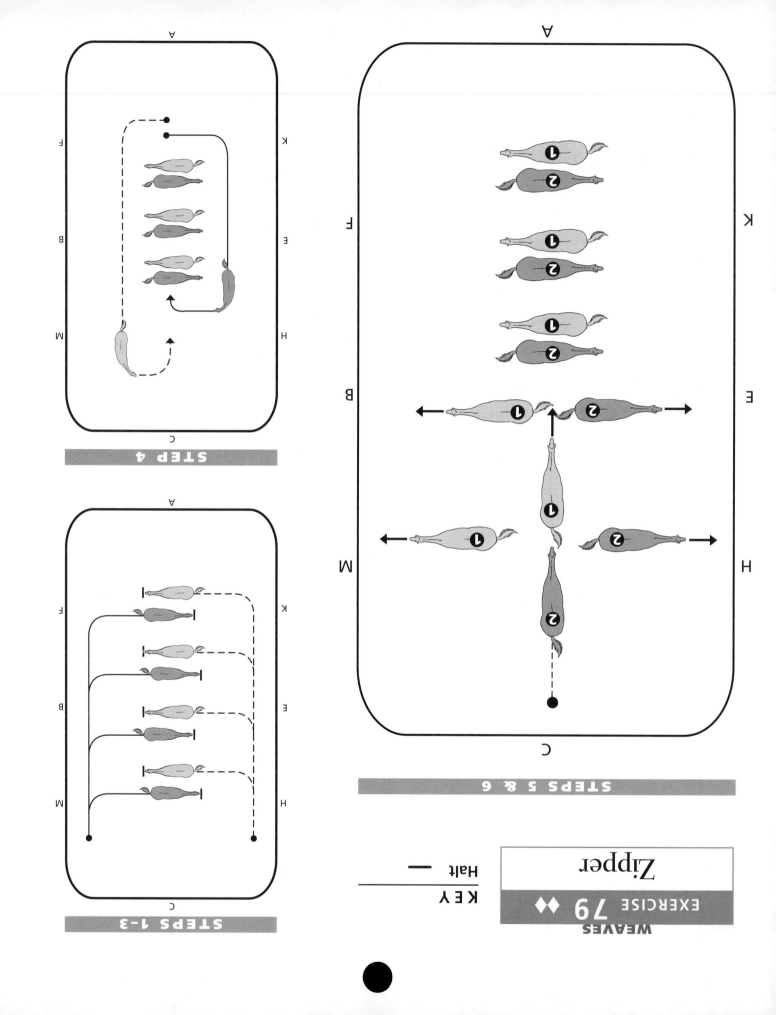

79. Zipper

STARTING POINT

- Form line 1 at **H** facing **E**, in closed formation.
- Form line 2 at **M** facing **B**, in closed formation.

HOW DO I RIDE THIS?

1 Ride forward.

2 The caller signals when all riders are on the long fence. At the signal, turn toward the centerline.

3 Halt so that riders line up on the centerline.

4 The partners closest to **A** move forward, turn, and ride toward **C**.

5 At **C**, the pair forms a single-file line and moves toward **A**.

6 As the pair meets riders on the centerline, centerline riders move forward and ride to the fence, then groups turn toward either **C** or **A**, forming a single-file line.

KEEP IN MIND

- Partners are left hand to left hand on the centerline.
- Partners "unzip" at the same time.

VARIATION

- Only one rider does the unzipping.

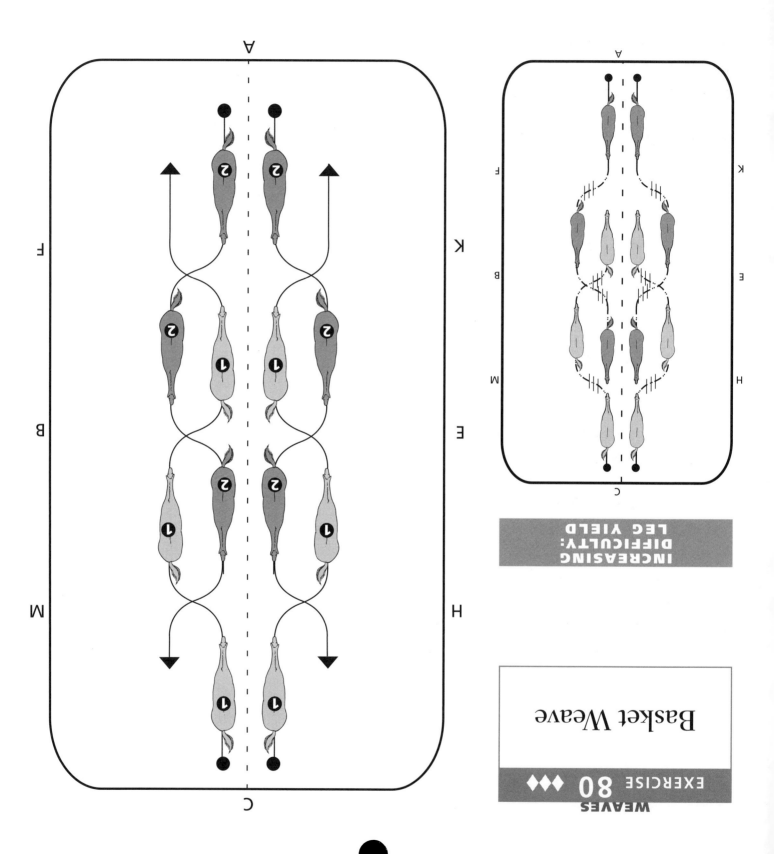

INCREASING
DIFFICULTY:
LEG YIELD

Basket Weave

WEAVES
EXERCISE 80 ◆◆◆

80. Basket Weave

STARTING POINT

● Group 1: Form pairs at **C** facing **A**, in open formation.

● Group 2: Form pairs at **A** facing **C**, in open formation.

HOW DO I RIDE THIS?

1 Pairs from groups 1 and 2 ride down the centerline.

2 The first group 1 pair splits to allow the first oncoming group 2 pair to pass between the riders.

3 Immediately, the first group 1 pair comes back together as a pair.

4 The next pair from group 2 splits to allow the first group 1 pair to pass between the riders.

5 Repeat this pattern, alternately splitting and closing formation, until everyone has completed the basket weave.

KEEP IN MIND

◆ Timid horses are given more space if needed.

◆ Riders of horses who are unhappy about riding close to other horses should do leg yields and change their bend through the weave.

INCREASING DIFFICULTY

◆ Increase the speed.

◆ Ride in closer formation, with less space between horses.

◆ Use a leg yield or a side pass (see small diagram).

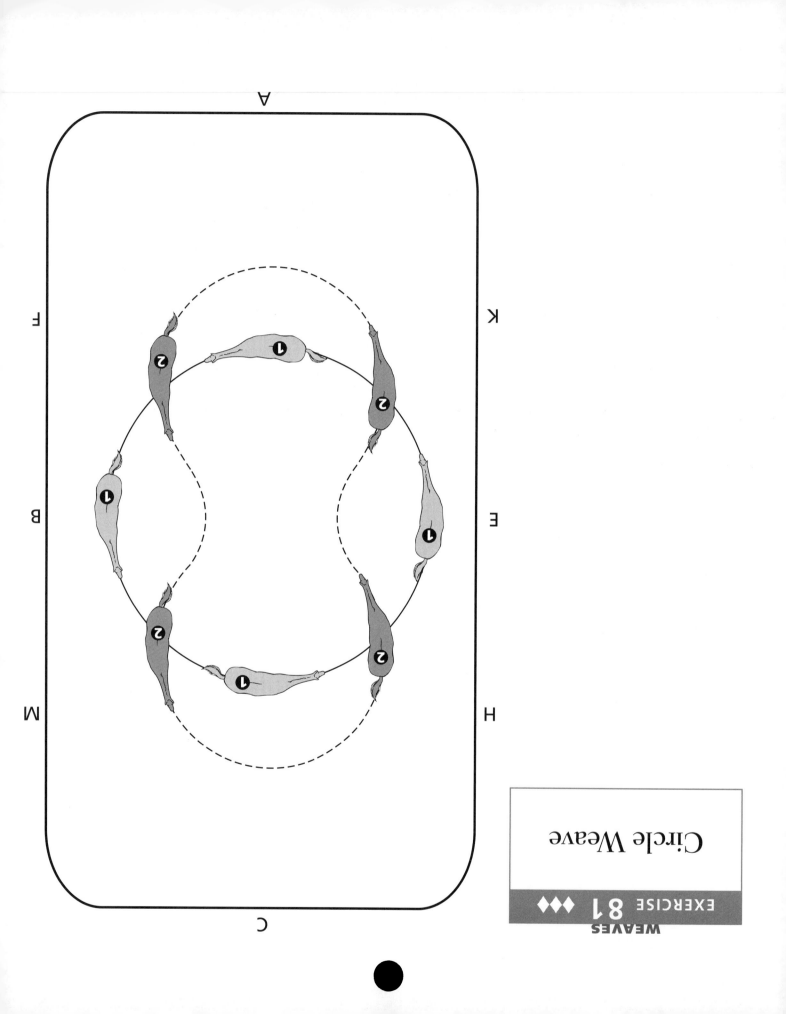

Circle Weave

81. Circle Weave

STARTING POINT

● Form a single-file line, in open formation, along the fence at **E** facing **K**. The first half of the line is referred to as group 1. The second half of the line is group 2.

HOW DO I RIDE THIS?

1 Number 1 riders walk a large circle between **B** and **E**.

2 Number 1 riders continue to circle at a walk as number 2 riders weave in and out of 1s at a trot.

KEEP IN MIND

◆ Riders are aware of the attitudes of others' horses, leaving more space for uncomfortable horses when they are near them.
◆ Riders maintain even spacing.
◆ Weavers watch fellow weavers to ensure that they reach the same point in the weave simultaneously.

INCREASING DIFFICULTY

◆ Number 1s trot or jog while number 2s canter or lope.
◆ Use a leg yield as you weave.

VARIATION
◆ ALTERNATING CIRCLE WEAVE

1 Count off 1, 2, 1, 2, in the single-file line. The exercise looks especially cool when the 1s are dark-colored horses and the 2s are light-colored horses.

2 Everyone makes one revolution on a large circle in closed formation.

3 Number 2s pull out of line and weave around the 1s until they reach their starting point on the circle.

4 Number 2s move back into line for one revolution.

5 Number 1s pull out of line and weave around the 2s until they reach their starting point on the circle.

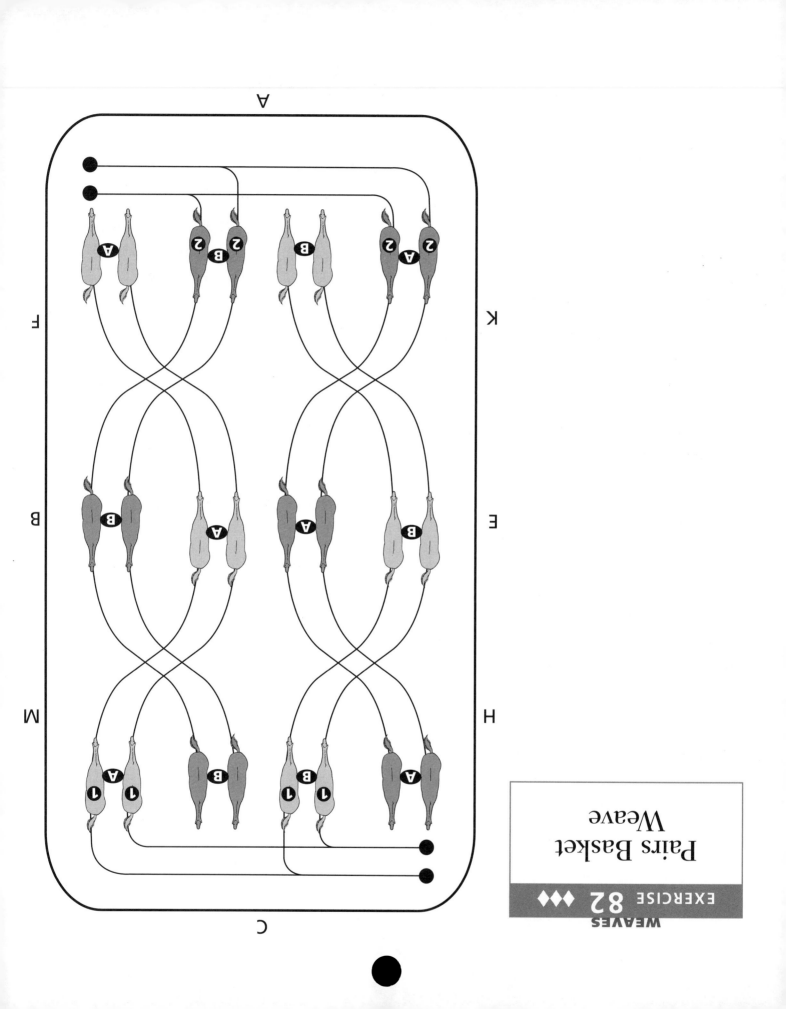

82. Pairs Basket Weave

STARTING POINT

● Form group 1 pairs in the corner between **H** and **C,** facing **C**, in open formation.

● Form group 2 pairs in the corner between **F** and **A**, facing **A**, in open formation.

● Each group counts off two types of pairs: pair A, pair B, pair A, pair B.

HOW DO I RIDE THIS?

1 Ride forward. The A pairs in both groups ride to the second quarter line. The B pairs in both groups ride to the first quarter line.

2 The first two pairs (A and B) in each group make an abreast turn and proceed down the arena to the left of the quarter line.

3 Pass the first letter on the long side.

4 The A pairs from groups 1 and 2 weave toward the centerline. The B pairs from groups 1 and 2 weave toward **E** and **B**, respectively.

5 Pairs from groups 1 and 2 pass each other and move back out to the left of the quarter line.

KEEP IN MIND

◆ When the first riders reach the first letter on the long side, the next pairs in line make their abreast turn down the long side.

◆ Pairs stay together.

◆ Horses are rated to meet the oncoming horses at **H-M**, **E-B**, and **K-F**.

◆ Be a BRATT (see page 23).

INCREASING DIFFICULTY

◆ Increase the speed.

◆ Use a leg yield.

VARIATIONS

◆ Ride more loops.

◆ Ride three or four abreast.

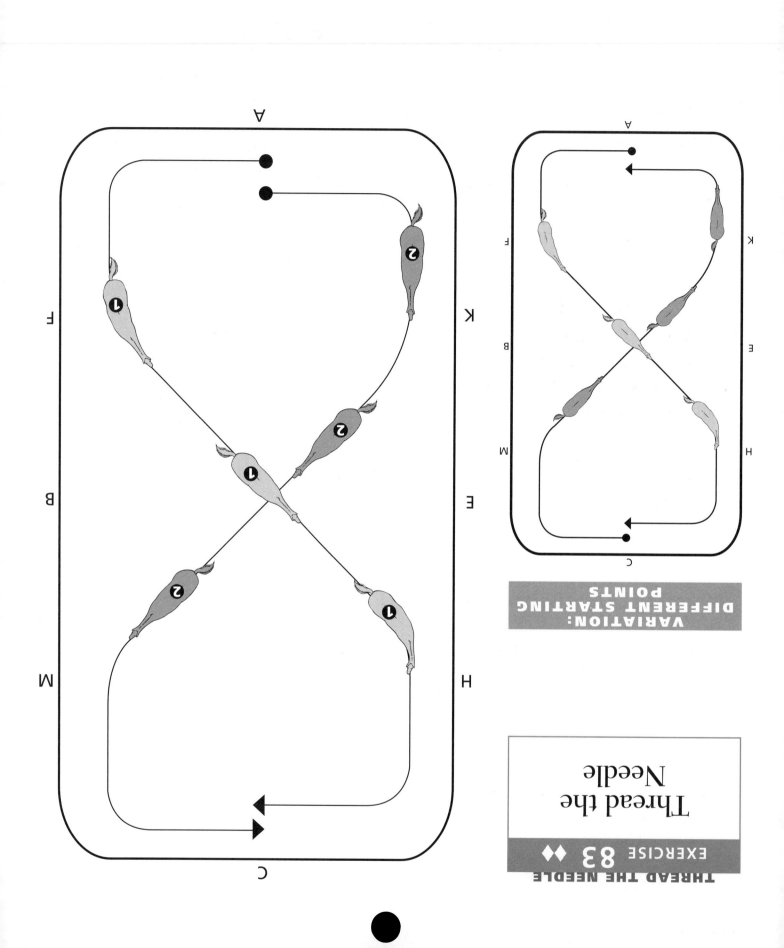

EXERCISE 83 ◆◆

Thread the
Needle

VARIATION:
DIFFERENT STARTING
POINTS

A

F

B

M

C

K

E

H

A

F

B

M

K

E

H

C

83. Thread the Needle

STARTING POINT

● Form a single-file line 1 at **A** facing **F**, in open formation.

● Form a single-file line 2 at **A** facing **K**, in open formation.

HOW DO I RIDE THIS?

1 Move forward past **K** and **F**.

2 Turn and travel across the diagonal.

3 Take turns with riders from the other line while crossing **X**.

4 Continue riding to the rail, then turn toward **C**.

5 Pass riders from the other line left hand to left hand at **C**.

KEEP IN MIND

◆ The team decides before riding the exercise which rider will cross **X** first.

◆ Lines stay straight.

◆ Riders turn onto the diagonal after their body passes the letter.

◆ Riders return to the fence before the letter so that they are parallel to the fence at the letter.

◆ Riders watch the other riders in the lines and rate their horses accordingly.

INCREASING DIFFICULTY

◆ Increase the speed.

◆ Ride in pairs.

VARIATIONS

◆ Line 1 starts at **A**. Line 2 starts at **C** (see small diagram).

◆ Two horses from line 1 pass over **X**, then two horses from line 2 pass over **X**. Repeat this pattern through the line.

pro tip

When threading the needle, try placing markers at each corner 6 to 10 meters (33 feet) from the end of the ring to use as reference points to which the leaders may ride. Everyone must follow that single-file line to the markers and not cut the corner.

— **Stephanie Dobiss**
Keystone Dressage and Combined Training
Association of Central Pennsylvania

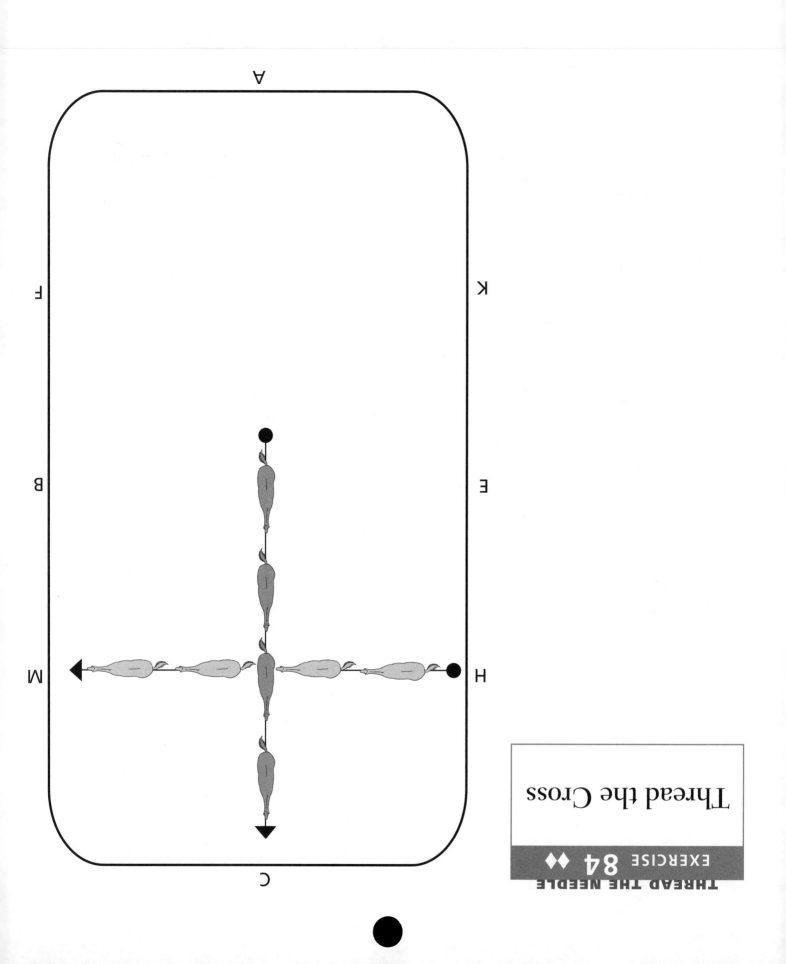

84. Thread the Cross

STARTING POINT

- Form line 1 at **H** facing **M**, in open formation.
- Form line 2 at **X** facing **C**, in open formation.

HOW DO I RIDE THIS?

1 Riders ride straight ahead.

2 The two lines intersect, with horses from one line passing through the spaces in the other line.

KEEP IN MIND

- Lines stay straight.
- Riders rate their horses to arrive at the intersection at the correct moment.

INCREASING DIFFICULTY

- Position every other horse haunches-in left or right.
- Position every other horse shoulder-in left or right.

VARIATIONS

- Ride this in pairs, threes, or fours.
- Number 1s cross from **B** to **E**.

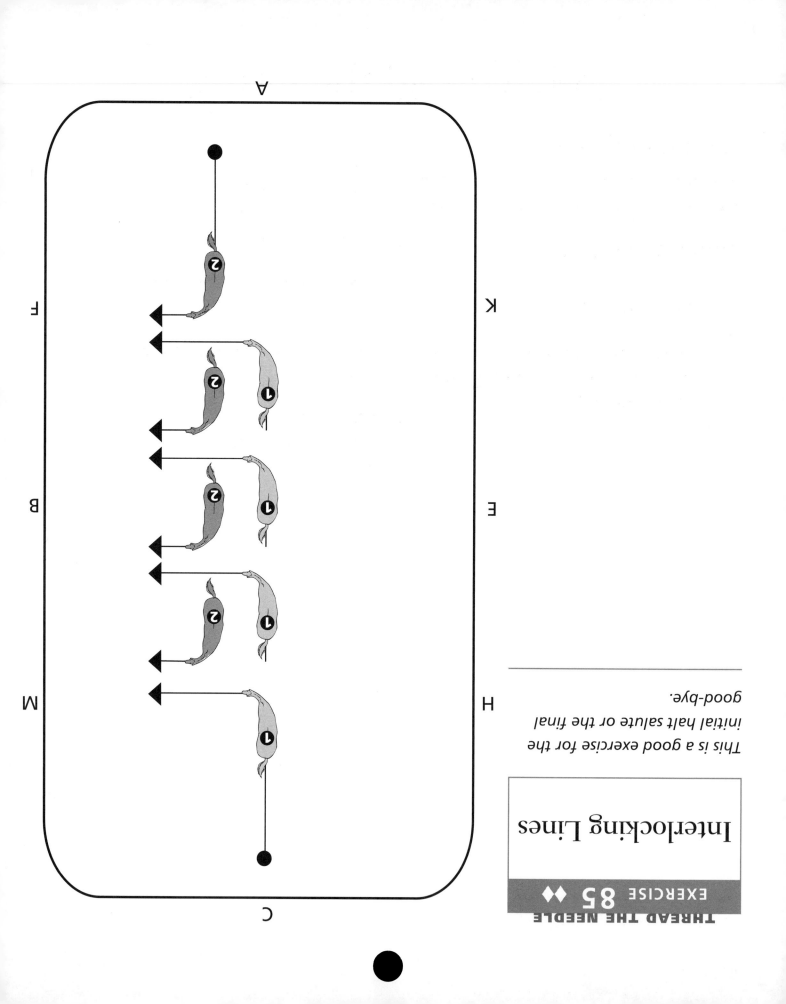

Interlocking Lines

THREAD THE NEEDLE

EXERCISE 85 ◆◆

This is a good exercise for the initial halt salute or the final good-bye.

85. Interlocking Lines

STARTING POINT

● Form line 1 at **C** facing **A**, in closed formation.
● Form line 2 at **A**, slightly to the right of the centerline and facing **C**, in closed formation.

HOW DO I RIDE THIS?

1 Ride down the centerline until your horse's nose has almost reached the nose of your partner's horse from the other line. The first horse from line 1 partners with the last horse from line 2, the second horse from line 1 with the second-to-last horse from line 2, and so on.

2 Turn toward **B** to form an abreast line.

KEEP IN MIND

◆ There has to be enough room for everyone to turn into the abreast line.
◆ In the abreast line, riders' bodies are parallel to each other.
◆ Riders halt facing the audience.

INCREASING DIFFICULTY

◆ Increase the speed.

VARIATIONS

◆ Ride this in open formation to make it easier.
◆ Turn toward **E** instead.
◆ Ride from **E** to **B** and turn toward **A** or **C**.
◆ Turn left behind your partner to continue the drill.
◆ **TRY DOMINOES:**

  1 Ride a single-file line down the centerline.

  2 The leader does a turn on the forehand or the haunches.

  3 The rest of the riders in line follow suit in domino fashion. Everyone turns in the same direction.

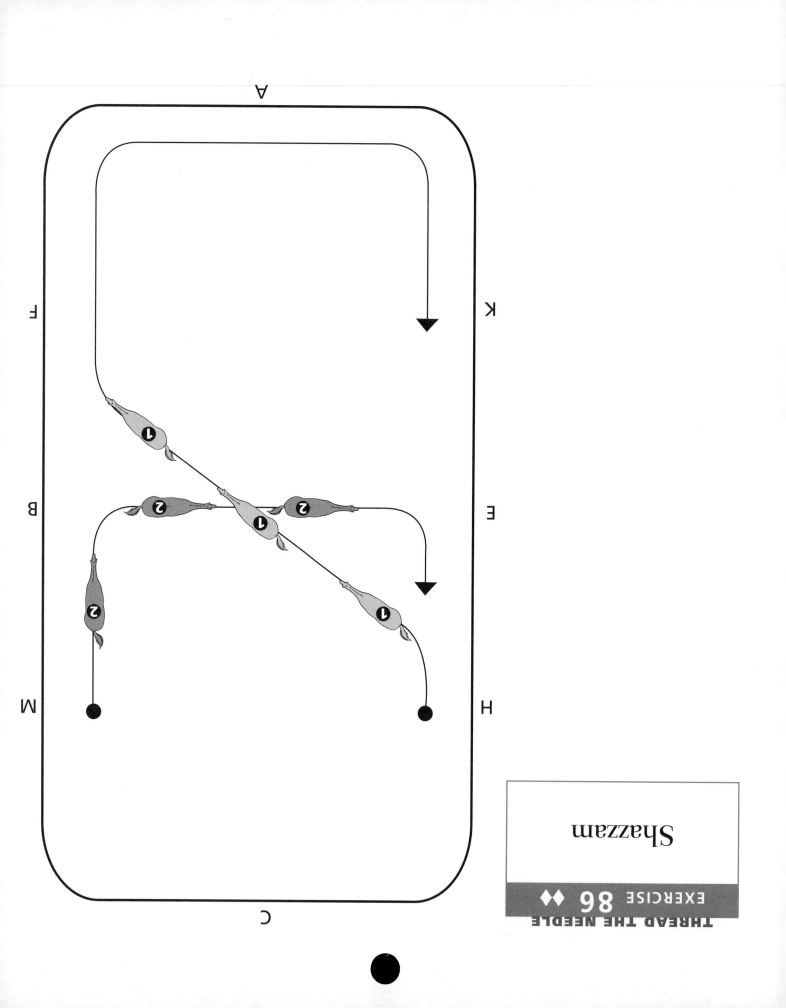

86. Shazzam

STARTING POINT

● Form line 1 at **H** facing **E**, in open formation.
● Form line 2 at **M** facing **B**, in open formation.

HOW DO I RIDE THIS?

1 Turn line 1 toward **F** and move forward on the diagonal. Move line 2 forward to **B** and turn toward **E**.

2 At **X**, the lines intersect, with riders from one line passing through the spaces in the other line.

3 Line 2 turns right at **E** and follows the fence. Line 1 turns right before **F** and follows the fence.

4 Line 1 catches up to line 2 along the fence near **E** to form one single-file line.

KEEP IN MIND

◆ Lines stay straight.
◆ Horses are not allowed to fall in around the corners.
◆ Be a BRATT (see page 23).
◆ The team decides before the exercise which rider will go first at **X**.

INCREASING DIFFICULTY

◆ Ride in pairs.
◆ Increase the speed.

VARIATIONS

◆ To end, line 2 turns left and passes line 1 left hand to left hand.
◆ To start, line 2 begins at **M** facing **K**. Line 1 begins at **K** and rides to **E**, then turns toward **B**, intersecting line 1.

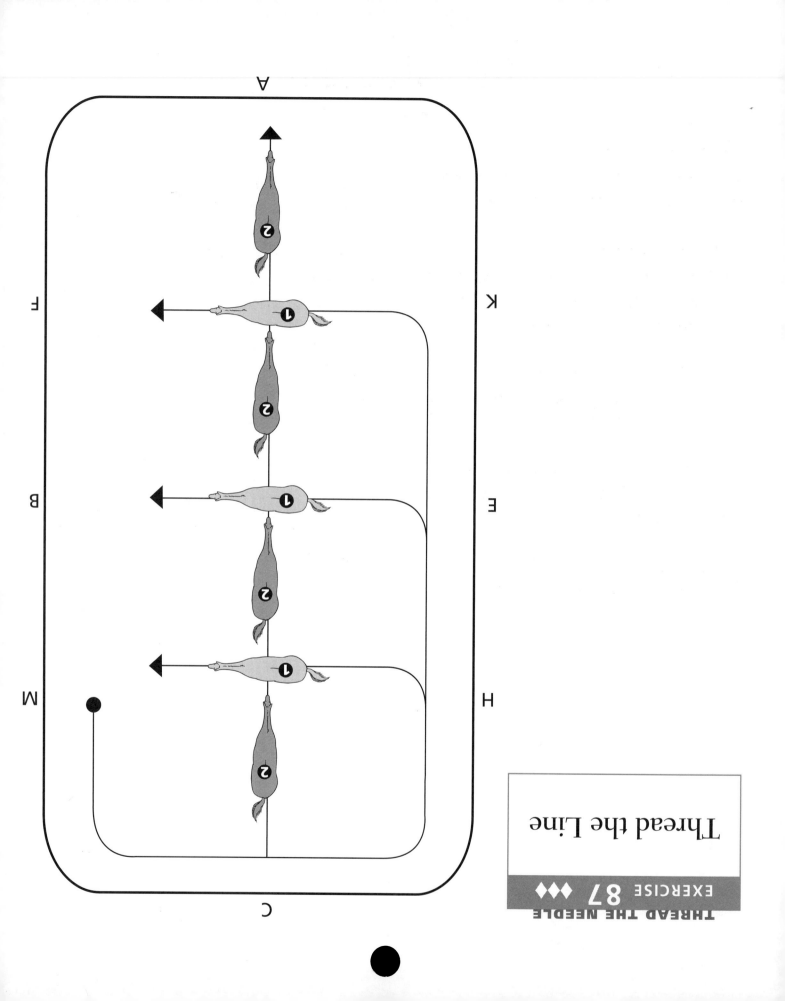

87. Thread the Line

STARTING POINT

● Form line 1 at **M** facing **C**, in open formation.
● Form line 2 behind line 1 in single file and open formation.

HOW DO I RIDE THIS?

1 Line 1 turns and rides along the fence toward **E**. Line 2 reaches **C** and turns down the centerline.

2 When the caller signals, line 1 makes an abreast turn left and rides through line 2.

KEEP IN MIND

◆ Line 1 is farther down the arena than line 2.
◆ Line 1 turns before line 2 reaches the point where they intersect.
◆ Riders focus on teamwork and timing.
◆ Riders' bodies are side-by-side in the abreast line.
◆ Riders ride a straight centerline.

INCREASING DIFFICULTY

◆ Increase the speed.
◆ Ride in pairs.
◆ Ride in passage (a very collected, cadenced, and elevated trot).

VARIATION

◆ Start line at **A**.

EXERCISE 88 ◆◆◆◆

The Box

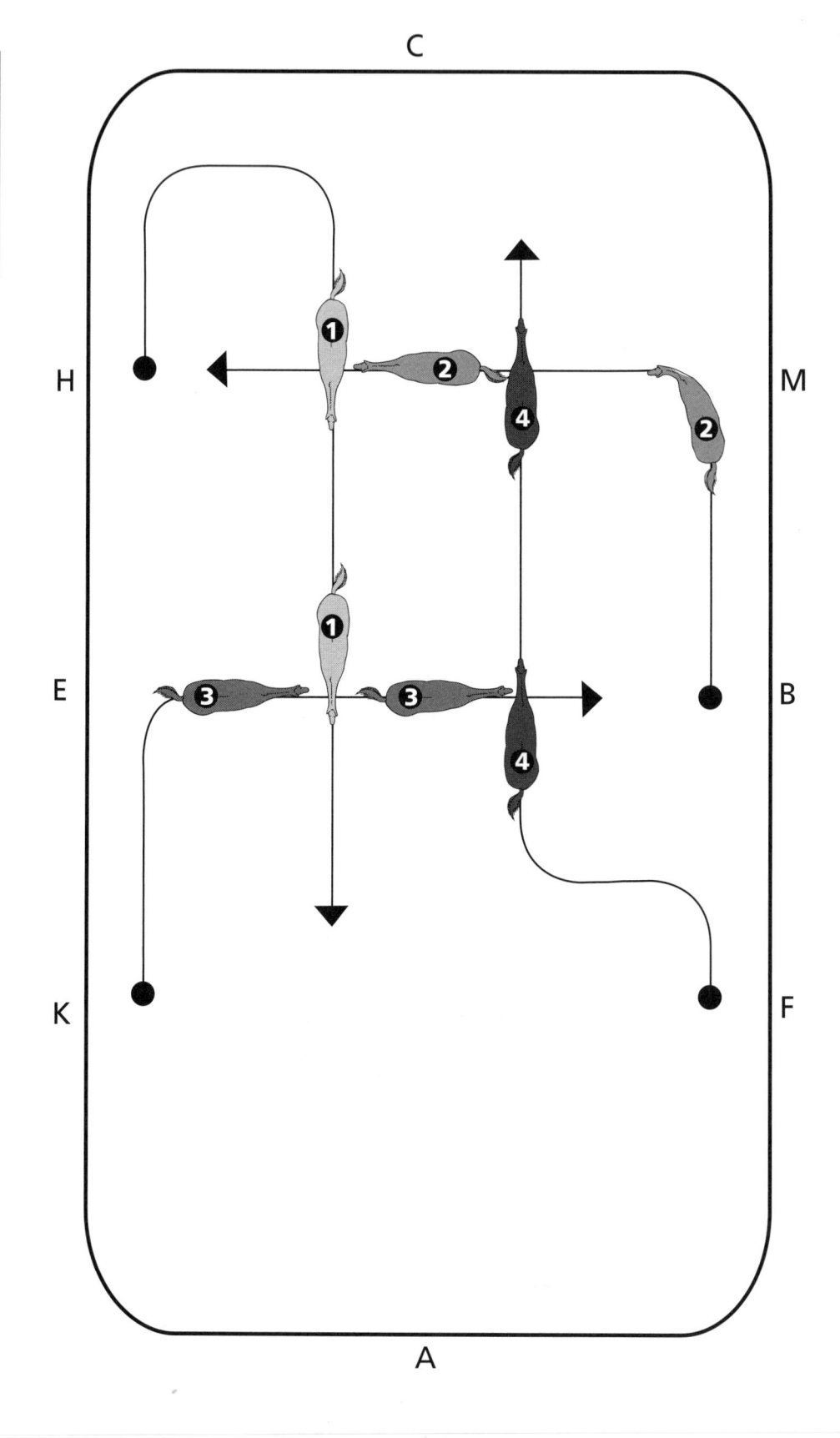

88. The Box

STARTING POINT

- Form line 1 at **H** facing **C**.
- Form line 2 at **B** facing **M**.
- Form line 3 at **K** facing **E**.
- Form line 4 at **F** facing **B**.

All horses should be in open formation.

HOW DO I RIDE THIS?

1 Riders ride forward.

2 Line 1 turns the corner toward **C**, then turns down the quarter line. Line 2 turns at **M** toward **H**. Line 3 turns right at **E**, heading toward **B**. Line 4 turns left between **B** and **F** and turns right on the quarter line.

3 Riders pass through each line that crosses their path.

KEEP IN MIND

- One horse at a time passes through each line to form a small box.
- Riders help to keep lines straight by focusing straight ahead.

INCREASING DIFFICULTY

- Ride in passage (a very collected, cadenced, and elevated trot).
- Ride in pairs.

VARIATION

- Form a large box by having two horses at a time pass through each line in single file. Spacing in all lines should be as follows: rider 1, rider 2, space, rider 3, rider 4, space, rider 5, rider 6.

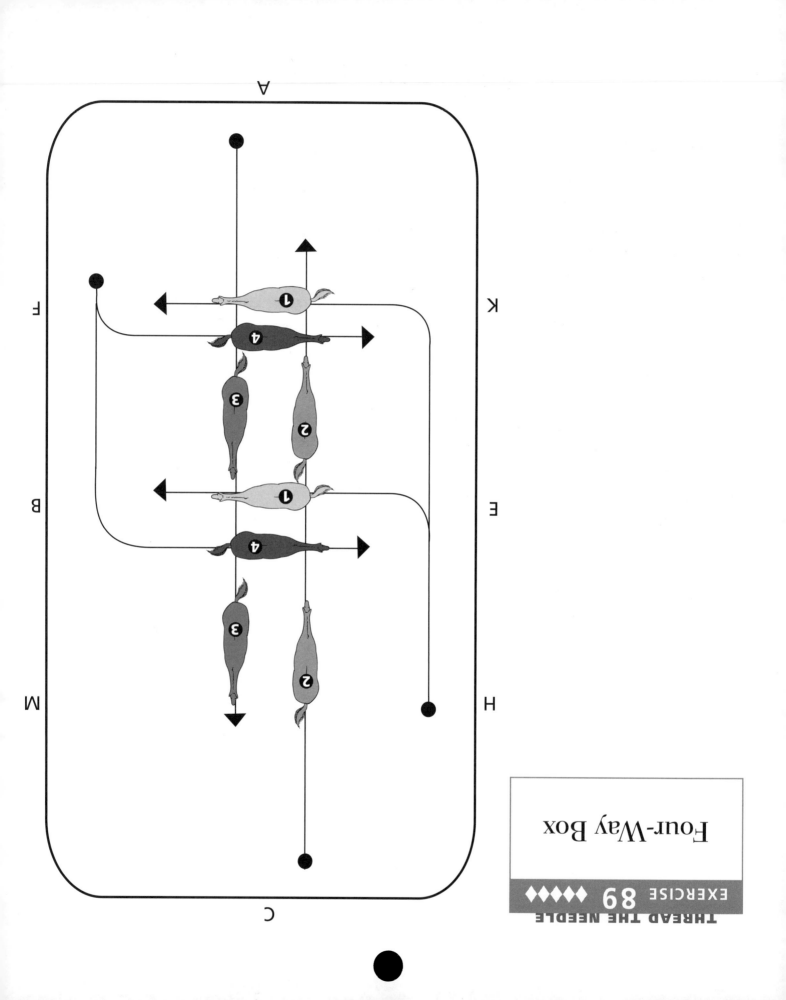

89. Four-Way Box

STARTING POINT

● Form line 1 at **H** facing **E**, in open formation.
● Form line 2 at **C** facing **A** to the right of the centerline, in open formation.
● Form line 3 at **A** facing **C** to the right of the centerline, in open formation.
● Form line 4 at **F** facing **B**, in open formation.

HOW DO I RIDE THIS?

1 All lines move forward.

2 When the caller signals, lines 1 and 4 make an abreast turn toward the centerline (be sure that partners in lines 1 and 4 leave enough space between them for oncoming and opposing horses).

3 Riders pass through the space in the opposing line at the same time as the oncoming horse.

KEEP IN MIND

◆ It is essential that your team has good timing, rating, and accuracy.
◆ Oncoming riders are passed left hand to left hand.

INCREASING DIFFICULTY

◆ Increase the speed.
◆ Do it in passage (a very collected, cadenced, and elevated trot).

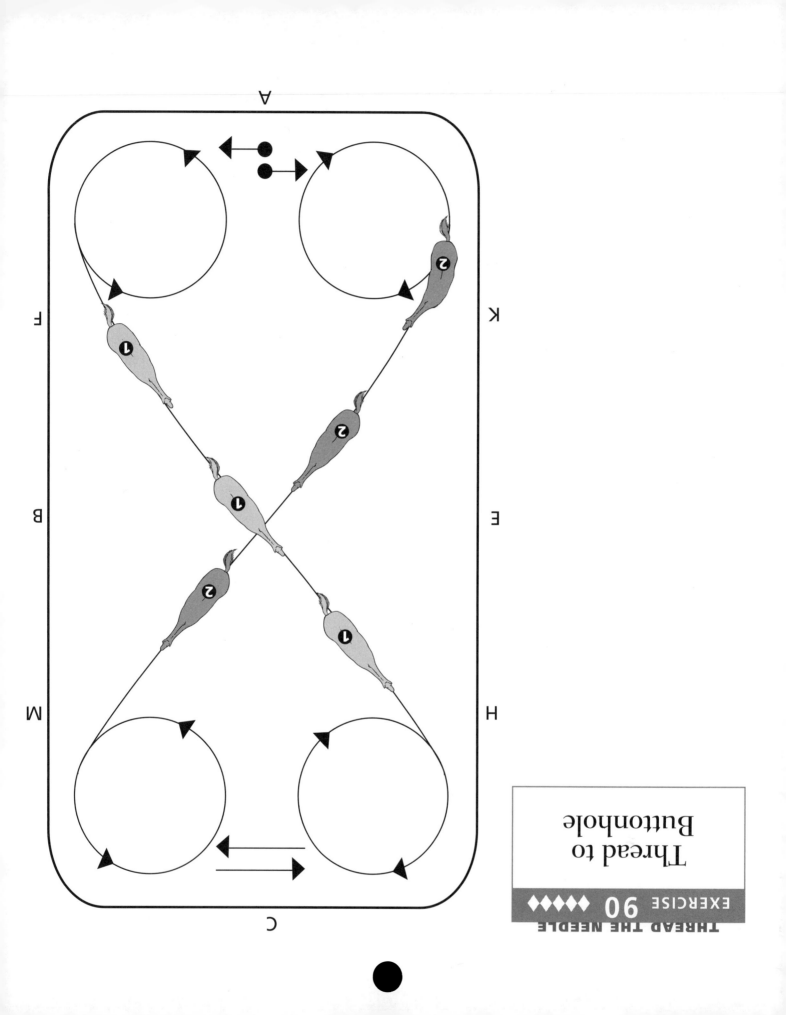

90. Thread to Buttonhole

STARTING POINT

● Form line 1 at **A** facing **F**, in open formation.
● Form line 2 at **A** facing **K**, in open formation.

HOW DO I RIDE THIS?

1 Ride to **K** and **F**.

2 Circle toward the centerline and back.

3 Ride across the diagonal.

4 Pass through the other line at **X**.

5 Ride to **H** and **M**.

6 Circle toward the centerline and back.

7 Ride straight to **C**. Pass left hand to left hand.

8 Repeat the exercise if desired.

KEEP IN MIND

◆ Circles are kept round.
◆ Partners maintain the same positions on the circle.
◆ During practice, partners give high fives at the centerline and on the circles.
◆ Lines are kept straight.
◆ Riders are aware of where their partners are.
◆ Be a BRATT (see page 23).

INCREASING DIFFICULTY

◆ Do reverses in the circles.
◆ Increase the speed.

VARIATIONS

◆ Position riders in the middle of the circles to do a spin or a pirouette.
◆ Put flag bearers in the center of the circles.
◆ Start at opposite ends of the arena.
◆ Ride in pairs.

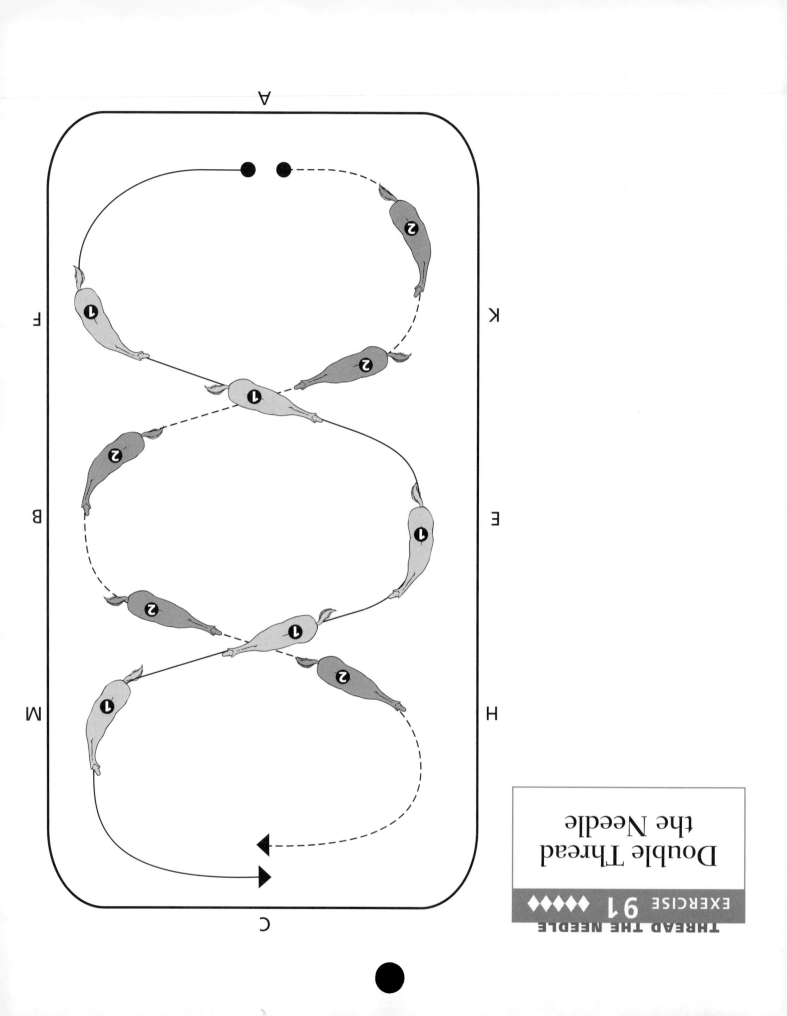

91. Double Thread the Needle

STARTING POINT

- Form line 1 at **A** facing **F**, in open formation.
- Form line 2 at **A** facing **K**, in open formation.

HOW DO I RIDE THIS?

1 Ride forward.

2 Pass **F** and **K**.

3 Cross on the diagonal to **E** and **B**.

4 Pass through the other line on the centerline.

5 From **E** or **B**, turn across the diagonal to **M** or **H**.

6 Pass through the other line on the centerline.

7 Turn at **M** or **H** and follow the fence.

8 Pass left hand to left hand at **C**.

KEEP IN MIND

- The team decides before the exercise which rider will cross the centerline first.
- The rider turns away from a letter after her body has passed it.
- The rider arrives at the fence about 2 meters (6.5 feet) before the letter and is parallel to the fence at the letter.

INCREASING DIFFICULTY

- Increase the speed.
- Do it in passage (a very collected, cadenced, and elevated trot).

VARIATIONS

- If you are in a very large arena, Thread the Needle more than twice.
- Ride in pairs.

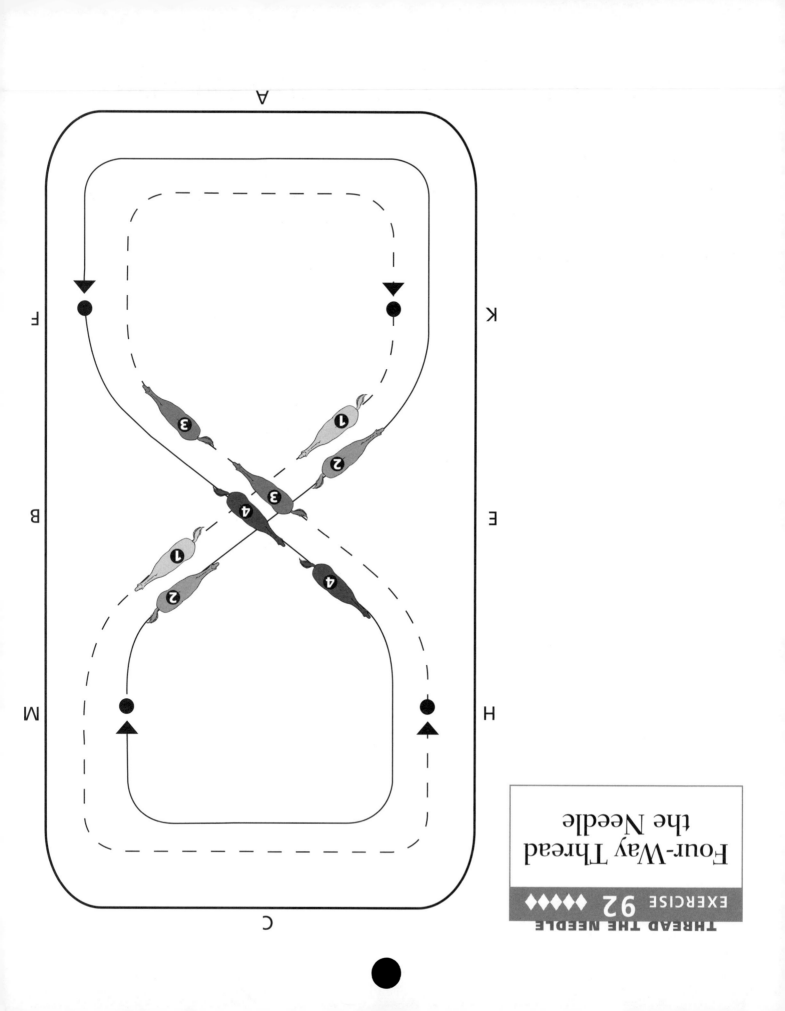

92. Four-Way Thread the Needle

STARTING POINT

- Form line 1 at **K** facing **X**, in open formation.
- Form line 2 at **M** Facing **X**, in open formation.
- Form line 3 at **H** facing **X**, in open formation.
- Form line 4 at **F** facing **X**, in open formation.

HOW DO I RIDE THIS?

1 Proceed toward **X**.

2 The first horses in lines 3 and 4 pass over **X** first, at the same time.

3 The first horses in lines 1 and 2 pass over **X** at the same time.

4 The second horses in lines 3 and 4 pass over **X** and through lines 1 and 2.

5 The second horses in lines 1 and 2 pass over **X** and through lines 3 and 4.

6 Repeat this pattern until all riders have threaded the needle.

KEEP IN MIND

- Partners watch each other so that they arrive at **X** at the same time.
- Riders watch the opposite line, rating their horses to pass through it at the correct time.
- Riders maintain spacing so that riders in the other line have room to pass through.
- Riders maintain a steady tempo.
- Riders do not stop, swerve, or yank on the reins.
- Be a BRATT (see page 23).
- Riders pass oncoming riders left hand to left hand.

INCREASING DIFFICULTY

- Increase the speed.
- Do this in passage (a very collected, cadenced, and elevated trot).

VARIATION

- Ride this two, three, or four abreast.

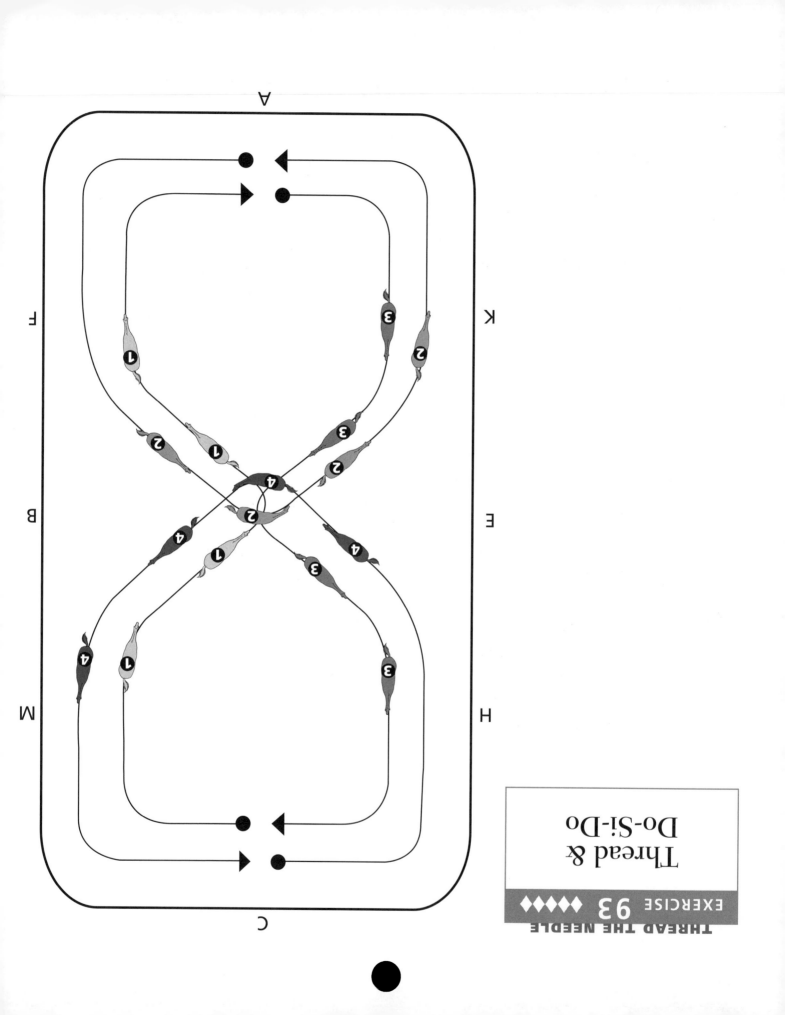

A

F

K

B

E

M

H

C

THREAD THE NEEDLE

EXERCISE 93 ◆◆◆◆◆

Thread &
Do-Si-Do

93. Thread & Do-Si-Do

STARTING POINT

- Form line 1 at **C** facing **M**.
- Form line 2 at **A** facing **F**.
- Form line 3 at **A** facing **K**.
- Form line 4 at **C** facing **H**.

All lines should be in open formation, with riders spaced two to three horse-lengths apart.

HOW DO I RIDE THIS?

1 Ride through the corner to the letter.

2 Cross the diagonal to **X**.

3 Ride a small one-quarter circle with your partner at **X**.

4 Ride to the corner to your left.

5 Pass the other line at **A** or **C** and repeat the exercise.

KEEP IN MIND

- Riders pass oncoming riders left hand to left hand.
- Riders watch their partners and rate their horses.
- Riders leave space for the pair ahead to circle and move out of the way.

INCREASING DIFFICULTY

- Increase the speed.
- Reduce the spacing between riders.

VARIATIONS

- Ride a half turn or a full turn at **X**.

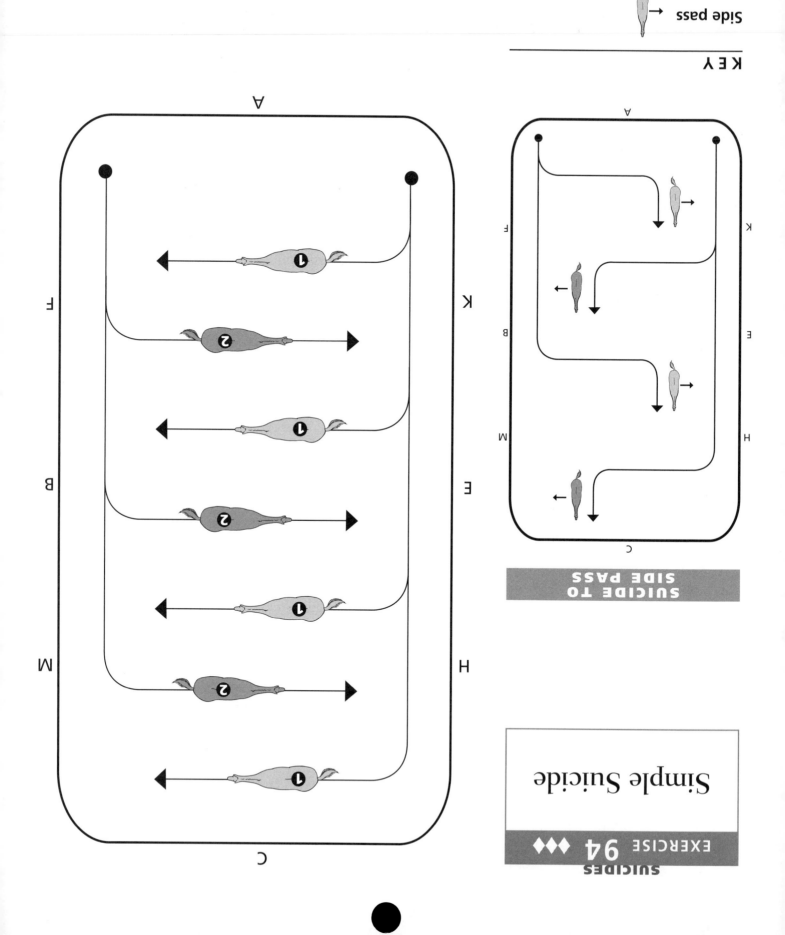

KEY

Side pass

A

F   K

B   E

M   H

C

SUICIDE TO
SIDE PASS

Simple Suicide

SUICIDES
EXERCISE 94 ◆◆◆

94. Simple Suicide

STARTING POINT

● Form line 1 at **K** facing **E**, in closed formation.
● Form line 2 at **F** facing **B**, in closed formation.

HOW DO I RIDE THIS?

1 Travel down the rail.

2 When the lines are centered along the rails, the caller signals for an abreast turn.

3 Pass the other riders on the centerline.

KEEP IN MIND

◆ Riders note which horses they will pass between.
◆ Riders stay aligned with the other riders in line as they travel down the rail.
◆ Riders rate their horses so that everyone arrives at the centerline at the same time.
◆ Riders maintain straight abreast lines by watching the bodies of riders beside them.

INCREASING DIFFICULTY

◆ The caller signals for horses to turn on the quarter line, then side-pass to the rail (see small diagram).
◆ Do the exercise in passage (a very collected, cadenced, and elevated trot).
◆ Increase the speed.

VARIATIONS

◆ Increase or decrease the speed at the centerline.
◆ Ride in open formation, to make it easier.

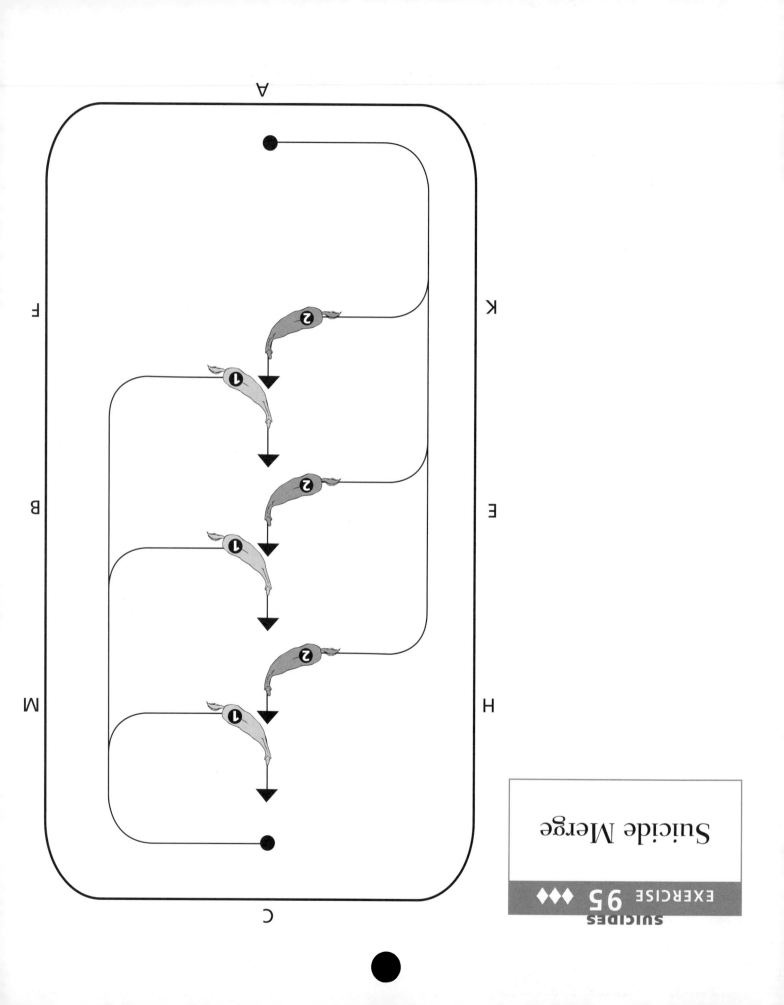

Suicide Merge

95. Suicide Merge

STARTING POINT

● Form line 1 at **C** facing **M**, in open formation.
● Form line 2 at **A** facing **K**, in open formation.

HOW DO I RIDE THIS?

1 Ride through the corner and down the fence.

2 When the caller signals, make an abreast turn.

3 At the centerline, turn toward **C** and merge into a single-file line.

KEEP IN MIND

◆ Riders note which horses they finish between on the centerline and rate their own horses coming down the fence to line up with them as they turn.
◆ The caller signals when all riders are on the long side and lined up with their partners.

INCREASING DIFFICULTY

◆ Do this shoulder-in or haunches-in.
◆ Increase the speed.

VARIATION

◆ Ride this in pairs, threes, or fours.

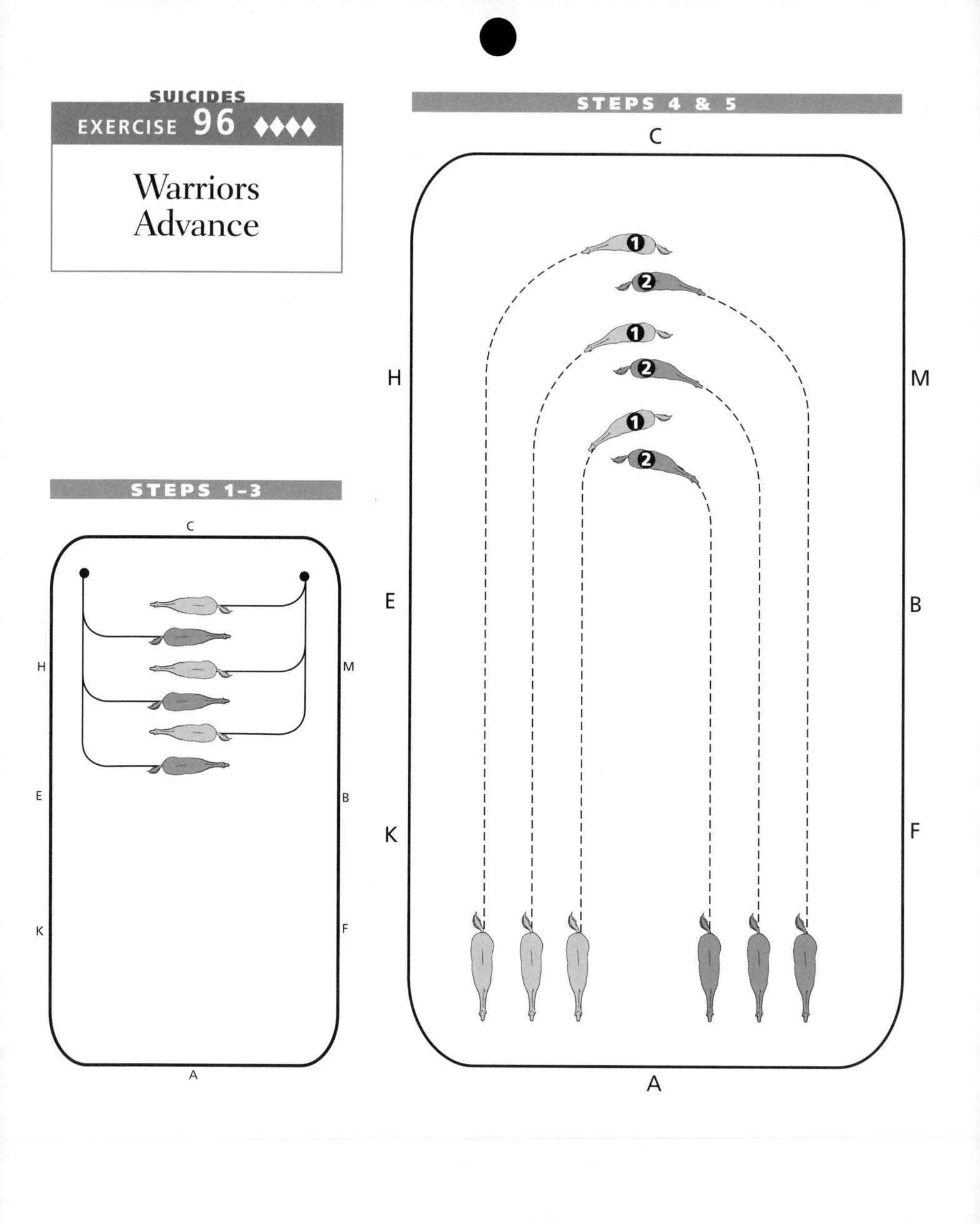

Warriors
Advance

STEPS 1-3

STEPS 4 & 5

96. Warriors Advance

STARTING POINT

- Form line 1 at **M** facing **B**, in closed formation.
- Form line 2 at **H** facing **E**, in closed formation.

HOW DO I RIDE THIS?

1 Ride forward.

2 When all riders are on the long side, the caller signals. At the signal, make an abreast turn toward the centerline.

3 Halt momentarily on the centerline in suicide formation.

4 Move forward and arc toward **A** in an abreast line.

5 Lines 1 and 2 ride forward in one abreast line.

KEEP IN MIND

- Riders watch the opposite line as they ride down the fence and rate their horses to reach the correct space on the centerline.
- In an abreast line, the bodies of the riders remain side by side.

INCREASING DIFFICULTY

- Ride a suicide wheel before proceeding down the centerline in an Abreast Sweep. (See Exercise 69.)

VARIATIONS

- Ride the abreast line to **K** and **F**, then do a Four-Spoke Suicide Wheel. (See Exercise 49.)
- Ride the abreast line to **B** and **E**, keeping the line closer to **B**. Pivot the abreast line around the horse on the far right. (See Exercise 45: Whip.)
- After forming the abreast line, ride to **B** and **E** and do a Whip Away. (See Exercise 46.)

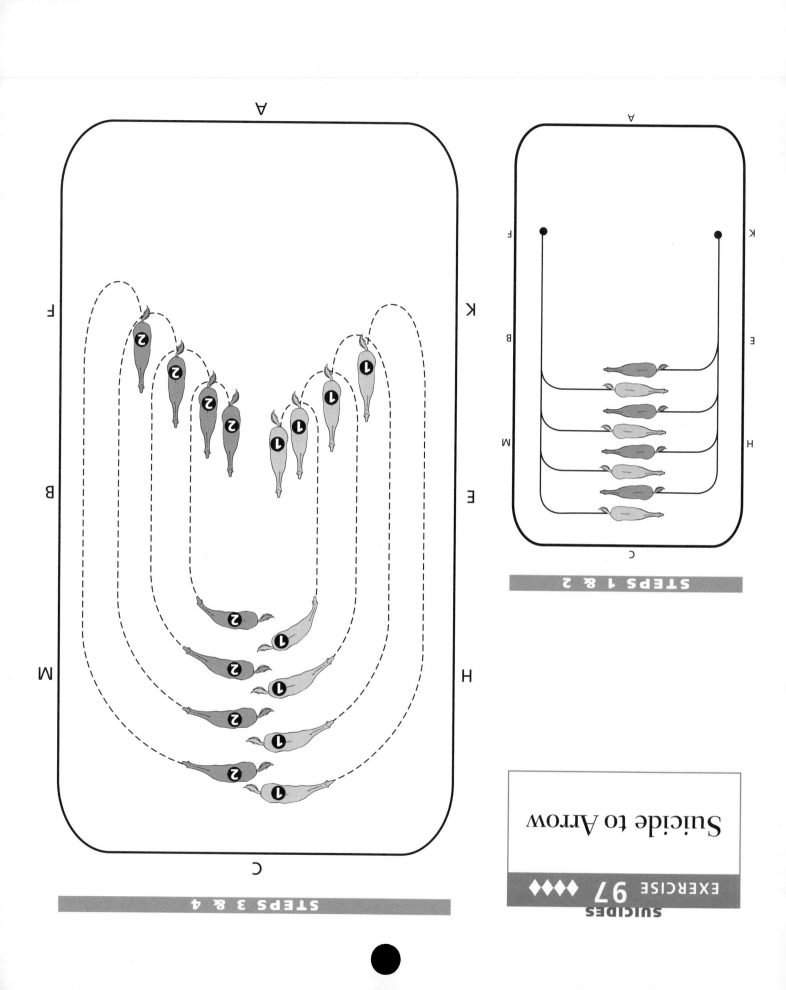

SUICIDES

EXERCISE 97 ♦♦♦♦

Suicide to Arrow

STEPS 1 & 2

STEPS 3 & 4

97. Suicide to Arrow

STARTING POINT

- Form line 1 at **F** facing **B**, in closed formation.
- Form line 2 at **K** facing **E**, in closed formation.

HOW DO I RIDE THIS?

1 When everyone is on the long side, close to **C**, the caller signals for an abreast turn toward the centerline.

2 Move forward and halt on the centerline between your partners. (See Exercise 94: Simple Suicide.)

3 When the caller signals, ride an arc forward and toward **A**.

4 When you are roughly between **K** and **F**, turn toward **C**. Stagger your line to form an arrow. (See Exercise 64: Arrow.)

KEEP IN MIND

- Riders watch the other riders in line, rating their horses to finish in the correct position on the centerline.
- Riders halt only momentarily on the centerline.
- In the arrow position, the horse's nose is beside the body of the rider ahead.

INCREASING DIFFICULTY

- Ride a Four-Spoke Suicide Wheel after you line up on the centerline. (See Exercise 49.)

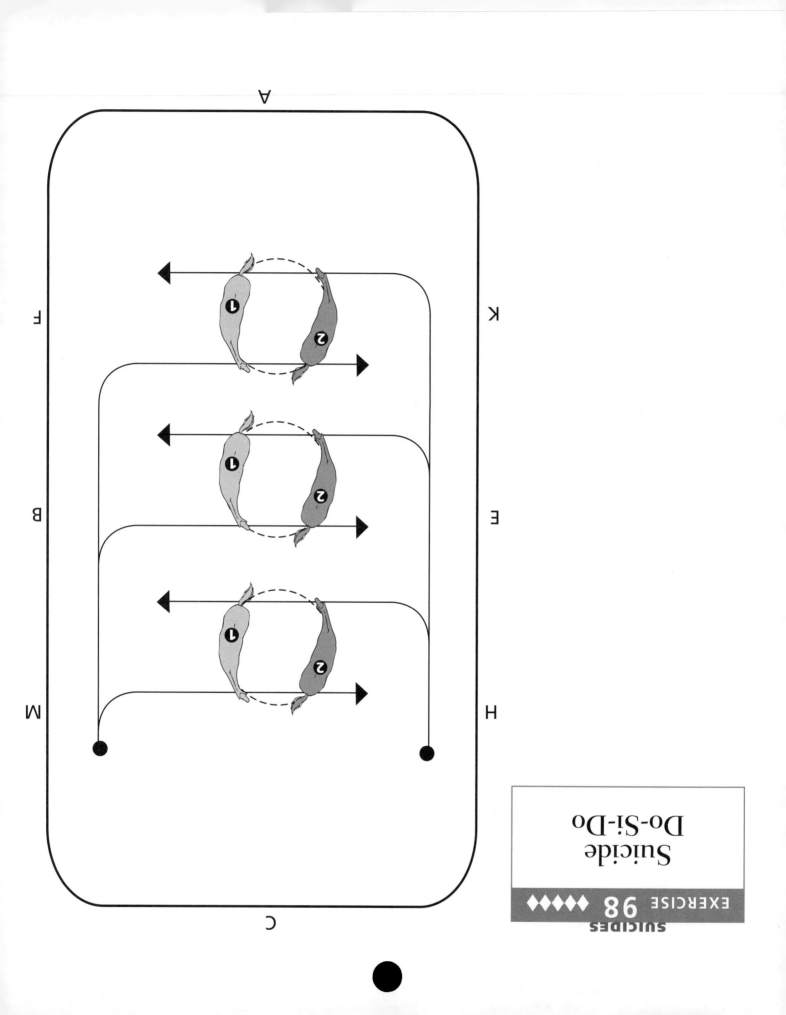

Suicide
Do-Si-Do

98. Suicide Do-Si-Do

STARTING POINT

- Form line 1 at **H** facing **E**, in open formation.
- Form line 2 at **M** facing **B**, in open formation.

HOW DO I RIDE THIS?

1 Proceed down the fence.

2 When the caller signals, make an abreast turn toward the centerline.

3 Meet your partner from the other line on the centerline, left hand to left hand.

4 Turn your horse's nose toward the tail of your partner's horse.

5 Make one complete circle.

6 Return to your original abreast line and ride straight ahead.

KEEP IN MIND

- The caller gives the turn signal when all riders are on the long side.
- In the abreast line, riders' bodies are aligned with the bodies of the riders on either side.
- Riders rate their horses to arrive at the centerline with the other horses.
- Circling riders are at the same point in the circle as the other team members.
- Riders exit the circle at the same time as the other riders.
- Be a BRATT (see page 23).

INCREASING DIFFICULTY

- Increase the speed.

VARIATIONS

- Do this on the diagonal.
- Ride from **A** and **C** toward **X** and Do-Si-Do between **E** and **B**.

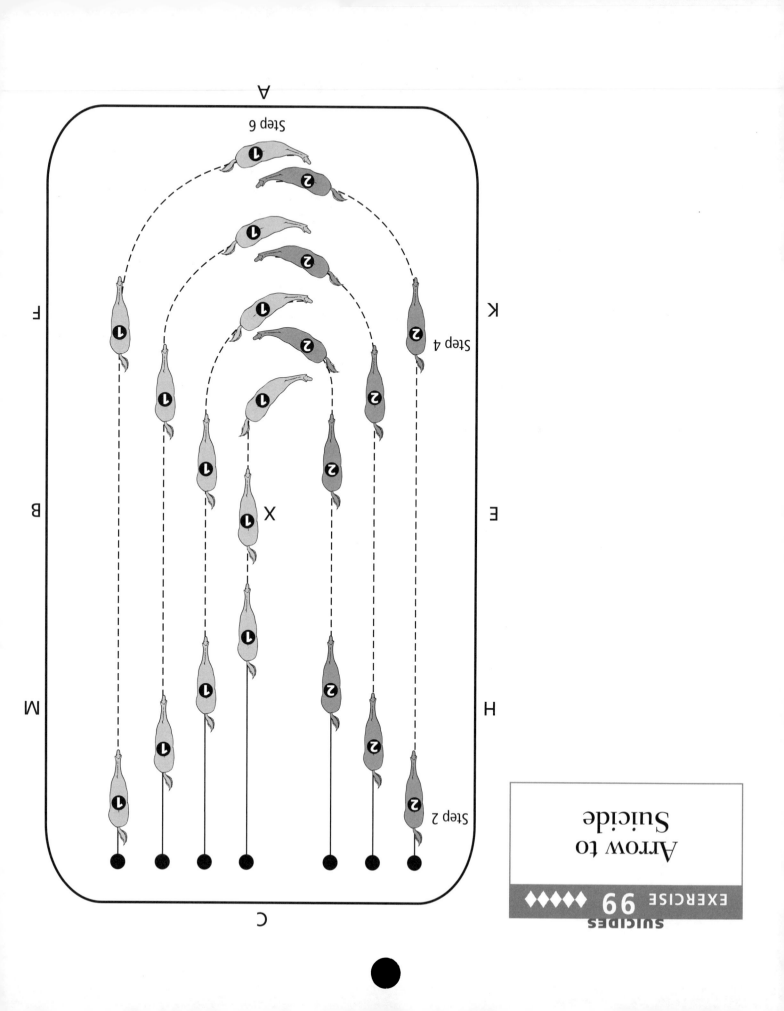

99. Arrow to Suicide

STARTING POINT

● Form line 1 between **C** and **M** facing **A**. Riders are abreast and in open formation.

● Form line 2 between **C** and **H** facing **A**. Riders are abreast and in open formation.

HOW DO I RIDE THIS?

1 Move forward as an abreast line.

2 Immediately, riders closer to the centerline pull forward to form an arrow. (See Exercise 64.)

3 Ride forward to **X**.

4 Near **X**, the rider at the point of the arrow stops or slows. Riders on the outside of the arrow speed up to form a backward arrow.

5 When the caller signals, lines 1 and 2 arc toward the centerline.

6 Pass riders in the other line left hand to left hand.

KEEP IN MIND

◆ Riders rate their horses to be in the correct place at the correct time.

◆ In arrow formation, the horse's nose is beside the leg of the rider ahead.

◆ Riders watch for their partners in the opposite line as they move from the backward arrow to the centerline.

INCREASING DIFFICULTY/ VARIATION

◆ Ride a Pinwheel after this exercise (see Exercise 47).

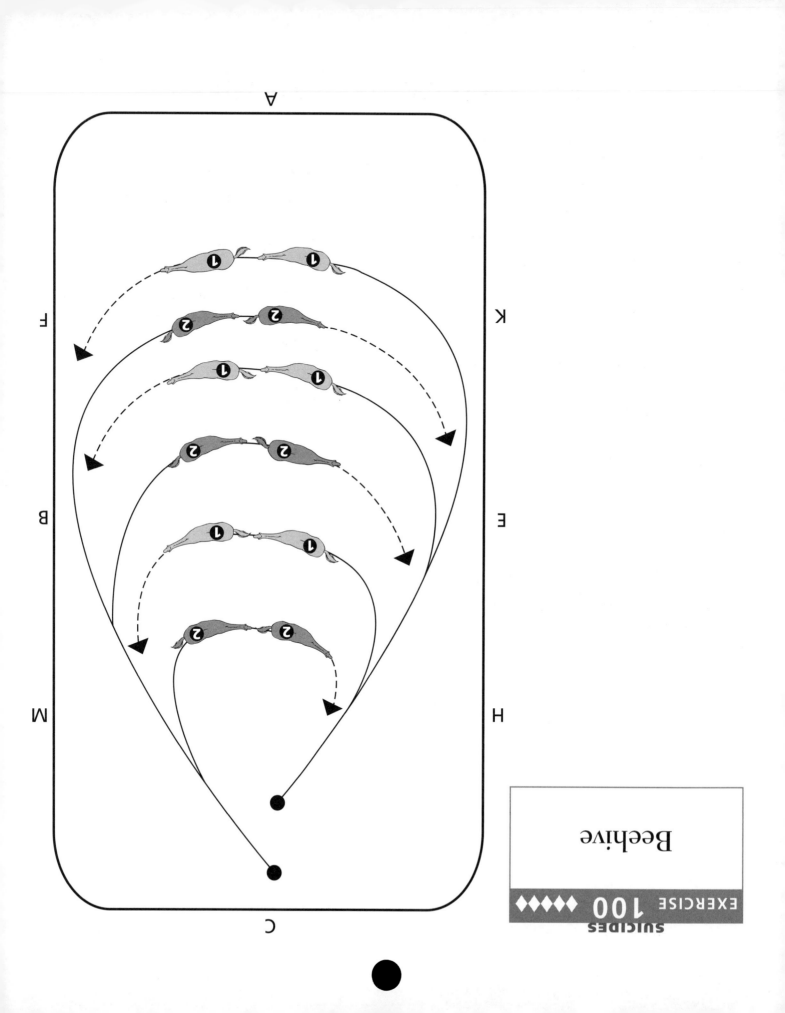

A

F   K

B   E

M   H

C

Beehive

SUICIDES
EXERCISE 100 ◆◆◆◆◆

100. Beehive

STARTING POINT

● Form line 1 at **C** facing **E**, in closed formation.
● Form line 2 at **C** facing **B**, in closed formation.
Divide your lines into thirds.

HOW DO I RIDE THIS?

1 Ride an arc toward **E** or **B**.

2 When the caller signals, each line turns toward the centerline and moves into three single-file lines.

3 At the centerline, pass your partners (the corresponding riders in the other lines) left hand to left hand.

4 Come together with other groups again into one single-file line and follow the arc back to **C**.

KEEP IN MIND

◆ Each third of the line turns together before forming a single-file line.
◆ Partners pass each other from the opposite line on the centerline.
◆ Be a BRATT (see page 23).

INCREASING DIFFICULTY

◆ Divide each line into a greater number of segments. Fill the whole arena with this exercise.

VARIATION

◆ Rather than turning in segments, have everyone turn individually.

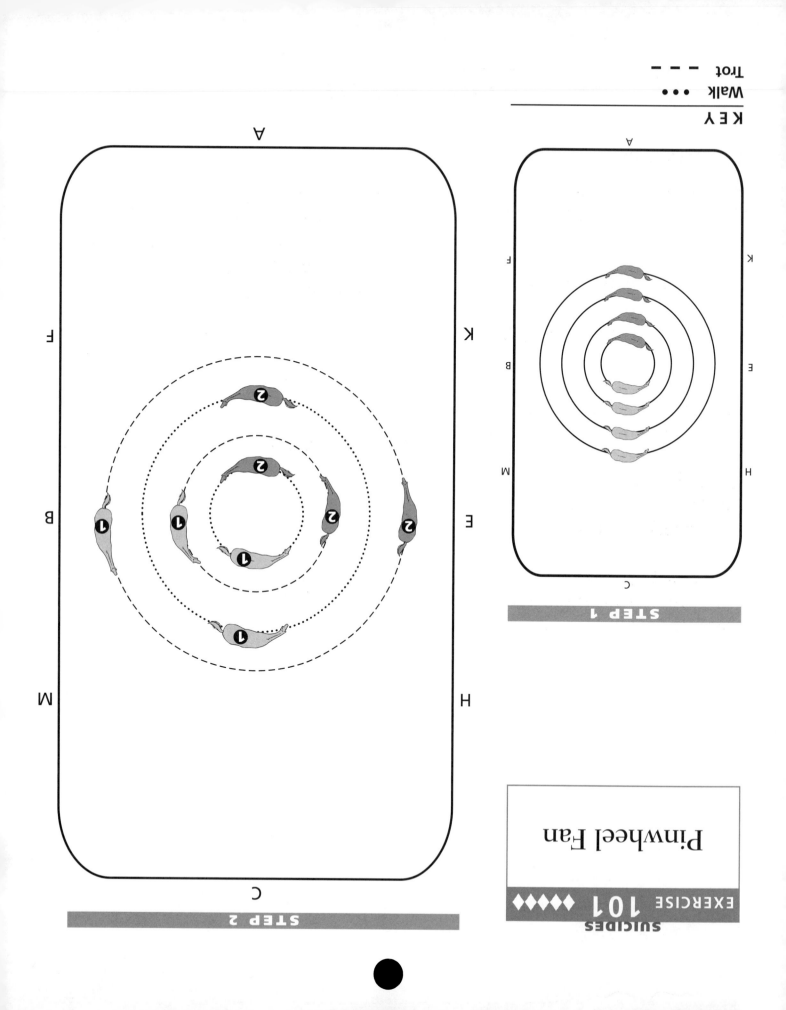

101. Pinwheel Fan

STARTING POINT

● Form line 1 on the centerline facing the fence between **H** and **E**. Riders should be abreast and in closed formation.

● Form line 2 on the centerline facing the fence between **B** and **F**. Riders should be abreast and in closed formation.

● Leave 8 to 10 meters (26 to 33 feet) of space between the lines.

HOW DO I RIDE THIS?

1 Do one full-circle rotation in abreast formation.

2 During the next rotation, the horses closest to the center walk, the horses second from the center trot or jog, the horses third from the center walk, and so on. This creates a fan effect, since the rings of the circle alternate between trotters/joggers and walkers.

KEEP IN MIND

◆ Riders in abreast lines watch each other's bodies to keep the lines straight.

◆ Walkers watch their walking partners in the other circle and trotters watch their trotting partners in the other circle to remain abreast and keep their lines straight.

◆ Riders ride their track.

◆ Outside horses may have to canter or lope.

◆ Riders keep the line open for the fan to pass through.

INCREASING DIFFICULTY/ VARIATION

◆ Do a walk and canter/lope or a trot/jog and canter/lope.

Arrows are a good way to add visual appeal to your drill routine.

CHAPTER 5

DRILLS

In this chapter, I have put together some of the previous exercises to form 10 drills for your team to try. Before you begin, go over the rules for drill team riding. Review the first seven exercises to add finesse to your drill team. Start with a simple drill and hone your drill team skills. Don't forget that you can also have a lot of fun building your own drills using different combinations of the 101 exercises in this book!

Types of Drills

Abreast drills. These consist of files of three or more abreast riders.

Combo drills. These combine a variety of aspects of different types of drills. Drills 5–10 are combo drills.

In-line drills. These are the simplest kind of drill because there is only a single-file line and everyone follows the leader. Good Vibrations (page 219) and The Accordion (page 221) are both in-line drills.

Mirror drills. These drills are based on pairs, but pairs mirror each other's moves. Threads & Pinwheels (page 225) is an example of this.

Pair drills. These consist of two single-file lines that work together as pairs.

Types of Drill Teams

Drama on horseback teams. Teams use the drill, music, costumes, and acting to tell a story.

Pas de deux. This is a ride for two. These are often mirror drills.

Quadrilles. These are performed in multiples of four horses (i.e., 4, 8, 12, 16, or 20). These complex patterns were usually ridden to music in the courts of Europe throughout the 17th, 18th, and 19th centuries.

Rodeo teams. Teams usually ride fast and furiously with western costumes.

Themed teams. Teams might dress as knights, ladies in waiting, Native Americans, hippies, or bandits. Only your imagination will limit you.

DRILL DESIGN POINTERS

- ◆ Use the whole arena. Balance your exercises so that they are not all at one end of the arena. This will make the drill more pleasing to the audience.
- ◆ Use the same-size arena each time you ride your drill. Use barrels, cones, or poles as markers to make an arena smaller.
- ◆ Use letters, cones, or colored tape as markers to help riders make accurate movements.
- ◆ Consider where your audience will be. If possible, face them at the beginning and the end of the drill. Hello and good-bye salutes are a nice touch.
- ◆ Show your team's strengths. Do what you are really good at.
- ◆ Don't make your drill any more difficult than your weakest horse and rider can handle.
- ◆ Your drill should be smooth and seamless. It should look easy.
- ◆ Allow preparation time for your next move. This should be short enough to keep the drill interesting.
- ◆ Be creative. Include a moment of surprise, such as an unusual combination.

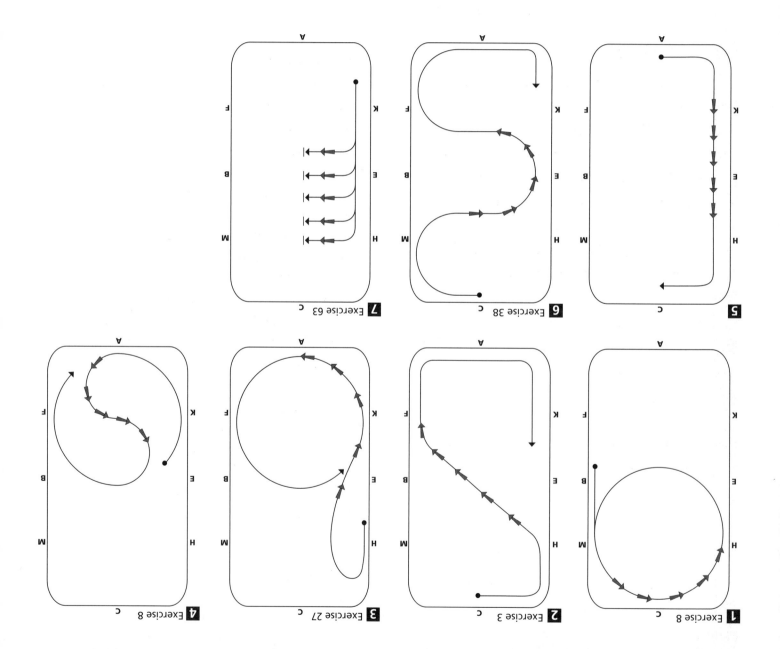

D1. Good Vibrations ♦

This is a fun drill set to the Beach Boys' song "Good Vibrations." The song needs to be played through twice. If you finish the drill before the music is finished, have your music coordinator fade out the music. If you run out of music, start the song again and fade it out when you are done with the drill.

Diagram	Instructions	Exercise
1	When music starts, walk from **B** toward **M** in closed formation. Trot when music picks up momentum. Turn at **M** and make a **circle** in half of the arena.	**8**
2	Do a **Z** from **H** to **F**. Follow along the rail at **A** and toward **E**. Walk when music slows and begins for the second time.	**3**
3	Do a **reverse** at **H** back to **E**. Make a **circle** in the lower half of the arena. Trot when music picks up again.	**27**
4	**Turn through the Circle.**	**8**
5	Ride along the rail from **A** to **C**.	**N/A**
6	Do a **serpentine.**	**38**
7	When the team is centered on the long side, make an abreast right turn and halt and **Salute** on the centerline.	**63**

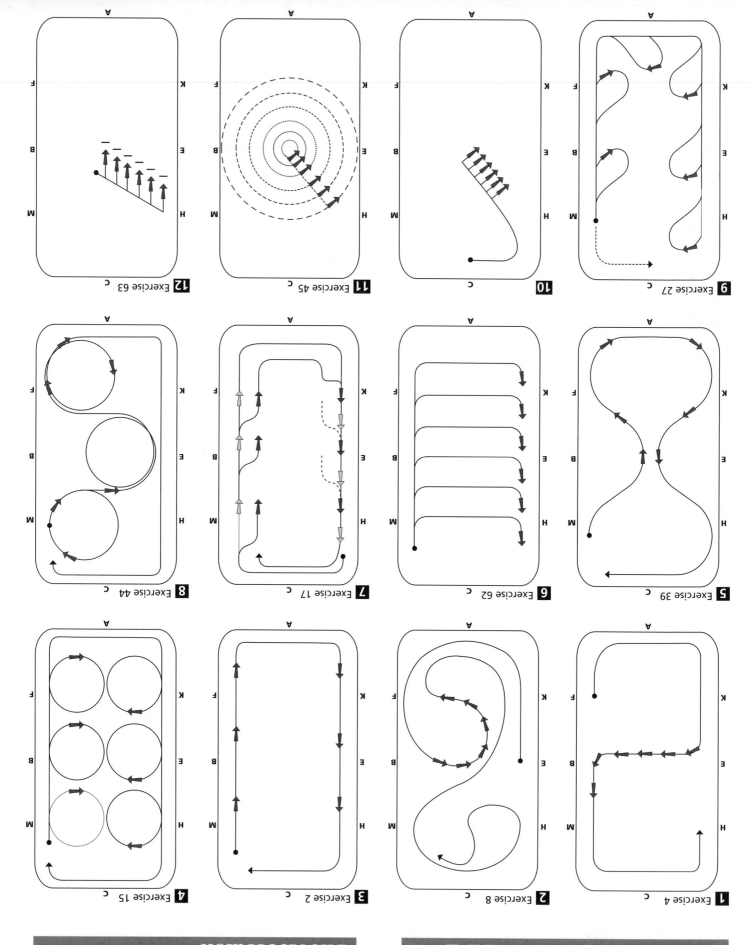

D2. The Accordion ♦♦

The purpose of this in-line drill is to help you learn to rate your horse. You will be challenged to open and close the line, ride side-by-side, and watch your partners as your group turns as a whole.

Diagram	Instructions	Exercise
1	Start in closed formation. Trot from **F** toward **A** when music starts. Turn right at **E** and turn left at **B**. Ride **Square Corners**. Ride along the rail.	4
2	Ride straight ahead from **E** toward **K**. **Turn through the Circle.** Ride a curving line from **K** toward **M** as if doing a **Figure 8**. **Turn through the Circle** again.	8
3	Beginning at **M**, ride along the rail in **open formation**.	2
4	Ride **Synchronized Circle Pairs** at each letter.	15
5	Ride a **Serpentine to Centerline**. Repeat the **Serpentine to Centerline**, making a mirror image. At **H**, ride straight ahead along the rail in **closed formation**.	39
6	When riders are centered on the long side near **B**, make an **abreast** turn right. Ride straight ahead toward the opposite rail. Turn right when you reach the opposite rail.	62
7	Ride **Add & Subtract**: When the caller signals, number 2 horses pull up to form pairs along the **M-F** rail. Ride straight ahead along the rail at **A**. When the caller signals, number 2 horses move behind number 1 horses along the **H-K** rail, forming a single-file line.	17
8	From **C** to **A**, ride a **Serpentine with Gopher Holes**. From **A** to **M**, ride along the rail in **open formation**.	44
9	Do simultaneous **reverses** at each letter. Ride along the rail to **C**.	27
10	Ride along the rail to **H**. At **H**, ride to **X** in a single-file line. Halt when the first rider reaches **X**. When the caller signals, turn to face **E**.	N/A
11	When the caller signals, do the **Whip**.	45
12	Halt and salute facing the audience.	63

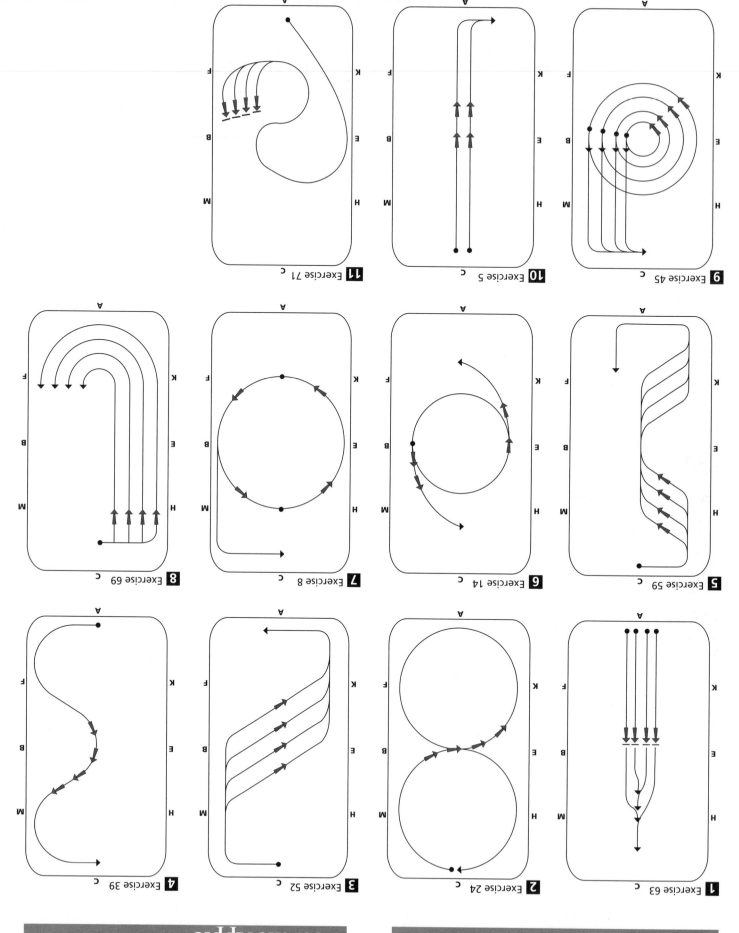

DRILL 3 ◆◆ ● Peel the Apple

D3. Peel the Apple ◆◆

This drill includes single-file lines and abreast work.

Diagram	Instructions	Exercise
1	At **A**, form an **abreast** line facing **C**. Ride forward. Halt between **E** and **B** and **Salute.** Ride forward in a single-file line on the centerline.	63
2	At **C**, turn right and do a **Figure 8.** Follow the leader.	24
3	Ride straight ahead from **C** to **M**. Between **M** and **B**, ride an **Abreast Oblique:** Make an **abreast** right turn and ride along the diagonal. Between **E** and **K**, turn left and return to a single-file line.	52
4	Do a **Serpentine to Centerline.**	39
5	Follow the instructions for **This Way & That.** When you pass **A**, turn down the quarter line closest to **F**.	59
6	Do a **Spinner Carousel.** Ride one revolution of a small **circle** around **X**. Line 1 spins off toward **C** in preparation to ride a large **circle**. Line 2 spins off toward **A** in preparation to ride the same large **circle**, behind line 1.	14
7	Ride a large **circle** in **open formation** between **E** and **B**. Ride in a single-file line in **closed formation** from **B** to **M** to **C**.	8
8	Ride an **abreast** turn between **C** and **H**. Make an **Abreast Sweep** on the rail.	69
9	Ride a **Whip** between **B** and **E**. Ride along the fence in **abreast** formation between **B** and **M**. At the corner between **C** and **M**, turn left into a single-file line.	45
10	Ride in **Partners** down the centerline from **C** to **A**. At **A**, turn right into a single-file line.	5
11	Ride from **A** toward **E**, then ride an arc toward **X**. Ride **Peel the Apple** between **E** and **B**. Halt and **salute**.	71

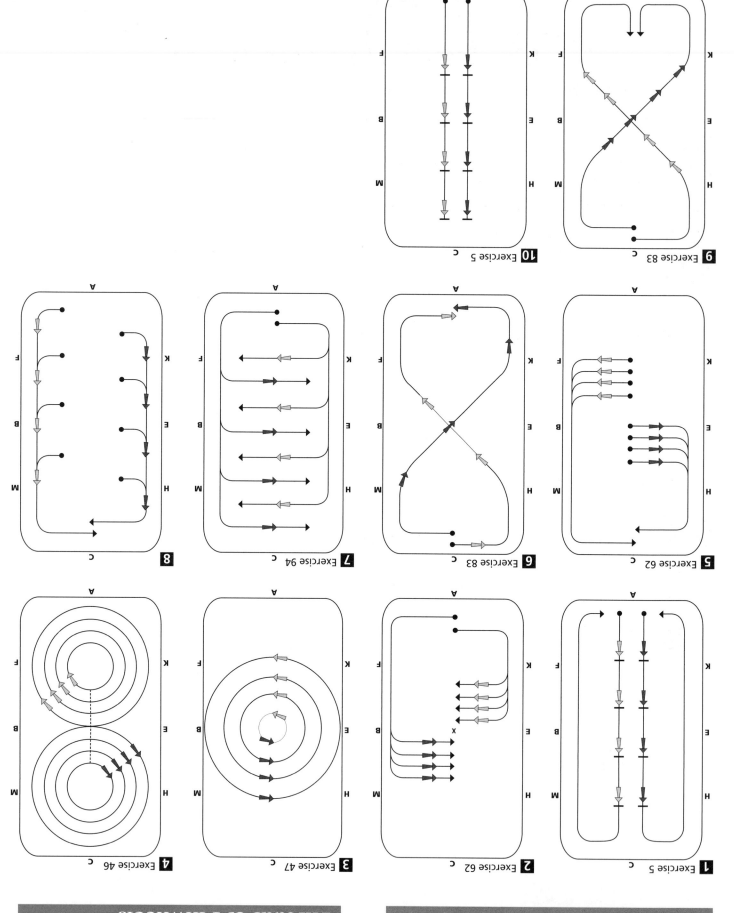

1 Exercise 5 C

2 Exercise 62 C

3 Exercise 47 C

4 Exercise 46 C

5 Exercise 62 C

6 Exercise 83 C

7 Exercise 94 C

8 C

9 Exercise 83 C

10 Exercise 5 C

D4. Threads & Pinwheels ◆◆◆

Wow your audience with this simple two-line mirror drill. Ride to "The Stars and Stripes Forever," or any music of your own choosing.

Diagram	Instructions	Exercise
1	Starting at **A**, ride as **Partners** down the centerline. When centered, halt and **salute**. Continue down the centerline and split at **C**. Follow the fence to **A**.	5
2	Pass left hand to left hand at **A** and continue along the fence. When centered on the long sides, make an **abreast** turn toward the centerline.	62
3	Halt on the centerline and ride the **Pinwheel**.	47
4	After one revolution, **Whip Away** from the centerline.	46
5	From the centerline, ride straight ahead in **Abreast Columns**. At the fence, turn toward **C** and form single-file lines.	62
6	Pass left hand to left hand at **C**. Cross the arena on the diagonal and **Thread the Needle**. Pass left hand to left hand at **A**.	83
7	Continue riding along the rail. When riders are centered on the long sides, make **abreast** turns to **Simple Suicide**.	94
8	At the fence, turn toward **C** and form single-file lines. Pass left hand to left hand at **C**.	N/A
9	Cross the arena on the diagonal and **Thread the Needle**.	83
10	At **A**, come together and ride as **Partners** down the centerline. **Halt and salute** in the center of the arena.	5

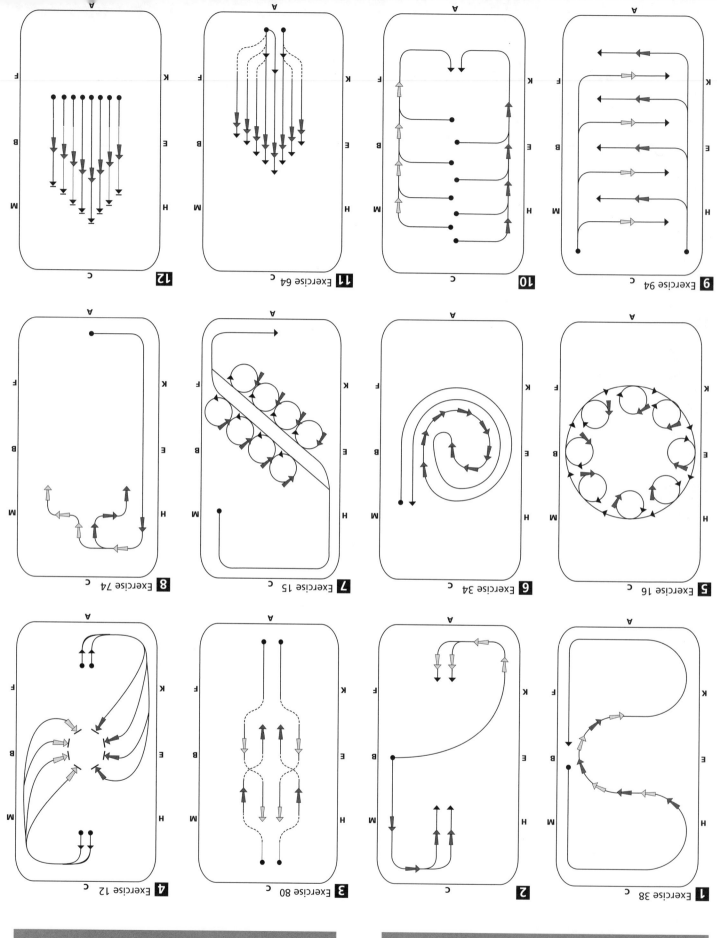

D5. Powwow ♦♦♦

You will form two lines for this drill. Use wallpaper music; it does not need to correspond with the movements of the drill.

Diagram	Instructions	Exercise
1	Form a single-file line along the fence between **B** and **M** in **closed formation**. Do a **Three-Loop Serpentine** between **C** and **A**. Ride straight along the fence from **A** to **B**.	38
2	At **B**, split into two lines. Line 1 turns left and arcs toward **K**. Line 2 rides straight ahead. At **A**, line 1 turns in pairs on the centerline. At **C**, line 2 turns in pairs on the centerline.	N/A
3	Lines 1 and 2 do a **Basket Weave** between **A** and **C**.	80
4	At **C** and **A**, respectively, lines turn right and form single-file lines. On long sides, both lines turn toward **X** and form a **Powwow** circle.	12
5	At the signal, each individual does a **Circle Right**. Come together single file into a large **circle**.	16
6	Do a **Simple Spiral** between **B** and **E**.	34
7	Follow the fence toward **C** in single file. At **H**, form pairs. Ride across the diagonal toward **F**. At the signal, ride **Synchronized Circle Pairs on the Diagonal**.	15
8	Ride along the fence in single file to **C**. At **C**, turn down the centerline in pairs. **Pairs Split** immediately. New line 1 turns left. New line 2 turns right.	74
9	Line 1 forms along the fence between **M** and **F**. Line 2 forms along the fence between **H** and **K**. At the signal, turn toward the centerline. Ride a **Simple Suicide**.	94
10	At the fence, turn toward **A** and ride straight ahead. At **A**, turn in pairs down the centerline.	N/A
11	Fan out to form an **Arrow**. Ride the centerline in **Arrow** formation.	64
12	When the lead riders are between **H** and **M**, halt and **salute**.	N/A

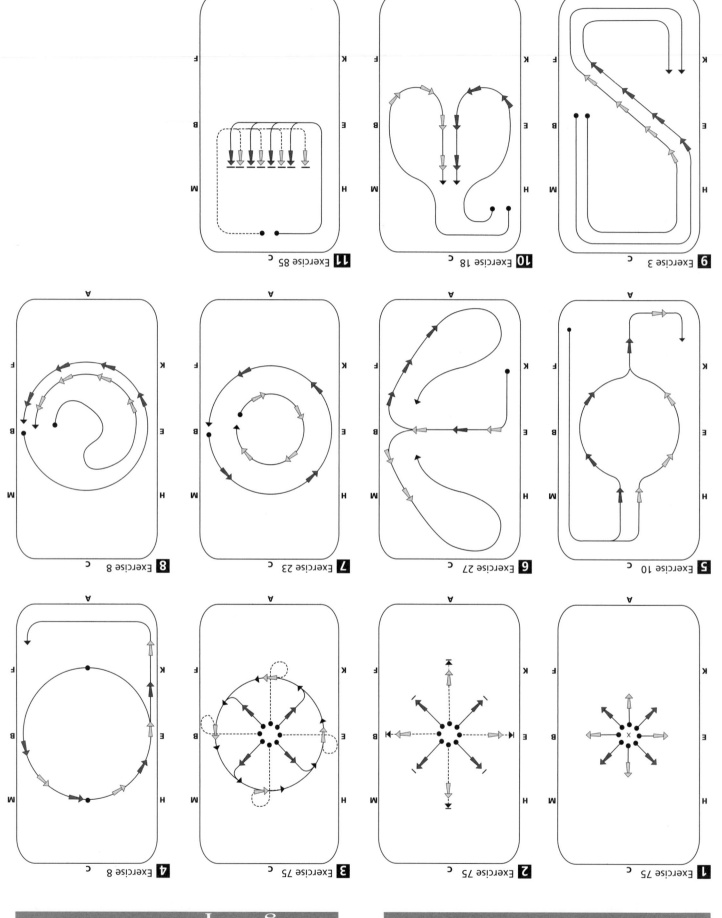

D6. Starlight Express ♦♦♦

This drill is designed to go with "Rolling Stock" by Andrew Lloyd Webber. Riders take their cues from musical changes during the first five frames. After that, the music becomes background music.

Diagram	Instructions	Exercise
1	Stand in the center in a **circle** with tails toward **X**.	setup for **75**
2	When chimes sound, 1s move forward to large **circle** and halt. Number 2s do not move.	setup for **75**
3	When the organ begins, form a **Star**: 1s circle right and 2s move to perimeter of large **circle** and turn left.	**75**
4	Ride a large **circle** between **B** and **E** when the music picks up trot. At **E**, follow the fence toward **F**.	**8**
5	Ride straight ahead toward **C**. Turn in pairs and form a **Bubble**. Between **K** and **F**, merge into a single-file line. At **A**, turn right and follow the fence.	**10**
6	At **E**, turn right and ride to **B**. At **B**, 1s turn left and 2s turn right. Number 1s do a **reverse** and stay to the inside as they approach **B**. Number 2s do a **reverse** and stay to the outside as they approach **B**.	**27**
7	Do one revolution of an **Opposing Carousel Turn-Through** with 2s on the outside and 1s on the inside.	**23**
8	Number 1s do a **Turn through the Circle** and pair up with a partner from line 2.	**8**
9	At **B**, ride straight ahead in pairs. Ride **The Z** in pairs. Ride straight ahead along **K-E**.	**3**
10	Ride along the fence from **H** to **C**. At **C**, turn down the centerline in pairs toward **A**. In the center of the arena, form a **Heart**.	**18**
11	Split at **C**. Number 1s turn right and 2s turn left. At **E** and **B**, turn toward **X**. Form **Interlocking Lines** between **B** and **E**. Halt and **salute**.	**85**

12 Exercise 62 C

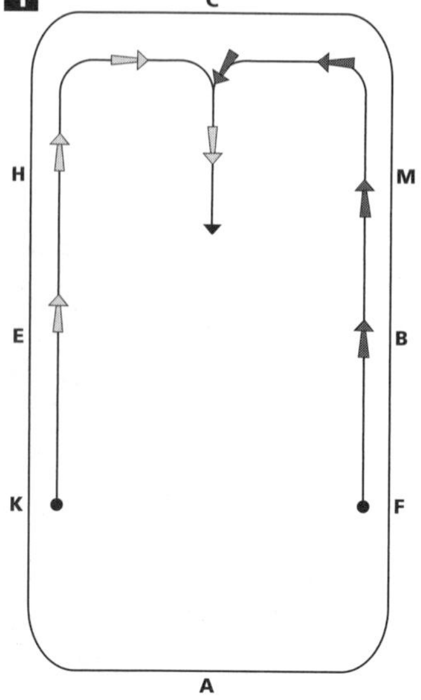

11 Exercise 8 C

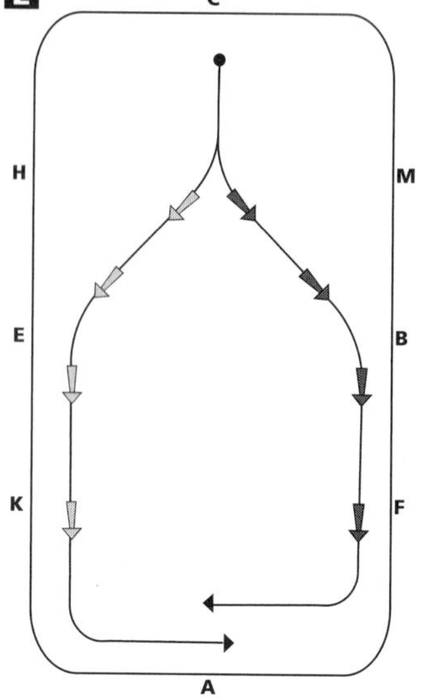

10 Exercise 30 C

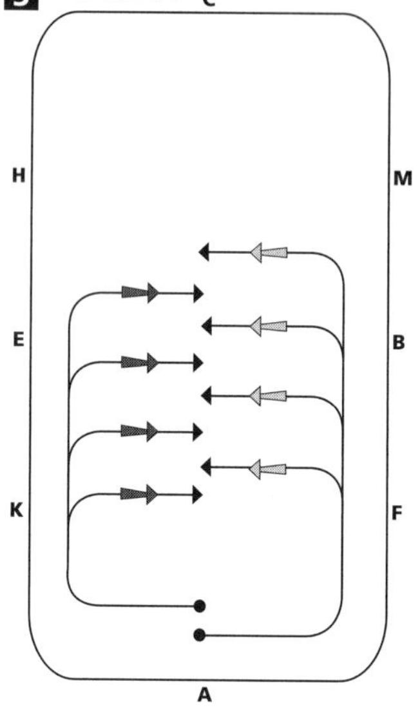

9 Exercise 9 C

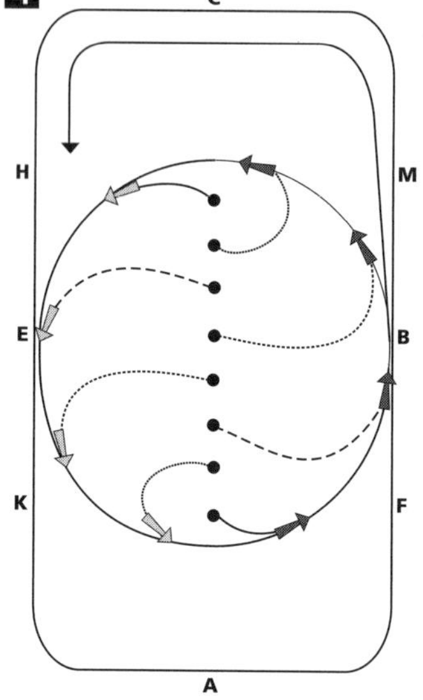

8 Exercise 52 C

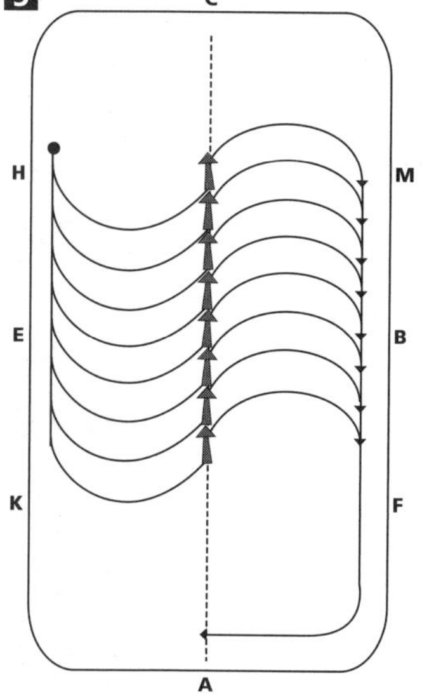

7 Exercise 52 C

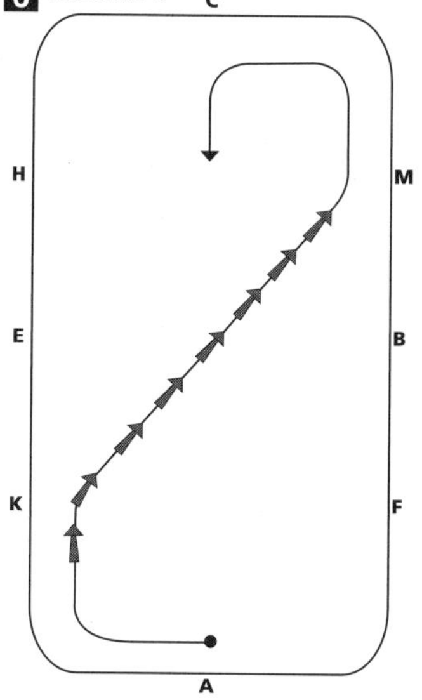

6 Exercise 3 C

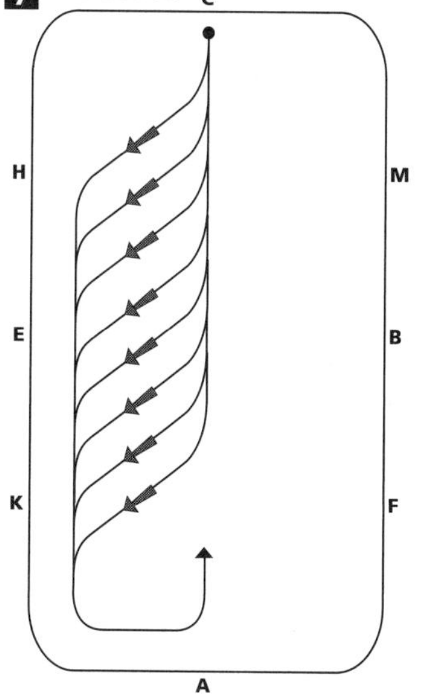

5 Exercise 11 C

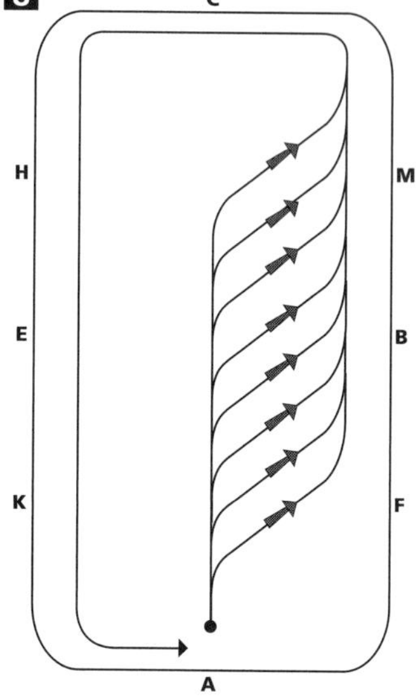

4 Exercise 8 C

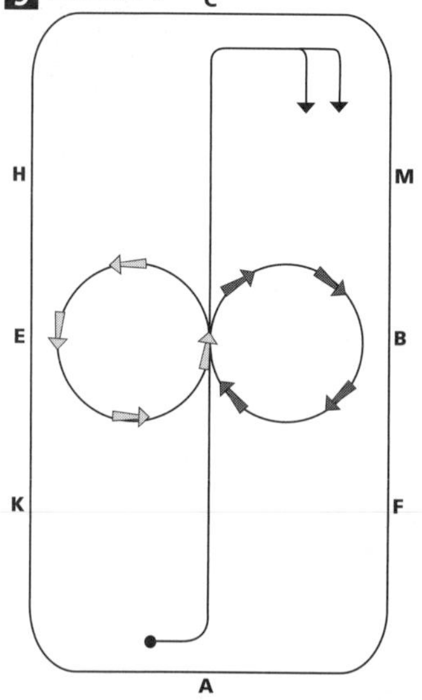

3 Exercise 94 C

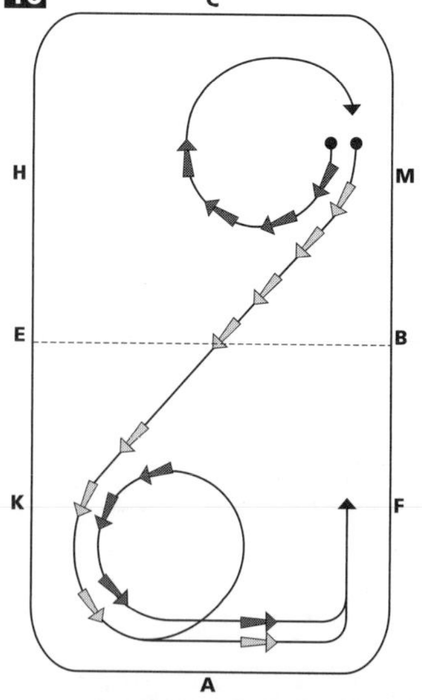

2 Exercise 56 C

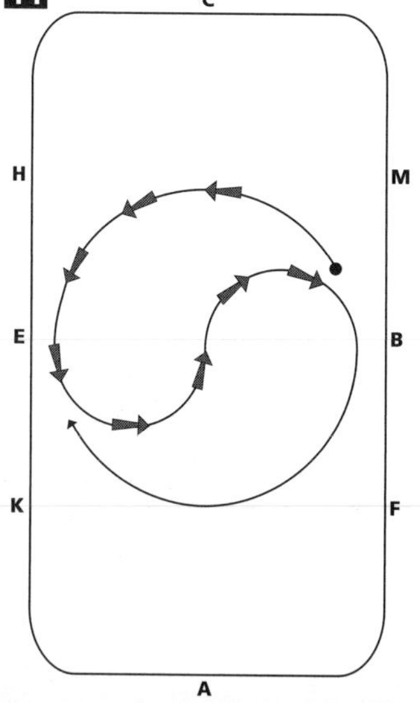

1 Exercise 2 C

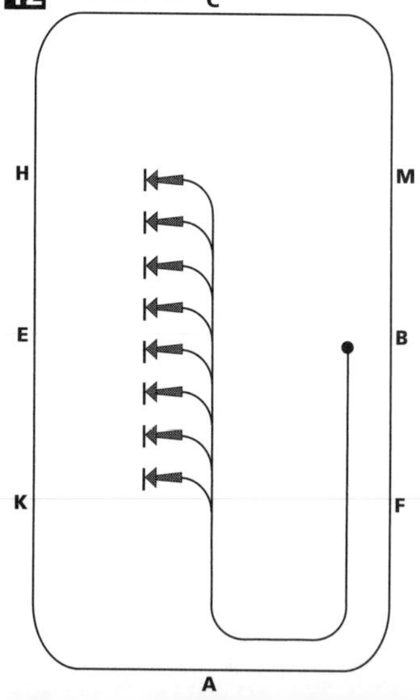

D7. Lines & Reels ◆◆◆◆

This drill combines simple and more-complex exercises.

Diagram	Instructions	Exercise
1	Line 1 lines up along the fence at **K**, facing **C**. Line 2 lines up along the fence at **F**, facing **C**. Ride along rail to **C** in **open formation.** At **C**, turn on the centerline and merge to single file.	2
2	Before **X**, the caller signals to split. Do a **Split Oblique.** At **A**, pass left hand to left hand.	56
3	When centered between **F** and **M**, line 1 turns left for a **Simple Suicide**. When centered between **K** and **H**, line 2 turns right for a **Simple Suicide**.	94
4	After crossing the centerline, turn left to form a large **circle**. Ride one revolution, then form a single-file line at **B** and ride the fence to **H**.	8
5	Ride **The Wave**: Between **H** and **K**, turn left and ride half-circles to the centerline. At the centerline, ride half-circles toward the opposite rail. Form a single-file line and follow the rail toward **A**.	11
6	Ride **The Z** to **C**. At **C**, turn down the centerline.	3
7	Between **C** and **A**, make an **Abreast Oblique** turn right to the fence. Ride along the fence. At **A**, turn down the centerline.	52
8	Between **A** and **C**, make an **Abreast Oblique** turn right to the fence. Ride along the fence to **A**.	52
9	Ride a single-file line down the centerline. At **X**, ride **Goggles.** At **C**, turn right in pairs.	9
10	Ride a **Reel to Reel.** Ride straight ahead along the rail at **F** in single file.	30
11	Ride a large **circle** with a reverse between **B** and **E**. Repeat large **circle**.	8
12	Ride along the fence from **B** to **A**. At **A**, ride down the centerline. When centered, make an **abreast** turn toward the audience. Halt and **salute**.	62

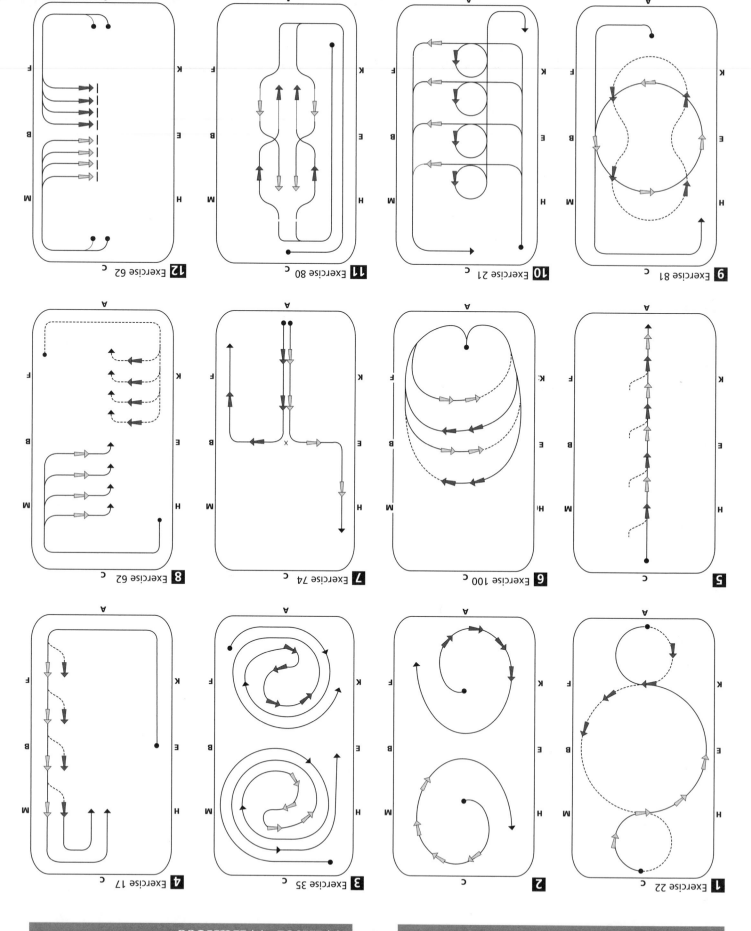

D8. Winter Wildness ◆◆◆◆

I use the Andrew Lloyd Webber song "Winter Wildness" as wallpaper music for this drill. This one will mix up the order of your team. If you want to keep the same order, you can adapt frames 6, 8, and 9.

Diagram	Instructions	Exercise
1	Form a line at **A** facing **K**. Form a line at **C** facing **M**. Ride **Mama & Twins**.	22
2	Beginning on the centerline, both lines ride a small half-circle to **A** and **C**, respectively. Then begin a large **circle**.	N/A
3	Ride **Cinnamon Buns**. Ride in open formation after the reverse.	35
4	At **E**, merge every other horse to form a single-file line. Ride **Add & Subtract**: Number 2 riders pull up to form pairs along the **F-M** rail. Pairs turn down the centerline.	17
5	Number 2s fall behind number 1s to form a single-file line along the centerline.	N/A
6	At **A**, the line splits left and right. Ride a **Beehive** from the long sides to the center and turn back to **A**.	100
7	At **A**, turn down the centerline in pairs. At **X**, **Pairs Split** to **E** and **B**, respectively, and turn right.	74
8	Follow the rail to **M-B** or **K-E**. When when the caller signals, make an **abreast** turn toward the centerline. On the centerline, turn into a single-file line and ride toward **A**.	62
9	At **A**, turn left and follow along the rail. Between **E** and **B**, ride a **Circle Weave**. Follow the rail from **B** to **H**.	81
10	When between **H** and **K**, turn to ride a **Freeway Ramp**. Line 1 turns left at the **M-B-F** rail. Line 2 turns right at **A**. Ride straight along the rail.	21
11	Lines 1 and 2 pass left hand to left hand on the long side. Both lines form pairs and ride down the centerline. Between **A** and **C**, do a **Basket Weave**.	80
12	At **C** and **A**, follow the rail to **B** in single file. Make an **abreast** turn toward the centerline. On the centerline, halt and salute in an **abreast** line.	62

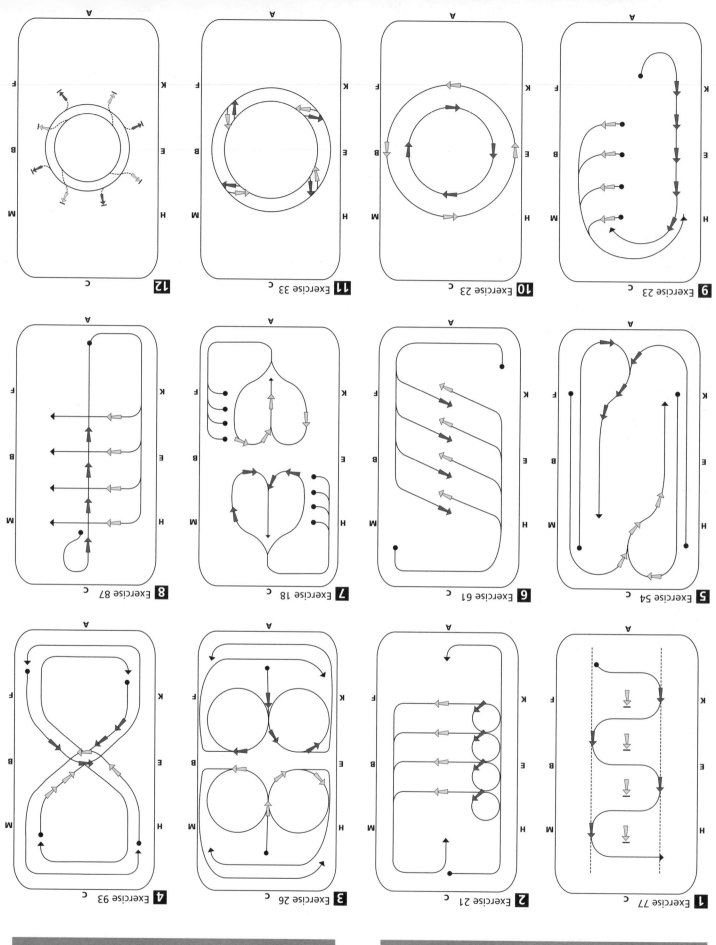

DRILL 9 ◆◆◆◆◆ ● Do-Si-Do

D9. Do-Si-Do ◆◆◆◆◆

This is a challenging drill that will wow your audience.

Diagram	Instructions	Exercise
1	Ride a **Sewing Machine** beginning at **A**: The first half of the line halts on the centerline (number 1s) and the second half of the line weaves between quarter lines (2s). Everyone forms a single-file line at **C**, with the 1s filing in behind the 2s.	77
2	Ride along the rail to **H-K-E**. Number 1s make an **abreast** turn left and ride across the arena, then turn left on the rail. On the long side, number 2s ride a **Freeway Ramp** along the rail. Number 1s turn on the centerline at **C**. Number 2s ride the rail and turn on the centerline at **A**.	21
3	Lines 1 and 2 ride a **Four-Leaf Clover** between **A** and **C**. Partners split at **B** and **E**. Riders follow the fence and pass left hand to left hand at **C** and **A**, respectively.	26
4	Ride a **Thread & Do-Si-Do.**	93
5	Ride along the rail toward the centerline, passing the oncoming line left hand to left hand. Do a **Centerline Meld**: Turn on the centerline and merge into single-file lines. Number 1s ride from **C** to **H**. Number 2s ride from **A** to **F**.	54
6	Follow along the rail. At the signal, ride an **Oblique Suicide**.	61
7	Numbers 1 and 2 turn right. Numbers 1 and 2 form single-file lines along the long sides. Number 1s ride toward **A** and number 2s ride toward **C**. Numbers 1 and 2 turn down the centerline and do two **Hearts**.	18
8	At **A**, 1s turn right in **open formation**. At **C**, 2s reverse in **open formation** and go down the centerline. When centered between **K** and **H**, 1s turn right. Number 2s ride the centerline and **Thread the Line.**	87
9	Between **F** and **B**, 1s turn left. Number 2s follow the rail toward **H**. At the centerline, pass left hand to left hand on an arch.	setup for 23
10	Ride an **Opposing Carousel**: Between **B** and **E**, 1s turn counterclockwise. Number 2s turn clockwise.	23
11	Ride a **Carousel Switch-Up** between **B** and **E**.	33
12	Between **B** and **E**, everyone turns to the outside circle. Halt and **salute**.	N/A

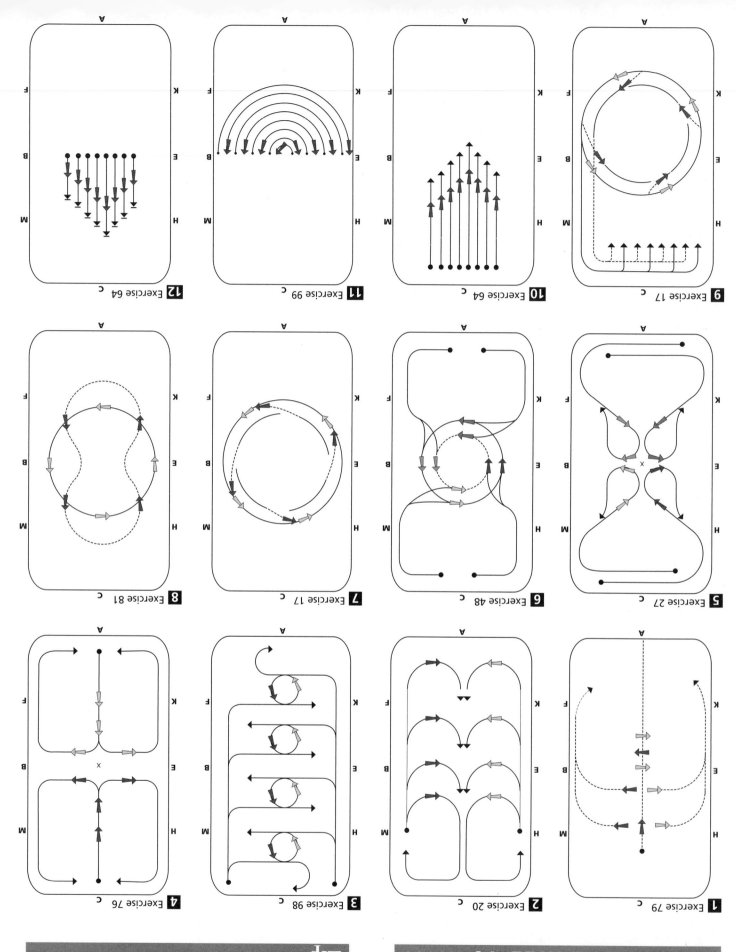

D10. Zip ♦♦♦♦♦

Once perfected, this will be an amazing drill.

Diagram	Instructions	Exercise
1	Ride a **Zipper**. Starting along the centerline facing **E**, 1s unzip to the rail and turn toward **A**. Starting along the centerline facing **B**, 2s unzip to the rail and turn toward **A**. The **zipper** separates the line, then splits left or right.	79
2	Ride **Half-Circles to Pairs** on the centerline. At **C**, 1s and 2s split.	20
3	When centered on the long sides, caller signals for lines to turn toward the centerline. Ride a **Suicide Do-Si-Do** and continue to the rail. At the rail, turn right.	98
4	At **A** and **C**, respectively, turn down the centerline in a single-file line. Ride a **Meet & Greet**, splitting four ways at **X**. Follow the rail after the split.	76
5	Pass left hand to left hand at **A** and **C**, respectively. Ride **Four Reverses** at **X**. Ride toward **A** and **C**, respectively, and pass left hand to left hand.	27
6	Turn the corner and form pairs out of your lines. Ride a **Four-Spoke Wheel**.	48
7	**Subtract on a circle**: The inside partner drops behind the outside partner. Ride one revolution.	17
8	Do a **Circle Weave** in the center of the arena. Riders who were previously on the inside weave one revolution. Nonweavers walk.	81
9	**Add on a circle**: Inside riders return to inside, forming pairs. Pairs ride down the rail from **B** toward **H**. When centered along the short side, the caller signals for an **abreast** turn.	17
10	Form **Arrow** toward **X**.	64
11	Ride an **Arrow to Suicide** and halt in an **abreast** line between **E** and **B**.	99
12	Ride **Arrow** to halt between **H** and **M**. **Salute**.	64

Glossary

abreast. Horses are side-by-side in a line, row, or column.

arrow. An exercise in the shape of an arrow.

caller. This person gives the signal for turns and specific moves. The caller is usually the last person in line, since that person can see when the whole line is in position to perform a move. The caller uses either a whistle or verbal signals. If the caller uses verbal signals, she must have a loud voice.

carousel. Two or more circles inside of each other.

centerline. The line between **A** and **C.**

closed formation. A line of horses in which there is about 4 feet (1.2 meters) of space between horses.

drillmaster. The person on the ground who is responsible for directing the team through the drill. His other responsibilities include seeing that the drill works efficiently, making sure that spacing is correct, and ensuring that the drill is aesthetically pleasing.

linear exercises. Moves composed of straight lines.

melding/merging. Putting two or more lines together to form one.

open formation. A line of horses in which there is one horse's length (about 2.5 meters or 8 feet) of space between horses.

quarter line. A line that is parallel to the centerline. There is one quarter line on each side of the centerline.

school. The arena or pen where both the horse and rider learn.

serpentine. An exercise that is made up of loops and looks like a snake.

spiral. Circling in or circling out to decrease or increase circle size.

suicide. An exercise in which one line of abreast riders rides head-on through another line of abreast riders.

thread. Riding through another line at a right angle.

weave. Moving in and out through another line of riders.

wheels. Circles with spokes of abreast riders.

whip. An exercise in which an abreast line of riders moves around a center rider who is semi-stationary.

x. The middle of the arena between **C-A** and **E-B.**

INDEX

Page numbers in *italics* indicate illustrations or photographs. Section titles, when not redundant, are indicated in parentheses next to exercise names.

Drill Teams!

Send your "pro tips" our way for a future printing of this book. E-mail your tips, including your team name and location, to deb.burns@storey.com.